What Your Colleagues Are Saying . . .

Too many of us perseverate on "fixing" our students and ourselves. Focusing instead on the strengths students bring to the classroom and redi~~~~~~~~~~~~~~ already employ, Kobett and Karp turn this thinking on its he~~~~~~~~~~~~~~~rotocols we can confront and unpack our beliefs, transform c~~~~~~~~~~~~~~tive and supportive learning environments our students des~~~~~~~~~~~~~~urce for educators committed to ensuring that each and ev~~~~~~~~~~~~~~der, and success in mathematics!

Matt Larson
Past President,
National Council of Teachers of Mathematics

Rarely does one find a text that provides both the aspirational vision and inspirational mission to transform both the striving mathematics educator *and* the student mathematician. Educators will be moved to embrace, then promote change through their work with Drs. Kobett and Karp's innovative strengths-based approach to teaching and learning mathematics. Kobett and Karp invite all math stakeholders to discover their own strengths from which to build a stronger foundation in the teaching and learning of mathematics.

Richard Cox, Jr.
Math Coordinator
STEAM Lab Facilitator
Bullitt County Public Schools, Kentucky

I love this book! More and more people are talking about the need to build on student strengths instead of focusing on their deficits, but doing this can seem unrealistic to a teacher. The authors not only elaborate what it means to build on student strengths, they offer concrete strategies for how to do it. Starting with the necessary step of looking at one's own teaching strengths, they offer practical guidelines and examples that lay out a path teachers can use to turn around their teaching and their students' learning.

Cathy Seeley
Mathematics Educator, Speaker, and Writer
Past President of the National Council of Teachers of Mathematics
Austin, TX

This book is a must-read for every stakeholder in the education system! The authors challenge us to acknowledge the damaging impact of deficit-based beliefs and provide concrete ways to leverage strengths in ourselves and in our students to create mathematics classrooms where students flourish.

Delise Andrews
Math Coordinator
s, NE

This book provides teachers with a wealth of resources for uncovering and nurturing students mathematical strengths. By focusing on recognizing and building on students' strengths rather than identifying their deficiencies, the authors have mapped out a pathway for creating instructional experiences that support the learning and identity development of each and every student. This is a must-have for all elementary teachers!

Margaret (Peg) Smith
Author of *The Five Practices for Orchestrating*
Mathematical Discussion

This book provides a clear, rich, strong rebuttal to "my kids can't." Kobett and Karp help us focus on our students' unique perspectives, talents, and strengths as well as our students' capabilities with mathematics practices and content. More important, they help us take stock of who we are. They help us identify aspects of our practice that are strong and those that are ready for a turnaround. They teach us about these turnarounds and describe how we can realize them effectively. This is a must-have for transforming "they can't" into "they can."

John SanGiovanni
Coordinator, Mathematics
Howard County Public School System, MD

Where do beliefs and pedagogy meet? In a world in which we are often asked to find flaws and weaknesses, this book is a breath of fresh air and reminds us that the best way to teach is to build from our strengths. Filled with research-based ideas, practical strategies, and tools, this book provides a comprehensive approach to creating asset-based learning environments by identifying and leveraging the strengths of students, teachers, schools, and caretakers.

Cathery Yeh
Assistant Professor, Mathematics Education
Chapman University, Orange, CA

This well-written book is a game changer! *Strengths-Based Teaching and Learning in Mathematics: Five Teaching Turnarounds for Grades K–6* goes beyond simply providing information by sharing a pathway for changing practice. The authors start with reflective activities allowing teachers to examine their beliefs and explore their teaching strengths. Using the Teaching Turnarounds will transform classrooms. Focusing on our students' strengths should be routine and can be lost in the day-to-day teaching demands. A teacher using these approaches can change the trajectory of students' lives forever. All teachers need this resource!

Connie S. Schrock
Emporia State University, KS
National Council of Supervisors of Mathematics President, 2017–2019

Drs. Kobett and Karp offer teachers a positive and practical way of using Appreciative Inquiry to put spotlight on teachers' instructional practices to celebrate their strength and support teachers to dream, design and deliver innovative ways to bring more equitable teaching practices to the forefront. By reimagining instruction focused on strengths-based teaching that leverage and put spotlight on students' abilities to use representations and reasoning, the authors unpack rich tasks by delving into the development of learning progressions in important mathematics as well as situate mathematics within contexts that students can relate to while bridging mathematics closer to students' lived experiences.

Jennifer Suh
Professor, Mathematics Education
George Mason University, Fairfax, VA

Strengths-Based Teaching and Learning in Mathematics: Five Teaching Turnarounds for Grades K–6 forces the reader to become extremely reflective about their own individual identity in mathematics and implementation of effective teaching practices/strategies. How many students have we lost or have allowed to feel defeated in learning mathematics because we didn't teach by harnessing the power of their strengths? This book intersperses time for this type of reflection as one identifies your own strengths, your individual math identity, as well as the inclusion of the numerous "spotlights on practices" to support successful implementation in the classroom. As one considers how to help students develop a growth mindset in mathematics, this book must become an essential resource. There are concrete examples to illustrate how this becomes visible in the classroom—all with the goal of helping students develop their identity, authority, and agency in mathematics. We lose too many students in mathematics; too many students hear that they have gaps, are deficit, or are stigmatized by having to endure endless intervention programs in mathematics. Instead this book uses subtleties, helps you focus on yourself as a teacher of mathematics, and provides explicit examples to harnesses the strengths of all students in mathematics. This will do a lot to change negative student self-images. I love this book!

Denise Walston
Director of Mathematics
Council of the Great City Schools, Washington, DC

Finally the book that good teachers have been waiting for: a book that focuses not on what students cannot do, but on what they *can*. This needed book offers teachers a positive, productive way to rethink teaching and learning in mathematics and would be ideal for a school- or districtwide book study.

Jeff Shih
Associate Professor of Elementary Mathematics
University of Nevada, Las Vegas

Anytime you purchase a resource book in mathematics, you hope that it does an inspirational delivery of its title. In *Strengths-Based Teaching and Learning in Mathematics: Five Teaching Turnarounds for Grades K–6*, the authors have gone above and beyond the book's high expectations. Kobett and Karp have masterfully tapped into the zeitgeist of contemporary math education and written a book that oozes with not just empathy, reflection, and candor but with clear and motivating practicality that will transform any math classroom into a place of community, hope, and unbridled strength.

Sunil Singh
Author of *Pi of Life: The Hidden Happiness of Mathematics* and
Math Recess: Playful Learning in an Age of Disruption

Strengths-Based Teaching and Learning in Mathematics
At a Glance

Turnaround Tips tied in with chapter topics include do-today activities that can begin impacting your classroom.

In the rush to complete mathematics prompts, some students equate speed with problem solving and often approach every kind of mathematics prompt with the same mindset about how much perseverance they will need and how much time they will need to solve it. As teachers, we casually use the word *problem* to indicate all kinds of mathematics work that we ask students to do. We say, "Please complete the next problem" when the problem looks like this:

- $8 + 5 =$ ____
- $5 \times 6 =$ ____
- $23.4 + 1.9 =$ ____
- Elena picked 14 flowers. She promised to pick 21 for her mother. How many more does she need to pick?
- Ellie and Tia are running a 10K race. Ellie and Tia started out together. Ellie runs every mile faster than Tia. What is happening to the distance between the two runners? Create a graph that represents the story (Williams, Kobett, & Harbin Miles, 2018).

Some of these prompts will cue students to engage at varying levels of problem-solving depth and perseverance. Therefore, it is critical that students recognize different kinds of problems, and tasks will require different ways of engaging with the problem. A true problem involves a question that cannot be immediately answered. What is a problem at one time to one person may be an exercise to another person depending on the students' developmental growth. Students truly enjoy opportunities to evaluate whether a mathematics prompt is indeed a problem and then determine what behaviors they will need to solve it. One way to help students differentiate between a problem and a nonproblem is to create a checklist.

Turnaround Tip

Support students' perseverance with problem solving by cutting out large letter Ps. Some teachers like to make the letter Ps using different kinds of paper, colors, and so on.

Place the Ps in a large jar for the students to see. As students are demonstrating perseverance, hand out a P to the student and describe what you are seeing. They may try to assemble a collection!

Source: Image created by Bob Ronau.

> A true problem involves a question that cannot be immediately answered.

Pull quotes highlight key topics of the chapter.

Exercise: A problem with a known solution path.

Marginal definitions provide clarity to novice and experienced teachers alike.

Try It! features aligned with each Teaching Turnaround introduce easy but impactful activities to use in the classroom.

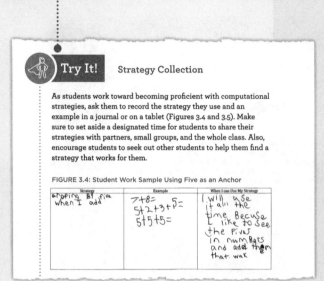

Try It!   Strategy Collection

As students work toward becoming proficient with computational strategies, ask them to record the strategy they use and an example in a journal or on a tablet (Figures 3.4 and 3.5). Make sure to set aside a designated time for students to share their strategies with partners, small groups, and the whole class. Also, encourage students to seek out other students to help them find a strategy that works for them.

FIGURE 3.4: Student Work Sample Using Five as an Anchor

Strategy	Example	When I can Use My Strategy
Groping BY five when I add	7+8= 5+2+3+5= 5+5+5=	I will use it all the time Becuse I like to see the Fives in num Bers and add them that wak

Try It! activities also include student facing surveys and templates to use directly in your classroom.

Try It!   Student Attitude Survey

- [ ] Math makes me curious.
- [ ] I enjoy doing math puzzles.
- [ ] I would rather avoid math classes.
- [ ] I never think about math unless I am in math class.
- [ ] Word problems are confusing.
- [ ] I am not very confident in math class.
- [ ] Working with numbers is fun.
- [ ] Using math materials helps me think about the problems.
- [ ] Math class makes me nervous.
- [ ] I have never liked math.
- [ ] I enjoy being challenged by math problems.
- [ ] Math tests are scary.
- [ ] When I get a hard math problem, I keep on working until I have a solution.
- [ ] My mind sometimes freezes up in math class.

Spotlight on Your Practice invites teachers to write, reflect, and make connections to their own practice.

SPOTLIGHT ON YOUR PRACTICE:
What Do You Believe?

We've spent some time unpacking some comments that we have heard; now it is your turn. Take a moment and really think about the students you teach. Shine the spotlight into your mathematics classroom on a student who is currently struggling and a student who is meeting expectations. Write down statements you have made or heard others make about each of the students in each box.

Student #1 _____   Student #2 _____

What kinds of underlying beliefs do you notice in these statements?

Next, select at least one alternative, asset-based belief for the student who is currently struggling and record it in each box.

Student #1 _____   Student #2 _____

- How does the asset-based belief redirect your thinking about the student who is currently struggling?

- How might an exercise like this promote strengths-based teaching?

This template can be downloaded for use at resources.corwin.com/teachingturnarounds.

Templates are available online to help track your progress and reflect as often as you'd like or start fresh with a new class!

FIGURE 2.6: Student Work Samples

MARVIN	LEO
$21 + 18 = \boxed{39}$ ✗ 7 what? 30 9	39 39 $21 + 18 = \boxed{32} + 7$ 20+10=30 39 1+9=9 −7 39 32

Jasmine: Wait a second! There are four numbers with the equal sign!

Katey: With an equals sign in the middle!

Jasmine: I don't think Marvin can cross out stuff. I think he did that because he wasn't sure what to do.

Katey: I agree. I did that one time.

Jasmine: Well then Leo must be right, but why is he right? Let's check his math!

Katey: Well, 21 + 18 = 39. But, why did he subtract the 7 when the problem says plus 7? Wouldn't we add 39 + 7?

Jasmine: Hmmm. Well let's add that. 39 + 7 = 46. But that doesn't make sense!

Student work samples and vignettes illustrate what strengths-based teaching and learning looks like in the classroom.

End-of-chapter summaries concisely tie up the key ideas and takeaways from the chapter.

Summary

As you venture into exploring how your own strengths can empower you to identify your own capabilities and, in turn, find strengths in your students, your proficiency as a change agent emerges. By creating a habit of identifying your own positives rather than teachers' all too frequent common focus on their weaknesses, the tenor of the instructional experience moves to more solid relationships with the content and the students. Using the tenets of the Appreciative Inquiry model builds productive change on top of a foundation of what's working well. As mathematics teacher educators, the two of us often encounter teacher candidates who come to student teaching seminars or classes feeling that they can't reach a student or don't know how to "handle" an instructional situation. They, like many teachers who care deeply about their students, report that they can't sleep over these concerns and even cry as they talk about particular children. By refocusing their attention to their strengths, we ask them to immediately start journaling about this student and the small (or big) successes they can claim each day. They are surprised when they feel better about these situations as the initial tendency to focus on their frustrations is great. It is these transfers in attention that match the Try It! activities found in this chapter. We know this first step is really a leap. Ready for the next footstep forward? Let's go!

Strengths-Based Teaching and Learning in Mathematics

Five Teaching Turnarounds for Grades K-6

Beth McCord Kobett

Karen S. Karp

Foreword by Francis (Skip) Fennell

A JOINT PUBLICATION

For information:

Corwin
A SAGE Company
2455 Teller Road
Thousand Oaks, California 91320
(800) 233–9936
www.corwin.com

SAGE Publications Ltd.
1 Oliver's Yard
55 City Road
London EC1Y 1SP
United Kingdom

SAGE Publications India Pvt. Ltd.
B 1/I 1 Mohan Cooperative Industrial Area
Mathura Road, New Delhi 110 044
India

SAGE Publications Asia-Pacific Pte. Ltd.
18 Cross Street #10–10/11/12
China Square Central
Singapore 048423

Publisher: Erin Null
Associate Content
    Development Editor: Jessica Vidal
Production Editor: Melanie Birdsall
Copy Editor: Gillian Dickens
Typesetter: Integra
Proofreader: Wendy Jo Dymond
Indexer: Integra
Cover and Interior Designer: Scott Van Atta
Marketing Manager: Margaret O'Connor

Library of Congress Cataloging-in-Publication Data

Names: Kobett, Beth McCord, author. | Karp, Karen S., author.
Title: Strengths-based teaching and learning in mathematics :
    five teaching turnarounds for grades K–6 / Beth McCord Kobett,
    Karen S. Karp; foreword by Francis (Skip) Fennell.
Description: Thousand Oaks, California : Corwin Press, Inc. [2020] |
    Includes bibliographical references.
Identifiers: LCCN 2019042502 | ISBN 9781544374932 (paperback) |
    ISBN 9781544374925 (ebook) | ISBN 9781544374918 (ebook) |
    ISBN 9781544374901 (adobe pdf)
Subjects: LCSH: Mathematics—Study and teaching (Elementary) |
    Student-centered learning.
Classification: LCC QA135.6 .K668 2020 | DDC 372.7—dc23
LC record available at https://lccn.loc.gov/2019042502

This book is printed on acid-free paper.

20 21 22 23 24 10 9 8 7 6 5 4 3 2 1

Contents

Find the Reader's Guide and other reproducibles
when you visit the companion website at
resources.corwin.com/teachingturnarounds

Foreword

Game changer! This book will change how you think about teaching children mathematics. The perspective provided by Beth Kobett and Karen Karp should literally rip deficit-based instructional decision making from our bookshelves, our conversations with colleagues, whether online, in schools, in professional development sessions, and, yes, from faculty room chats as well. It's time! Over 60 years ago, J. Fred Weaver (1954/1970) noted that diagnosis is relevant to all elements of mathematics instruction. However, he also indicated that "only when we have diagnosed the difficulties and determine the needs of children, can we provide the kinds of instruction designed to remedy those difficulties and meet those needs" (Kramer, 1966, pp. 334–335). Yes, diagnosing and determining instructional expectations and needs are ongoing, but focusing on "what's missing?" has provided our schools and, frankly, our culture with funding opportunities and related support, instructional techniques and materials, grouping practices, a myriad of assessments, and so much more, all with a seemingly singular focus—identifying, intervening, addressing, and remediating "what's missing?", a deficit model driving instructional thinking and, sadly, the teaching of mathematics.

Again, it's time! *Strengths-Based Teaching and Learning in Mathematics: 5 Teaching Turnarounds for Grades K–6* operationalizes an instructional paradigm shift that truly provides access to effective teaching and the instructional support needed to maximize the learning opportunities for every student. Yes, this book thoroughly and convincingly presents the case for teaching that begins with and consciously and consistently considers student strengths. What such an instructional focus requires, of course, is changing the way many of us think about instruction, hence the need to "turn around"—to approach instruction based on what students know and care about. In essence, a teaching turnaround is a reflective reminder to consider elements of your teaching differently. Let's consider the teaching turnarounds necessary to not just acknowledge and value but that truly define *Strengths-Based Teaching and Learning in Mathematics*.

Chapter 1 starts with you. Teaching Turnaround One: Identify Your Teaching Strengths engages teacher readers in identifying and exploring their strengths, recognizing that many teachers would rather not openly "share" and, as noted earlier, would prefer to discuss their instructional deficiencies. So, right in the first chapter, Kobett and Karp expose the deficit model. Teaching Turnaround One offers appreciative inquiry (Cooperrider & Whitney, 2005) as a process designed to discover and highlight teaching strengths. This book, in its initial chapter, launches an instructional focus that frankly is much more than "things for you to try." No, what Kobett and Karp have provided is a full tapestry related to accessing instruction that fully engages you and your colleagues in strengths-based instructional considerations, with each turnaround chapter providing activities titled Turnaround Tip, Spotlight on Your Practice, and Try It!—all designed to directly connect you to the intent of each turnaround and support both your understandings and teaching.

Teaching Turnaround Two: Discover and Leverage Your Students' Mathematical Strengths establishes the importance of determining and addressing student strengths mathematically. It addresses mathematical proficiencies, processes, and practices (Chapter 2) and critical mathematics content strands (Chapter 3). Classroom-connected activities that address the mathematical proficiencies defined and emphasized in *Adding It Up* (National Research Council & Mathematics Learning Study Committee, 2001), the mathematical processes of *Principles and Standards for School Mathematics* (National Council of Teachers of Mathematics [NCTM], 2000), and the *Common Core State Standards for Mathematics* (National Governors Association Center for Best Practices & Council of Chief State School Officers, 2010) shape the emphasis of Chapter 2. Chapter 3 emphasizes a selected collection of content topics from standards within Number and Operations, Fractions, and Geometry. This content focus is not about identifying computational deficiencies or error patterns, analysis of test results, perceived misconceptions, or other considerations of "what's missing?"; rather, it's directed toward truly capitalizing on what's known, what students can do, and their interests within critical mathematics topics and standards.

I might, in fact, argue that Teaching Turnaround Three: Design Instruction From a Strengths-Based Perspective presents the greatest challenge for teachers as they consider moving away from an instructional focus that spends an inordinate amount of time on identifying and attempting to address (I often see the word *remedy*) "what's missing?" in a learner's mathematical background and experiences to an emphasis on determining student strengths and then using the strengths to truly influence instruction. This teaching turnaround addresses grouping (Chapter 4), tasks (Chapter 5), and feedback (Chapter 6). The Mathematics Teaching Practices (NCTM, 2014) are used to launch Chapter 4, which then addresses challenges related to fixed versus flexible grouping, ability grouping, mixed-strength whole-group instruction, and targeted small-group instruction, among other grouping-related topics. Any teacher interested in ensuring that their students have everyday access to mathematics tasks will appreciate the Chapter 5 focus, which includes, among many valuable instructional tools and activities, a strengths-based task discussion protocol, as well as attention to task personalization. I have often felt that feedback is far too often the missing element of a plan for and implementation of a lesson's classroom-based formative assessment. Chapter 6's attention to teacher-to-student feedback prior to, during, and within the close of a lesson, as well as student-to-student feedback, is important to the strengths-based perspective. In addition, the chapter's attention to classroom-based formative assessment presents, for many, a first-time consideration of connections to planning, instruction, and assessment from a strengths-based perspective. Teaching Turnaround Three: Design Instruction From a Strengths-Based Perspective is a professional development *must* for many schools and school districts.

Teaching Turnaround Four: Help Students Develop Their Points of Power presents, in Chapter 7, a thorough analysis of the importance of the emergence of student identity. And yes, the intent is for students to both develop and identify their Points of Power, to understand what they can do to essentially know and value their mathematical self. The activities provided in this chapter help teachers to not just consider but address, instructionally, student disposition. Students who recognize their Points of Power are independent and confident thinkers and collaborators. What we know is that children begin to dislike mathematics toward the end of their elementary school years. Consider such findings as yet another "what's missing?"—in this case, a positive attitude. A strengths-based approach will use activities like those presented in this chapter (e.g., talent showcase, windows and mirrors, translation task) as a foundation for students developing their Points of Power—their mathematical me!

Teaching Turnaround Five: Promote Strengths in the School Community is the concluding teaching turnaround and provides strong recommendations with regard to the importance of professional learning opportunities and communities (Chapter 8) and family communication (Chapter 9). In essence, this turnaround is all about communication and the support needed to truly sustain a strengths-based approach to teaching and learning. Let's first consider professional learning. First, Chapter 8 begins with the premise that in promoting a strengths-based approach to teaching and learning, all teachers are leaders. The chapter then appropriately champions the potential of Appreciative Inquiry and Whole-School Agreement as paradigms for professional learning that not only engages teachers but also offers a focus for the development of collaborative school-based teams. What a welcome and appropriate change for many! Chapter 9 is all about thinking differently about developing and sustaining family connections. Recognizing that many family members are seemingly lifetime-attached to mathematics topics and the methods they used for learning them, it's imperative that a viable partnership among teachers, schools, and families be nurtured, supported, and sustained.

The chapter's suggestions and related multilingual activities will engage teachers, students, and families and expand and extend the access to strengths-based teaching to include families and the larger school community, thus providing the necessary support for both mathematics learning and developing and maintaining a positive and productive mathematical disposition.

You need this book right now! The NCTM states that "an excellent mathematics program requires that all students have access to a high-quality mathematics curriculum, effective teaching and learning high expectations, and the support and resources needed to maximize their learning potential" (2014, p. 59). Actually, every student's access to appropriate learning experiences in mathematics every single day is a right! Considering teaching and learning from the perspective of "what's missing?" is more than antiquated. Kobett and Karp not only recognize and discuss the importance of starting with and building on strengths instructionally, but this masterful effort has actually defined the teaching turnarounds that must be addressed as teachers truly embody a strengths-based approach to teaching and learning. In short, this book not only talks the talk, through the identification of the teaching turnarounds and activities to be used to support them, but, more important, truly walks the walk. It's your game plan.

—**Francis (Skip) Fennell, PhD, DHL**

L. Stanley Bowlsbey Professor of Education and Graduate and Professional Studies Emeritus

Project Director, Elementary Mathematics Specialists and Teacher Leaders Project

Past President, National Council of Teachers of Mathematics

Past President, Association of Mathematics Teacher Educators

McDaniel College, Westminster, MD

About the Authors

Beth McCord Kobett is an associate professor in the School of Education at Stevenson University, where she works with preservice teachers and leads professional learning efforts in mathematics education both regionally and nationally. She currently serves on the board of directors for the National Council of Teachers of Mathematics and is the former president of the Association for Maryland Mathematics Teacher Educators. She is a former classroom teacher, elementary mathematics specialist, adjunct professor, and university supervisor. At the undergraduate level, Beth teaches early childhood, elementary, and middle school mathematics methods and content courses. Beth has coauthored nine peer-reviewed teaching and coaching mathematics books in addition to numerous book chapters and articles. Dr. Kobett is a recipient of the Mathematics Educator of the Year Award from the Maryland Council of Teachers of Mathematics and Johns Hopkins University Distinguished Alumni award. Beth also received the Johns Hopkins Excellence in Teaching Award as a part-time instructor and Stevenson University's Excellence in Teaching Award as both an adjunct and full-time faculty member.

Karen S. Karp is a professor in the School of Education at Johns Hopkins University. Previously, she was a professor of mathematics education in the Department of Early and Elementary Childhood Education at the University of Louisville, where she received the President's Distinguished Teaching Award and the Distinguished Service Award for a Career of Service. She is a former member of the board of directors of the National Council of Teachers of Mathematics and a former president of the Association of Mathematics Teacher Educators. She is a member of the author panel for the What Works Clearinghouse Practice Guide on assisting elementary school students who have difficulty learning mathematics for the U.S. Department of Education Institute of Educational Sciences. She is the author or coauthor of approximately 20 book chapters, 50 articles, and 30 books, including *Elementary and Middle School Mathematics: Teaching Developmentally*, *Developing Essential Understanding of Addition and Subtraction for Teaching Mathematics*, and *Inspiring Girls to Think Mathematically*. She holds teaching certifications in elementary education, secondary mathematics, and K–12 special education.

Acknowledgments

Our strengths-based journey has been filled with self-examination, experimentation, and exploration that began several years ago with an initial exploration of appreciative inquiry. Since then, our strengths-based work with students, preservice teachers, beginning and experienced teachers, families, and leaders has revealed the power in learning to look for another person's strengths, including those we teach, work alongside, learn from, and lead. We continue to be fortified by how this work positively affects members of the educational community who have embraced this way of planning and teaching mathematics. We are grateful to our critical friends, Delise Andrews, David Nicholson, Avonshae Rounds, Denise Walston, and Jon Wray, for their valuable feedback and to the countless preservice teachers from Stevenson University who developed lessons and designed instructional plans using strengths-based approaches for students. We wish to give a special thank you to Skip Fennell for reading and responding to the earliest versions of this work. His thoughtful suggestions made this a stronger book!

From Beth Kobett: I wish to thank my husband, Tim Kobett, and my daughters, Hannah Kobett and Jenna Kobett, who are my greatest cheerleaders and who always provide the epitome of strengths-based support! I also want to thank my sister, Kitty McCord, and mother, Pam Allen, for their constant encouragement. I would also like to thank my youngest reviewers, Jocie and Jake Janowich, for giving me incredibly insightful and thoughtful feedback and student samples.

From Karen Karp: I wish to thank my husband, Bob Ronau, who created many of the figures for this book and as a mathematics educator offered many reviews and insights. I also especially thank two of my grandchildren, Jack and Emma, for their responses to several tasks and their parents, Matthew, Christine, Jeffrey, and Pamela, for their assistance in making space in their busy lives for those projects to happen.

We are very thankful to our publisher at Corwin, Erin Null. She championed this project from the beginning, celebrated our thoughts, and questioned us to make our ideas clearer and practical. Her thoughtful edits and recommendations have made this a better book for school communities. We appreciate her dedication throughout the entire process. Thank you to

Jessica Vidal for translating the family letters and activities to Spanish. We also want to thank Natasha Bhogal, Gillian Dickens, Margaret O'Connor, and the whole production team. We would also like to thank the reviewers for their time and extremely helpful feedback.

Publisher's Acknowledgments

Corwin gratefully acknowledges the contributions of the following reviewers:

Avital (Tali) Amar
Math Consultant
Centre for Leadership and Learning
Curriculum and Instructional Services for York Region District School Board
Newmarket, ON

Delise Andrews
Mathematics Coordinator
Lincoln Public Schools
Lincoln, NE

Richard Cox Jr.
STEAM Lab Facilitator, Instructional Coach
Bullitt County Schools, Old Mill Elementary
Mt. Washington, KY

Francis (Skip) Fennell, PhD, DHL
L. Stanley Bowlsbey Professor of Education and Graduate and Professional Studies Emeritus
Project Director, Elementary Mathematics Specialists and Teacher Leaders Project
Past President, National Council of Teachers of Mathematics
Past President, Association of Mathematics Teacher Educators
McDaniel College, Westminster, MD

Lori Mueller
Mathematics Consultant
Great Prairie Area Education Agency
West Point, IA

John W. Staley
National Council of Supervisors of Mathematics President 2015–2017
Coordinator, Division of Research, Accountability, and Assessment
Baltimore County Public Schools, MD

Introduction

An Invitation to Turn Around

The spirit of hope, inner strength, enthusiasm and persistent determination are the pillars for any success.

—Lailah Gifty Akita

What if it were possible to capture all the words that we said to and about each and every student and put them in a giant word cloud? Furthermore, what if the giant word cloud floated above and followed the student throughout the school day and accumulated year after year? What would those words look like? Sound like? Feel like? Look at the two word clouds in Figure i.1. What comes to mind? How would you respond to having each of these word clouds floating above your head as you went about your day?

FIGURE i.1: Word Clouds

Source: Word clouds created using wordcloud.com. Images courtesy of iStock.com.

Unfortunately, the word clouds for some students may be filled with negative, deficit-based words that drain students' motivation and interest in learning, such as those you see on the left. However, teaching with a strengths-based conviction, more often using the language you see on the right, isn't easy. As teachers, particularly teachers of mathematics, we have been carefully taught that our role is to diagnose, eradicate, and erase students' misconceptions—in other words, even in the best of classrooms with the best formative assessment practices, we are taught to focus on the aspects of a child's work that demonstrate their challenges in order to determine where to take them next. Rather than viewing teaching as what Paulo Freire (1972) compared to banking, by making deposits in children, he prompts the educational community to recognize the knowledge and expertise that exist within the learner. He eloquently explains, "The teacher is of course, an artist, but being an artist does not mean that he or she can make the profile, can shape the students. What the educator does in teaching is to make it possible for the students to become themselves" (p. 181). Learning, in its natural state, invites the learner to bring forth experiences, ideas, culture, feelings, passions, and interests into the learning experience. When students learn this way, they flourish. This is the essence of strengths-based instruction. Looking for and showcasing students' strengths recognizes the learner as valuable, competent, and important.

> **Strengths-Based:** The strong points and the internal fortitude that students and teachers can build from; they are the collection of assets that support learning and teaching.

Why Strengths-Based Instruction?

Children may regularly hear:

> *"You didn't do well on the math test we had yesterday."*
> *"You need to listen more carefully."*
> *"Take your time with this test, it is important that you do better this time."*
> *"Your work showed you still do not know your facts."*

What if teachers heard each day:

> *"Your students are not learning the math standards."*
> *"I hope your math lesson is better today."*

What if we regularly were only told what we don't do well? That environment would make it hard to stay in our chosen profession. We would likely be discouraged, be disheartened, and feel inadequate for the task. How can children who are likely less equipped with emotional strategies do any better?

If you think they can't, you're right. What we are proposing in this book is that shifting from an attention to students' weaknesses to an emphasis on their strengths is an essential revolution. We believe this revolution holds a great deal of promise to fill classrooms with the following:

- Students eager to learn more mathematics
- Students who are more willing to persevere and engage in productive struggle
- Students who build agency that they can solve problems and think mathematically
- Students who think about what they are learning in mathematics at other times of the day—besides math class
- Teachers and students who develop a passion for the possibilities that mathematical literacy facilitates
- Teachers who relish the deeply positive and productive relationships they develop with students
- Families who grow in their desire to have their children become mathematical thinkers
- Families who enjoy mathematics at home in ways they didn't experience when the they were in school
- Communities that are filled with members who understand mathematics and can use it to solve problems at home and at the workplace
- Community members who will not be scammed because they didn't grasp mathematical ideas important to function in our economy
- Community members who believe they "can do math"

As the pebble of this idea of strengths-based teaching is tossed into the lake—the ripples are endless.

Who Is Strengths-Based Mathematics Teaching For?

Strengths-based mathematics teaching is for each and every educator or family member in all school contexts. Teachers and leaders can use strengths-based mathematics teaching to design lessons, organize their classrooms, provide feedback, engage in professional learning communities, and communicate with families. This approach benefits all students, including those who repeatedly have difficulty in mathematics, those who sometimes need support, multilingual learners, those with specific learning challenges, and those who may not exhibit learning challenges but instead relish challenges. In other words, strengths-based instruction supports students to recognize their value, develop an identity as a competent learner, increase their confidence, and engage in learning with clarity and purpose (Anderson, 2000).

For students, having a teacher—any teacher—who sleuths out and capitalizes on their strengths in mathematics can stimulate more engagement and eagerness to learn and make for a more positive and productive learning environment as a whole.

Look at Figure i.2. What do you think these data represent? What is the story behind them?

FIGURE i.2: Tally of Comments

STRENGTH COMMENTS	DEFICIT COMMENTS
IIII	HHT HHT HHT HHT HHT IIII

Imagine the conversations you hear daily about students' mathematics ability. In a study by one of the authors (Kobett, 2016), teachers were asked to describe the mathematics strengths of several of the students who were experiencing challenges with learning mathematics in their classes. The teachers were unable to describe any. Then the students' family members were asked the same question. The parents, extended family, or guardians were able to provide details of multiple strengths their children had in mathematics. Some of the family comments included

- Charlie loves to count everything! He is always counting and comparing amounts.
- Nyia tells me that she likes when they do fractions at school. She cooks with me at home a lot and says fractions make sense to her.
- Alonso plays checkers with his grandpa and is learning to play chess. He beats everyone but his grandpa!

Fourteenth-century Persian poet Shams-ud-din Muhammad Hafiz (ca. 1320–1389) wrote, "The words we speak become the house we live in." This phrase illustrates the power of the words we use. As we describe children in varying ways, we situate their position as learners in an instructional environment. The late, well-known influential thinker about business management Peter Drucker (2005) stated, "And yet, a person can perform only from strength. One cannot build performance on weaknesses, let alone on something one cannot do at all" (p. 100). If our goal is to deliver excellent mathematics instruction to each and every one of our students, we need to heed these words and think of ourselves as strength detectives. To explore this idea more deeply, first imagine a learner you have worked with in the past year who has struggled in mathematics. Write three to five words below that you have heard others use to talk about or describe this student.

What do you notice about the words? If you are like many people we have posed this task to, the words can be perceived as negative, maybe even derogatory, and they tend to detail what the student cannot do. In a recent workshop, we asked teachers and counselors to write the words they had heard about students who were currently struggling in mathematics (Figure i.3).

FIGURE i.3: Deficit-Based Descriptors of Students

low slows	Under-achieving	"Too Slow"	Bad Attitude Apathetic
Confused	Can't/don't get it	Doesn't Know Basic Facts	"Regular Class"
Struggling	Lack Basic Skills	Doesn't show her work!	Language Barrier
low level	Difficulty Communication	"Can't do Word problems"	don't want to work
low levels			

Now, imagine what hearing these phrases might be like for a student who is struggling. Imagine if you were the student they were describing. Of course, you wouldn't necessarily have heard those words spoken about you, but you might have overheard a conversation or two. Or, you might just get the feeling that the educators you are working with don't think you can be successful in mathematics or even have low expectations about your ability to learn any new mathematical ideas. If we call attention to the idea that the words teachers use to describe their students might influence how other professionals respond to them, we understand the power of Shams-ud-din Muhammad Hafiz's quotation. Consider these descriptions in Figure i.4 and reflect about how you might respond as a teacher to each of these students.

FIGURE i.4: Teacher Descriptions

"This student is never prepared for class! He rarely does homework. He is easily distracted and gets off track all the time. He doesn't know many of the basic addition facts and still counts on his fingers! He is very physical and seems to be moving all the time."	"This student will persevere through anything. He never gives up. He responds well to redirection and is very well liked among the other students. He is very athletic and loves to move around the classroom to work in different spots. He responds really well to collaborative activities."

Would it surprise you to learn that the *same* teacher wrote these descriptions about the *same* child? The first was written before engaging with the notion of a strengths-based approach in a professional development experience and the second after an extensive professional development experience. As the teacher began to focus on the student's assets rather than his deficits, there was a shift not only in her words but also in her actions. The teacher then used those assets in designing lessons based on the strengths the student brought to the learning experience. She shared, "Before [strengths-based work] I would perseverate on what he couldn't do—and I often reminded him of that! He would just slump down in the chair. Oh, yes, I was positive and told him he could learn, but I was so focused on building off his weaknesses, I couldn't see beyond that." Ron Kral (1995), author of *Strategies That Work,* explains: "If we ask people to look for deficits, they will usually find them and their view of situations will be colored by this. If we ask people to look for successes, they will usually find them and their view of situations will be colored by this" (p. 35).

We have a natural tendency to bolster students' performance by identifying their challenges, describing them in great detail, and focusing on what students do not know. After all, the business of education is to promote student learning. It will always be important to understand students' learning, academic, and social-emotional challenges. However, leveraging their strengths to address their challenges yields greater success than marshaling efforts into overcoming weaknesses and deficits (Clifton & Harter, 2003).

We believe that each and every teacher possesses mathematics teaching strengths and that every student possesses mathematics learning strengths. Our goal is to help you discover, embrace, and grow your mathematics teaching strengths to best support your students. Equally important, we want you to uncover and nurture your students' mathematics strengths.

Rather than having teachers and families who fixate on the lowest grades and ignore the higher scores, students need teachers to invest more time in using their areas of strength to build bridges to areas that need attention. Otherwise—with consistent negative messaging—children will feel disheartened, be disenfranchised, and ultimately may begin wanting to avoid going to school. It's a slippery slope that we as teachers are in the best position to prevent.

> With consistent negative messaging—children will feel disheartened, be disenfranchised, and ultimately may begin wanting to avoid going to school.

What Are Mathematics Strengths We See in Students?

When we first started doing this work, we were asked for a list of mathematics strengths and we resisted. Why resist, you may wonder? We worried that students might be pigeonholed into particular strengths, much like the myth of specific learning styles (Riener & Willingham, 2010). But then we found we enjoyed sharing the multiple strengths of different students we knew and worked with. The activity actually pointed to new ways of thinking about strengths in mathematics beyond the idea that strengths equaled mathematics content knowledge. We found that some strengths on our list were dispositional, others related to processes and practices, and then others were specific to content knowledge. We know this is not an exhaustive accounting of all options, and hence, our original caution remains. But, we'd like to share our initial thoughts with you and hope you will send to us and share with your colleagues lists of other strengths that you identify from your practice (Figure i.5).

Once we began the strengths-based work with students, we discovered more strengths that students possess, and more important, students identified their own and one another's strengths. We also noticed that students possessed multiple strengths that ebb and flow within and around particular content areas and within particular contexts. It is important to recognize that this strengths-finding work is dynamic—ever changing in response to the beliefs and expectations of those who teach and support the students.

FIGURE i.5: Student Strengths

DISPOSITIONAL	PROCESSES AND PRACTICES	CONTENT
• Perseveres	• Creates varied representations (e.g., manipulatives, drawings, numberlines)	• Understands concepts
• Works well with other students	• Sketches mathematical ideas	• Understands and uses procedures
• Uses novel or creative approaches	• Links manipulatives to abstract concepts	• Uses number sense
• Compromises with others when working on strategies and solutions	• Explains strategies and ideas	• Identifies and understands patterns
• Knows when to ask for help	• Explains thinking	• Converts measurements
• Asks good questions	• Connects mathematical concepts and procedures	• Connects real-world problems
• Takes risks	• Listens to others' ideas	• Regularly estimates quantities
• Recognizes making mistakes is part of learning	• Uses and applies appropriate mathematical vocabulary	• Has algebra sense
• Can teach/mentor others	• Identifies and understands patterns	• Has graph sense
• Demonstrates a positive attitude towards mathematics	• Enjoys solving puzzles	• Has fraction sense
• Enjoys mathematics	• Enjoys finding another way to solve a problem	• Has spatial sense
• Sees mathematics as a way to understand the world	• Regularly seeks multiple ways to solve problems	• Has number sense
• Listens to others' ideas	• Uses reasoning	• Visualizes mathematics
• Works well with other students	• Uses manipulatives well	• Knows basic math facts
• Works independently	• Perseveres	• Understands and regularly uses mental math
• Is curious about mathematical ideas		• Interprets information from a chart, table, or graph
		• Converts measurements

DISPOSITIONAL	PROCESSES AND PRACTICES	CONTENT
• Enjoys finding another way to solve a problem • Creates mathematics problems • Brainstorms new approaches	• Works analytically • Knows when responses are reasonable • Thinks and works logically • Explains mathematical information • Identifies important and unimportant information • Justifies results • Translates data into different forms • Thinks flexibly • Organizes information • Uses novel or creative approaches • Appropriately sequences multiple steps or directions • Asks probing questions • Regularly seeks multiple ways to solve problems	• Remembers and uses previously learned mathematics ideas • Understands concepts • Identifies the correct operation • Regularly estimates quantities • Explains the meaning of procedures

Exploring Your Own Math Identity

Before we can think further about how we identify our students' strengths, take a moment to consider your own experiences with learning mathematics. What do you remember most? What messages did you hear about your mathematics performance? Before reading further, write a memory down. Don't censor your memory; just let it come to you.

_____

_____

_____

What do you notice about the memory? Were you judged? Coaxed? Reassured? Championed? Shamed? Supported? Praised? Energized? Take a moment to feel what it felt like in your memory. If you had to identify one feeling that matches that moment, what would it be?

Now, consider how that one memory may have shaped your beliefs. Did you emerge from this experience with a belief that you were a mathematics learner, adept problem solver, and capable of achieving the highest levels of mathematical understanding? Or did you feel that you were "not a math person" or "just not smart in math" or maybe you began to identify as someone who struggles with learning mathematics?

Finally, we wonder, did you have people in your life who acted as mathematics role models? Did you see math learners who looked like you in school or in your community? Did you have a teacher or family member who encouraged you to study higher levels of mathematics? At a mathematics teachers' conference, a panel of people who work in STEM (science, technology, engineering, and mathematics) fields were asked what was their trajectory to getting to this job they hold. Each panel member pointed directly back to a teacher they had who inspired them or in some cases pushed them to continue in mathematics. To a person, they felt that their teacher lighted and fueled a flame from a spark. Did you have such a teacher? Or possibly a family member? If yes, how did they support your math identity? If no, how did the absence of a mathematics role model affect your notion about who excels at mathematics?

Our own teaching decisions are influenced by so much of our own experiences. We carry our lived experiences of learning mathematics into our classrooms. Our mathematics identity is constructed through our own very special and curated collection of involvements inside and outside of the classroom, through our interactions around mathematics learning, and through the relationships we have formed with our families, peers, teachers, and communities. Imagine that this identity begins from our earliest moments experiencing mathematics, is still formulating now, and extends to the future. **Mathematical identity** can be defined as "the dispositions and deeply held beliefs that students develop about their ability to participate and perform effectively in mathematical contexts and to use mathematics in powerful ways across the contexts of their lives" (Aguirre, Mayfield-Ingram, & Martin, 2013, p. 14). Given this definition, we wonder, do you find yourself feeling powerful about the role of mathematics in your life? Fortunately, mathematical identity is not a fixed trait. It is malleable (Boaler, 2013) and can be changed at any time—for better or, unfortunately, for worse. You play an important role in not only the advancement of students' mathematics knowledge but also the process of their development of a positive math identity instead of an identity of failure. Let's harken back to the words of the members of the STEM panel described earlier and realize that as a teacher, you have the opportunity—and the responsibility—to help shape students' mathematical identity into one of success and empowerment, rather than failure. You are a critical piece of their evolution. We hope that as you build a positive, energetic, and strengths-based approach for your students that your own mathematical identity will flourish, in tandem, with your students seeing themselves as a "math person."

> Mathematical Identity: The dispositions and deeply held beliefs that students develop about their ability to participate and perform effectively in mathematical contexts and to use mathematics in powerful ways across the contexts of their lives (Aguirre, Mayfield-Ingram, & Martin 2013, p. 14).

Moving to a Strengths-Based Perspective

Let's revisit the word clouds we introduced at the beginning of this chapter. There are any number of well-intended assessment and instructional practices that can actually turn into unproductive, harmful, deficit-based cycles. We call these vicious cycles because they do not help children grow mathematically. Let's explore three vicious cycles we commonly see.

First, let's consider how mathematics learners are often assessed. Far too frequently, progress monitors and screening tools are used to shallowly assess computation skills only, and we find that children have problems with computation skills. Unfortunately, these practices lead to interventions that only attend to computational skills and not the underlying conceptual understandings. We call this the Vicious Assessment Cycle, as illustrated in Figure i.6.

FIGURE i.6: The Vicious Assessment Cycle

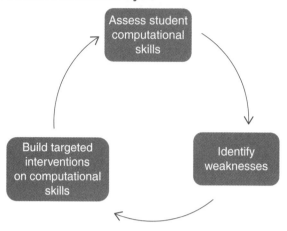

The heavy emphasis on "math facts" and computation as being the definition of mathematical learning is a century-old norm that measures children against a dominant and possibly antiquated and obsolete notion of what mathematics really is for a student at the elementary level. What would mathematics look like if computation with whole numbers was not the only implied major expectation for most classrooms? Should children learn the same way their parents and teachers learned to be deemed "successful" at mathematics? In essence, is there benefit to keeping the status quo? We think not. Such heavy emphasis on knowing the math computational facts through multiple years of instruction and interventions may hide students' abilities to learn other, deeper mathematical ideas. Although we agree that computational skills are critical, they will not be the only understandings students need to advance toward college and career goals. Instead, students may be limited by this oversimplification of what they are to learn and miss out on building their ability to communicate and reason mathematically. If some experts have described algebra as a gatekeeper for the high school student (Schoenfeld, 1995), fluency with basic facts is the gatekeeper for the elementary school student who struggles—particularly a student with disabilities. Many students who are challenged by mathematics never "get to" the more engaging mathematics and therefore never experience the beauty and joy of doing mathematics—two features of the discipline that could be motivating and energizing.

We see another vicious cycle around students' completion of classwork or homework. Students who struggle to complete classwork may be challenged for a variety of reasons. Students may not complete homework because they have other, more demanding responsibilities at home, including caring for siblings or other obligations. They may not understand the homework or the scope of the homework is overwhelming. Other students may not be able to access the homework because of language or learning differences. These homework challenges can create inequities by inequitably rewarding some students. When students are then required to miss recess or more engaging learning activities because they have not completed the work, they can become defeated by the overwhelming deluge of work stacking up. They may then believe that learning mathematics, and even school, is not for them. Not unlike how we often feel as teachers. We call this the Vicious Classwork or Homework Cycle (Figure i.7).

> **Many students who are challenged by mathematics never "get to" the more engaging mathematics and therefore never experience the beauty and joy of doing mathematics.**

FIGURE i.7: The Vicious Classwork or Homework Cycle

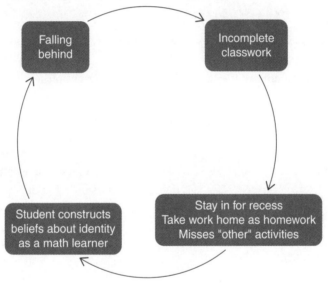

We often see a third vicious cycle occur when multilingual students are engaging in mathematics problem solving. Sometimes, well-intentioned teachers reduce the cognitive challenge of the problem in an effort to provide more access for multilingual learners when, in fact, this action reduces the students' access to rich mathematics learning opportunities. We call this the Vicious Low-Access Cycle (Figure i.8).

FIGURE i.8: The Vicious Low-Access Cycle

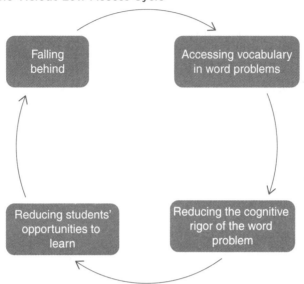

Practices That Build a Strengths-Based Cycle

Focusing attention solely on students' weaknesses or deficits can be mind-numbing and is neither professional nor ethical. Instead, how can we spot, target, and develop students' strengths? When students focus on their strengths as they often do with extracurricular activities like soccer, painting, dancing, or skateboarding, they are motivated and engaged. How can a similar transformation occur in the mathematics classroom?

> **"** . . . .
>
> Focusing attention solely on students' weaknesses or deficits can be mind-numbing and is neither professional nor ethical.

We need to initiate a model of "what's going right" and define what our strengths-based launching pad may be. What can we can build on rather than focusing exclusively on where the breakdowns are for students?

We suggest reframing this effort to one that emphasizes strengths and a problem-solving approach. This model is called the Strengths-Based Cycle.

This cycle begins with identifying strengths to support students' mathematics learning. By unpacking how a strength can be used to leverage a challenge, teachers and students are empowered in that moment and for a lifetime.

Following are two different examples of this cycle in action. In the first cycle (Figure i.9), students' strengths are identified first, and then teachers can develop targeted interventions or lessons. From there, students use their strengths to engage in and learn mathematics.

For example, Timmy struggles with timed assessment of basic multiplication facts. Instead of timing Timmy on a worksheet of basic facts, hoping he'll miraculously get faster, his teacher, Mandi, conducts an interview with Timmy to identify the strategies he uses to solve these facts. She first determines which facts he knows and those he struggles to remember. She discovers that he knows all his doubles, twos, and fives by memory. She shows him all that he knows, and then she introduces the near doubles strategy next, beautifully leveraging what he knows to access those facts that currently stump him. Next, she selects a fact that he doesn't know, 4 × 6, and asks him to make a 4 × 6 array using cubes. She then probes, "Let's see if we can find one of the doubles facts that you know in your 4 × 6 array." Timmy immediately notices the 4 × 4 array (Figure i.9).

FIGURE i.9: 4 × 6 Array

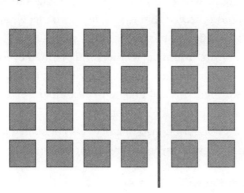

Mandi then asks, "What other fact represents the other part of the array?" Timmy replies, "Oh it is my two fact: 2 × 4 = 8! So, 4 × 6 is the same as 4 × 4 and 4 × 2!" She says to Timmy, "You used the facts you knew to learn a new fact! Let's see if we can try that for another fact!" As this scenario illustrates, Mandi engages Timmy in the Strengths-Based Cycle (Figure i.10) by first designing a concept-based assessment to identify his strengths, build a targeted intervention that engages him in doing mathematics, and develop connections from prior knowledge to new knowledge.

FIGURE i.10: Strengths-Based Cycle

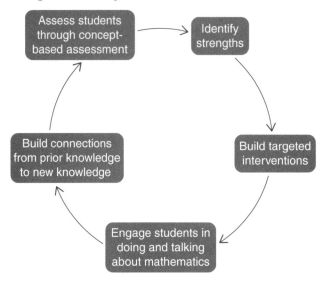

Figure i.11 illustrates another example of the Strengths-Based Cycle. Bob discovered through individual assessments that his multilingual students demonstrate their strengths when they can use visual images to accompany the problems. He also has observed that his students thrived when they had opportunities to talk about the problem with other multilingual learners first before discussing with nonmultilingual learners. He planned every lesson for students to engage in multiple discourse opportunities throughout every lesson. In addition, he designed visual images to accompany each lesson. For example, he created visual images for mathematics vocabulary such as add, subtract, problem, and so on. These two practices also benefited all his students and, therefore, became a regular part of his teaching practice.

FIGURE i.11: Strengths-Based Cycle in Action

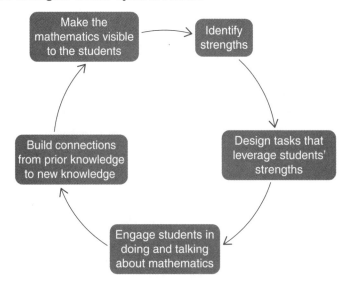

Again, Bob started with his students' strengths, recognizing when his multilingual students were strongest. He made a conscious effort to look for moments of brilliance, strength, competence, and confidence. When he saw those moments, he collected data about what the students were doing at that exact moment. Next, he designed mathematics tasks that were rich with visuals and that integrated opportunities for the students to engage in discourse with multilingual and nonmultilingual peers. As the students were working, he circulated about the room, listening in on their conversations and observing their representations. He paired students to present mathematical ideas to the rest of the class, giving them time to prepare their representation and rehearse their presentation. Finally, he recognized the contributions of the students, highlighted their strengths, and publicly posted their mathematical thinking.

These examples highlight strengths-based classrooms, where teachers see their students' brilliance and use their strengths to build confident, thoughtful mathematical thinkers.

The Five Teaching Turnarounds

It's time to turn those vicious cycles around! We have organized this book around five Teaching Turnarounds that promote strengths-based mathematics teaching and learning.

These Teaching Turnarounds are based on practices in which we have firsthand experience turning around for ourselves and that we have facilitated for educational communities. Through these five Teaching Turnarounds, we explore how to promote a positive and productive learning environment that will illuminate the strengths, resources, knowledge, brilliance, and power that students and teachers hold. Join us on this mathematical strengths-finding adventure to seek out and celebrate your students' individual and collective mathematical superpowers.

Teaching Turnaround One: Identify Your Teaching Strengths

Understanding your own teaching strengths is a bit like putting on an oxygen mask in an airplane when you are traveling with a child. You must first know your own teaching strengths before you can

> " Understanding your own teaching strengths is a bit like putting on an oxygen mask in an airplane when you are traveling with a child.

begin the work of supporting your students' strengths. Chapter 1 will help you explore your own teaching strengths and capitalize on those strengths in productive and positive ways. Leveraging your strengths can help you capture and sustain joy in mathematics teaching, which leads to student learning success for your students and for you—a positive and productive career.

Teaching Turnaround Two: Discover and Leverage Your Students' Mathematical Strengths

This teaching turnaround will help you strategically discover your students' many mathematics strengths. Changing our mindsets from peering through the deficit lens we've been taught to use to instead locating assets requires specific shifts in thinking and teaching practices. You will be invited to discover your students' strengths by carefully observing and recording the moments when your students shine and by asking them, "What are you good at in _____?" Remarkably, once we hone our strengths-based observation skills, we find that the strengths spotting multiplies. In Chapter 2, you will explore the dispositions, processes, and practices that teachers facilitate and that the students exhibit while learning mathematics. Chapter 3 focuses on content and explores how students demonstrate strengths when learning and accessing mathematics concepts and procedural understanding.

Teaching Turnaround Three: Design Instruction From a Strengths-Based Perspective

This teaching turnaround focuses on designing mathematics instruction—primarily through grouping practices, content-specific task design, and feedback practices—that leverages students' strengths to achieve mathematics goals. Students who struggle with mathematics often do not frequently experience mathematics success. Without these successful moments, they may not build the network of understanding that connects mathematics strategies and promotes learning. By strategically designing instruction that promotes students' strengths, teachers leverage those strengths to counteract and respond to areas where students struggle most. Explore this turnaround in Chapters 4, 5, and 6.

Teaching Turnaround Four: Help Students Develop Their Points of Power

This teaching turnaround positions students as the central force in identifying and celebrating their strong points: Points of Power. Many students (and adults) wrongly perceive their mathematical abilities as weak, and often this belief is reinforced by messages about their test performance. Here, in Chapter 7, we emphasize the importance of improving students' positive attitudes toward mathematics as a discipline and their ability to persevere and guide their own visualization of a future where mathematics plays a key role. Possessing a positive vision makes jumping into investigations and problem solving with a can-do approach as appealing as the next level on a video game—"I will try and I can do it!"

Teaching Turnaround Five: Promote Strengths in the School Community

This teaching turnaround focuses on specific steps that you can take to promote a strengths-based perspective with colleagues (Turn Around Professional Learning Communities, Chapter 8) and families (Turn Around Family Communication, Chapter 9) in your school and school district. These strategies can be supported through professional learning communities or networks and be the impetus working as teams through Whole-School Agreements.

In the following chapters, we explore each of the Teaching Turnarounds in depth. We also invite you to explore the ideas in four distinct ways: Turnaround Tip, Spotlight on Your Practice, and Try It!

- *Turnaround Tip* includes brief suggestions or reflections that you can make to transform the way you might think about or approach your teaching.

- *Spotlight on Your Practice* activities are deep dives into your current teaching practice. These activities often require recording or charting your current practices and considering ways to change or refine your future practice. Questions will prompt you to reflect on how you can promote a strengths-based learning environment for your students. Many of these are available for download.

- *Try It!* has activities that you can try with students, families, and your learning community. Many of these are available for download.

- You will also find a companion website to this book (**resources .corwin.com/teachingturnarounds**) that includes many tools and printables for easy download and use as well as a Reader's Guide that you can use to reflect with a group on how some of what you learn in this book may apply to your practice as individuals and as an educational community.

Don't delay—your strengths-based classroom is a Turnaround away!

Notes

_____

_____

_____

_____

_____

_____

_____

_____

_____

_____

_____

_____

_____

_____

_____

_____

_____

_____

_____

_____

PART ONE

Teaching Turnaround One
Identify Your Teaching Strengths

Turnaround One: Identify Your Teaching Strengths is the topic of Chapter 1. It focuses on you, the teacher, the change agent, the classroom leader, and the champion for children who sets the tone and establishes the learning environment for each and every one of your students. While you may be tempted to move to the next Teaching Turnaround because you want to know how to help your students, we ask you to take a deep breath and focus on **you** for a moment.

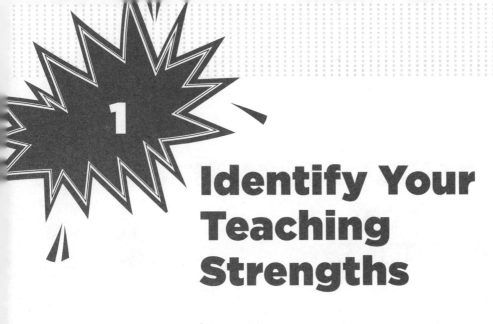

Identify Your Teaching Strengths

With the new day comes new strengths and thoughts.

—Eleanor Roosevelt

When we ask teachers to identify their strengths, we often hear a deafening silence roll like a wave across the room. Inevitably, someone calls out, "How about if we tell you our weaknesses?" The teachers chuckle and, almost in perfect unison, breathe relief as they wait hopefully to see if we will redirect our question. We never do. Teachers aren't in the practice of identifying and exploring their strengths and less so publicly labeling them as such. They are, however, fully comfortable discussing what is not going well. In many ways, teachers and students have been conditioned to continuously and frequently unpack their deficits. To combat this mindset and to shift the focus on the inevitable, we use a process-oriented protocol workshop approach (Stratton-Berkessel, 2010) called Appreciative Inquiry (AI), to engage teachers in discovering their strengths in all aspects of teaching. Appreciative Inquiry is an organizational change theory that uses inquiry questions to focus on what is going well to create new possibilities (Cooperrider & Whitney, 2005). Appreciative Inquiry focuses us on the positive aspects of our lives and leverages these characteristics to address the negative aspects (White, 1996). The process includes a five-step approach (Define, Discover, Dream, Design, and Deliver) that

> In many ways, teachers and students have been conditioned to continuously and frequently unpack their deficits.

> **Appreciative Inquiry:** An inquiry process that focuses on what is working well to implement change.

we have adapted for preservice and inservice teachers to begin the process of identifying and leveraging their strengths for success. This process is most productive when you can engage with other teachers in sharing your thoughts and ideas.

SPOTLIGHT ON YOUR PRACTICE:
Your Strengths

Gather together in a professional learning community, find a partner, or reflect on your own to begin this important process.

EXPLORING YOUR TEACHING STRENGTHS FROM AN APPRECIATIVE INQUIRY PERSPECTIVE	
AI Stage: *Define*	*AI Define* **Prompt**
• Arrange yourselves in pairs to conduct interviews. • With a partner, share your story following the prompts to the right. (Actively listen and be prepared to retell your partner's story in the **Discover** stage that comes next.)	Think back on a point in your mathematics teaching. Think about a peak experience when you felt fully engaged and successful. 1. Tell your story (Paired Interviews). • Describe what was happening. • Who was involved? • What were you doing? • In what ways was this experience meaningful, energizing, engaging, and valuable to you and your students? • What strengths did you bring to this experience? 2. What are the characteristics you value most about yourself in this experience?

AI Stage: *Discover*	*AI Discover* **Prompt**
• Rearrange your pair into groups of four or six. • As you listen, record themes you noticed from the paired interview discussion on sticky notes. • Discuss how the themes might be grouped, organized, and named.	Share your partner's story in your small group. Think about the successful mathematics teaching stories you just heard. What can we discover about the common themes in our stories? In your groups, discuss 1. What themes do you notice in the stories about our mathematics teaching strengths? 2. What themes do you notice in what characteristics we **value about ourselves** in our successful mathematics teaching? 3. How can we organize these themes?
AI Stage: *Dream*	*AI Dream* **Prompt**

• Remain in groups of four to six.
 	
• Chart, draw, or record the group's ideas.
	Let's build on the themes we developed. What if you were regularly using your teaching strengths? Imagine what this teaching would look like. Imagine what you would be doing. Imagine what students would be doing.
	
	1. As you imagine, consider the following:
	
	  • Particular structures in the classroom environment
	
	  • Student engagement
	
	  • Selection of tasks
	
	2. Discuss with your group your thoughts and ideas from your imagining.
	
	3. What do you notice about the groups' ideas?
	
	4. Are these dreams out of reach or within grasp?

AI Stage: *Design*	*AI Design* **Prompt**
• Remain in your groups of four to six. • Make sure you have some chart paper and markers on hand. You may want additional materials such as construction paper.	Using the ideas from the group and the discussion of your teaching strengths, design a mathematics classroom environment where you regularly plan ways to use your strengths. Include as many details as possible. Be ready to share your design.

continued >>

>> continued

AI Stage: *Deliver*	*AI Deliver* Prompt
• Locate your original partners to discuss and reflect.	Think about your group's design for strengths-based instruction and all the designs that you heard about from the other groups. With your partner, discuss the following questions: 1. What can you do to bring your idea to a reality? 2. What is the smallest step you can take tomorrow? 3. How can you ensure that you will take this action?

 This template can be downloaded for use at resources.corwin.com/teachingturnarounds.

Reflect: How did this process help you identify your teaching strengths? How can you continue the work you started here?

 Turnaround Tip

Every day, challenge yourself to tell one person about at least one teaching strength you experienced and ask at least one other colleague to share a teaching strength from the day. Or, record your teaching strengths in a My Teaching Strengths Journal.

What Do You Believe About Your Students' Learning?

If asked explicitly to do so, most educators would state positive beliefs about their students. It is the comments made when, perhaps, teachers feel most vulnerable, tired, and even frustrated that underlying beliefs may slip out. Take a look at some comments (Figure 1.1) we have heard in our work with teachers, and also likely made ourselves, about students we teach.

FIGURE 1.1: Comments Made About Students

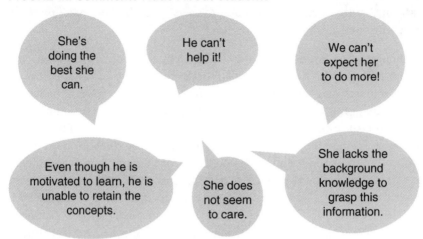

Each of these comments describes an underlying belief that a teacher has about students. While some of these comments might, at first, seem like they are caring and the teacher may describe them as such, they unintentionally undermine the work that teachers do to support students at the highest level. More important, they can—by word or behavior—potentially affect the students' beliefs about themselves.

A well-known study conducted by Rosenthal and Jacobson (1968), titled *Pygmalion in the Classroom*, examined how teachers' beliefs about their students and their teaching practices were influenced by the information they received about the first- and second-grade students they were going to teach. These teachers were told that about 20% of students had been tested and were found to be smarter and more able to learn at greater rates than other students. In reality, the students were randomly selected. Remarkably, the students perceived as "advanced" outperformed the other first and second graders!

Rosenthal and Jacobson's study sparked other researchers to test the Pygmalion effect in multiple contexts, including the preschool (Alvidrez & Weinstein, 1999) and college classrooms (McLeod, 1995). Even in these varied contexts, the teachers' beliefs about their students influenced their teaching practices and, ultimately, student

> The teachers' beliefs about their students influenced their teaching practices and, ultimately, student performance.

performance. In a recent study, Klehm (2014) found that teachers' attitudes about their students with disabilities to "learn and achieve higher level thinking was a significant predictor" (p. 236) of student performance on national assessments. Clearly, these studies help educators understand the critical role that teacher beliefs and expectations play for students in the teaching and learning environment.

Although often unintended, our beliefs may reflect biases, particularly about students who have different cultural, gender, language, and economic backgrounds than we do. Some groups of students have experienced discrimination in schools and suffer when their teachers make assumptions about their learning capabilities because they are different. Some schools create structures and policies that may "dehumanize" students and make it difficult to recognize the valuable contributions that each and every student makes to the mathematics classroom (Gutiérrez, 2017). Understanding our own biases and beliefs is the first critical step in uncovering, nurturing, and cultivating our own strengths as educators (Berry, 2008). Gutiérrez (2017) explains: "Not until we seek to stand in the shoes of our students, to understand their conceptions, will we will be on the path to recognizing and embracing their humanity" (p. 2).

Like a detective, it can be helpful to first examine a statement, determine the underlying belief, and then create an alternative, asset-based belief that contradicts or even challenges the initial belief. Through examination of these statements and beliefs, teachers, administrators, families, and other school leaders can begin the work of identifying key instructional practices that will address students' needs based on their strengths and potential.

Take a look at the statements, the underlying beliefs inherent in the statements, and alternative beliefs that emphasize assets and strengths (Figure 1.2). What do you notice?

> **"**
> The first step in changing the narrative is to consciously hear the language that we and others use to describe our students.

When we work to identify a belief that focuses on moving in a positive direction, we are more likely to interact with other teachers, our students, and families in more positive and productive ways. The first step in changing the narrative is to consciously hear the language that we and others use to describe our students. Truly examining the words that we use to describe our students will help us identify underlying and harmful beliefs that sabotage good teaching practices. In the Spotlight that follows (page 30), we invite you to explore your own beliefs about your students.

FIGURE 1.2: Shifting to Beliefs That Emphasize Students' Strengths

STATEMENT	UNDERLYING BELIEF	ALTERNATIVE BELIEF
She is doing the best she can.	She can't learn more.	She can learn math. We just need to find an entry point into her learning.
He can't help it.	He doesn't have self-control or self-regulation skills.	He has better self-control when he is able to select manipulatives, tools, and a place to work.
We can't expect her to do more.	She cannot learn more mathematics than she is currently learning. She is incapable of learning more.	If we raise our expectations and set success criteria in collaboration with the student, she will be able to achieve.
She lacks the background knowledge to grasp this information.	How much students can learn depends on the background knowledge they hold. Students are unable to learn without the right background knowledge.	She has solid knowledge about money. Let's use that knowledge to develop ideas about place value.
She does not care.	This student's behavior indicates that she does not value school.	The student's behavior indicates that we need to show her how much we care about her learning.
Even though he is motivated to learn, he is unable to retain the concepts.	Students who struggle with retention cannot learn mathematics.	I notice that he retains more when he is able to work with his peers to solve problems. Let's try pairing him with a classmate.
He can do this—he is just lazy.	Students choose to not work.	We need to find out why he does not complete his work.
You just need to tell them how to do it because they can't think on their own.	Direct instruction is best for students who struggle.	My students are capable of higher-level thinking and problem solving.
His parents don't care and can't help him.	Families that cannot attend conferences don't care about their child's learning.	Families care very much about their children's school success but don't always show it in the same way or in ways that resonate with teachers' own families.

SPOTLIGHT ON YOUR PRACTICE:
What Do You Believe?

We've spent some time unpacking some comments that we have heard; now it is your turn. Take a moment and really think about the students you teach. Shine the spotlight into your mathematics classroom on a student who is currently struggling and a student who is meeting expectations. Write down statements you have made or heard others make about each of the students in each box.

Student #1 _____   Student #2 _____

[ ]   [ ]

What kinds of underlying beliefs do you notice in these statements?

Next, select at least one alternative, asset-based belief for the student who is currently struggling and record it in each box.

Student #1 _____   Student #2 _____

[ ]   [ ]

- How does the asset-based belief redirect your thinking about the student who is currently struggling?

- How might an exercise like this promote strengths-based teaching?

 This template can be downloaded for use at resources.corwin.com/teachingturnarounds.

Consider this Turnaround Tip to empower the relationships you are building with your students.

 Turnaround Tip

Share your strengths-based belief with the student who is currently struggling and with other teachers who work with this student. Sharing our strengths-based beliefs with our students can improve our relationships with them.

What Do Students Think You Believe?

We know and observe regularly that teachers work diligently to develop positive relationships with all their students. Teachers who develop these close connections report that their students are more cooperative, demonstrate more self-directed behaviors, and exhibit higher levels of engagement (Birch & Ladd, 1997; Decker, Dona, & Christenson, 2007; Klem & Connell, 2004).

Students want their teachers to know them as special and unique learners who possess an array of strengths, weaknesses, and interests (Daniels & Perry, 2003). Not surprisingly, students' interest in classroom learning and their perception of their own abilities as learners are associated with their beliefs about the degree to which their teacher cares about them and recognizes them as unique learners (Daniels, Kalkman, & McCombs, 2001). Learning new content in innovative ways motivates students to not only engage in the learning at hand but also work harder. On the flip side, students express concerns about their mathematical skills when they are required to do repetitive work and as a result engage less in the task, perhaps associating the repetition with negative beliefs about the value of these tasks (Daniels & Perry, 2003). Being understood as a unique learner is clearly important to our students. While we have the most desirable intentions, we may unintentionally communicate unintended messages about what we believe our students are able to accomplish. These beliefs are often reinforced through the current heavy emphasis on standardized testing.

> Students want their teachers to know them as special and unique learners who possess an array of strengths, weaknesses, and interests (Daniels & Perry, 2003). 99

We can discover what our students believe about our behaviors as mathematics teachers by inviting conversations with them about the teaching and learning practices that they desire. You can start these informal conversations with individual students or with small groups, or more formally through a whole-class meeting. Record students' ideas on chart paper for later reference. Try the following conversations starters in your next class.

Try It! **Conversation Starters**

These conversation starters can be posed with individual students, small groups, or as a part of a community circle.

What do teachers do

- To help you feel encouraged to do your best in math class?
- To show you that they care about your learning?
- To help you learn math?
- To help you feel comfortable in speaking up to answer questions during math instruction?
- To get to know your likes and dislikes?
- To learn about what you are good at in math?
- To challenge you in math class?
- To help you when you don't understand math?
- To make you excited to learn more math?
- To help you work with your classmates and learn from others?

Surveys can also offer great opportunities to learn about students' beliefs about their teachers, schools, and learning environment. The Bill and Melinda Gates Foundation conducted a large-scale Measures of Effective Teaching (MET) project to determine which teacher and school factors contributed to student success and discovered that student survey results revealed that students were able to identify when and how they were challenged by their teachers, teacher clarity, expectations, and care for their students. Remarkably, the teachers who had higher student survey scores were linked with higher student achievement (MET Project, 2010). Not surprisingly, students recognize good teaching when they experience it! Surveys can be administered and data can be collected electronically through free survey options (Google Form, surveymonkey.com) or in paper format. While there are many validated survey instruments that can be purchased (e.g., Tripod, www.tripodproject.org; YouthTruth, www.youthtruthsurvey.org; My Student Survey, https://mystudentsurvey.com; and iKnowMyClass, www.iKnowMyClass.com), you can also design a survey of your own to learn more about what your students believe about your teaching.

The next Try It! is an example of questions that you can ask your students. If you choose to survey your students, it is important to collect this information anonymously so they can answer more openly. If you do not have access to technology, you can ask someone else to administer the survey to your students to soften any sense that there is an answer they should give.

 **Try It!**   **Students' Beliefs**

1. My teacher encourages me to do my best in math class.
    Always   Usually   Sometimes   Never

2. My teacher cares about me.
    Always   Usually   Sometimes   Never

3. My teacher knows what I am good at doing in math class.
    Always   Usually   Sometimes   Never

4. My teacher knows what I need help with in math class.
    Always   Usually   Sometimes   Never

5. My teacher knows what I like to learn in math class.
    Always   Usually   Sometimes   Never

6. My teacher thinks I can learn challenging math.
    Always   Usually   Sometimes   Never

7. During math instruction, my teacher is best at

    _____

 This survey can be downloaded for use at resources.corwin.com/teachingturnarounds.

SPOTLIGHT ON YOUR PRACTICE:
Monitoring Your Message

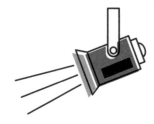

Video or audio record your classroom in five- to ten-minute segments throughout the day or over the course of the week. Make sure that you capture moments in your classroom during both mathematics teaching and transitional times.

As you watch or listen to your recordings, write down particular statements that you make that may indicate your underlying beliefs about your students. For example, you might say, "I know that you will be able use lots of strategies to solve this problem." Or "I am going to put you in groups to work on this task because you think of great ideas when you work together."

```

```

Statements: After recording these statements, consider the beliefs that you are communicating to the students and write them down.

Select one statement that you want to ensure that you continue to foster. How will you make certain that students continue to receive this important message?

```

```

Select one statement that you want to ensure that you change. How will you make certain that you change this message?

```

```

online resources ➤ This template can be downloaded for use at
resources.corwin.com/teachingturnarounds.

Implement this Turnaround Tip as a formative assessment about your own teaching practice.

Understanding the ways in which we communicate can be better interpreted by collecting evidence about our teaching practices. In the following Spotlight activity, teachers are invited to gather and analyze teaching data.

Sometimes it is helpful to develop visual reminders about our affirmative beliefs to help us focus on the positive messages we want to convey to our students.

Finally, we ask you to consider how your beliefs about your students, your own teaching strengths, and the messages you communicate to your students form a network of strength-building ingredients. In the Spotlight on the next page, we ask you to develop an action plan for each of the areas explored in this chapter.

 Turnaround Tip

Collect and share the results with your students and explain to them how you plan to either continue and/or improve a particular teaching practice. Include a list of action steps for implementation.

 Turnaround Tip

Develop your own affirmative belief statements and post them around the room. Share your belief statements with your students, families, and colleagues.

Summary

As you venture into exploring how your own strengths can empower you to identify your own capabilities and, in turn, find strengths in your students, your proficiency as a change agent emerges. By creating a habit of identifying your own positives rather than teachers' all too frequent common focus on their weaknesses, the tenor of the instructional experience moves to more solid relationships with the content and the students. Using the tenets of the Appreciative Inquiry model builds productive change on top of a foundation of what's working well. As mathematics teacher educators, the two of us often encounter teacher candidates who come to student teaching seminars or classes feeling that they can't reach a student or don't know how to "handle" an instructional situation. They, like many teachers who care deeply about their students, report that they can't sleep over these concerns and even cry as they talk about particular children. By refocusing their attention to their strengths, we ask them to immediately start journaling about this student and the small (or big) successes they can claim each day. They are surprised when they feel better about these situations as the initial tendency to focus on their frustrations is great. It is these transfers in attention that match the Try It! activities found in this chapter. We know this first step is really a leap. Ready for the next footstep forward? Let's go!

SPOTLIGHT ON YOUR PRACTICE:
Making Connections

In the first box, record an example. In the second box, consider an action plan item to implement in your classroom as a result of your learning.

What I Learned About My Beliefs	How Can I Ensure That I Believe in the Mathematics Ability of Each and Every Student?
What I Learned About My Strengths as a Mathematics Teacher	How Can I Continue to Showcase My Strengths in My Mathematics Classroom?
What I Learned About My Mathematics Teaching	How Can I Build on My Best Teaching Practices?

Notes

PART TWO

Teaching Turnaround Two

Discover and Leverage Your Students' Mathematical Strengths

Teaching Turnaround Two: Discover and Leverage Your Students' Mathematical Strengths is made up of two chapters that focus on the ways that teachers can build and support students' mathematics proficiencies, processes, practices, dispositions, and content strengths. In this chapter, we explore the ways students showcase their mathematical strengths within the mathematics processes and Standards for Mathematical Practice either from the Common Core or developed by your state (National Governors Association Center for Best Practices & Council of Chief State School Officers [NGA & CCSSO], 2010). This Turnaround focuses on searching for your students' mathematical strengths in terms of both their mathematical habits of mind and practices, as well as development of their content understanding. You'll find a number of activities to help you through this process as it relates to the mathematics standards in Grades K through 6 for number, operations, fractions, and geometry. We chose to highlight these conceptual areas as they represent some of the most challenging topics for students and teachers alike. We hope these activities help you to immediately hit the ground running looking for student strengths to build on every day.

2

Turn Around Mathematical Proficiencies, Processes, and Practices

Everytime I shoot a turnaround, I feel like nobody can block it.

—DeMar DeRozan

As we embark on the charge of strengths finding in mathematics, we must first challenge our own ideas about what it means to be "smart" in math. When most of us were learning mathematics as children, the title "Smart in Math" was often reserved for those students who could calculate quickest. Unfortunately, this trait is still commonly prized as the singular pinnacle of performance, and that is an unfortunate fallacy. This belief that *fast in calculating* equals *"smart in math"* can send a strong and incorrect signal to very talented mathematics students that they don't belong on the mathematics playground.

> This belief that *fast in calculating* equals *"smart in math"* can send a strong and incorrect signal to very talented mathematics students that they don't belong on the mathematics playground.

Cathy Seeley (2009), former president of the National Council of Teachers of Mathematics, explains,

> *Some students are good at seeing relationships among numbers, quantities, or objects. Others may be creative problem solvers, able to come up with nonroutine ways to approach an unfamiliar problem. Still*

others may be good at visually representing relationships or problems or translating from one representation to another—from a graph to a table, from an equation to a graph, or from a word problem to a pictorial model, for example. All of these students—and others—should have the opportunity to access mathematics from different entry points and become successful math students. A comprehensive mathematics program not only makes room for and nurtures all kinds of smart students, it also creates opportunities for students to expand the strengths they have to help them access other dimensions of mathematics. And it offers such opportunities to all students—even those who may be disenfranchised or disengaged with mathematics, often hidden in remedial programs or special classes. (p. 8)

There isn't one right strategy to solving mathematics problems, and there isn't one strength that qualifies someone as "smart" in mathematics. In this chapter and the next, we will explore how to recognize and build on your students' strengths in using and applying mathematical process, dispositions, and through a select set of content examples including operations, fractions, and geometry. While we know that the elementary mathematics content topics list is extensive, we hope that the collection of ideas presented here can be applied and adapted to your needs.

The variety and richness of mathematics dispositions, processes, and content offer many opportunities for teachers to design learning experiences for students to discover and build their strengths within particular mathematics concepts and support classmates' learning as strengths are revealed.

Turnaround Tip

Reflect on your own perceptions of what "smart" in mathematics means:

- What messages did you receive about who was "smart" in mathematics when you were in school?

- What might your own students say about what it means to be "smart" in mathematics in your class?

- How can we shift from the word *smart*? What is another term that we can get others to use?

Building Mathematical Proficiency Through a Strengths-Based Lens

Across mathematics content areas, students must develop a repertoire of understandings, skills, and dispositions to become doers of mathematics. We call these mathematical processes, practices, or habits of mind. The well-respected report titled *Adding It Up: Helping Children Learn Mathematics* (National Research Council & Mathematics Learning Study Committee,

2001) describes five components of mathematical proficiency that are central to successful mathematics learning: Conceptual Understanding, Procedural Fluency, Strategic Competence, Adaptive Reasoning, and Productive Disposition (p. 5). Each of these components offers particular and specific opportunities for students to showcase their strengths. While people may sometimes imagine that the students who learn mathematics quickest will be considered the strongest in mathematics, we want teachers to think about how their students *respond to* and *interact with* mathematics learning via each of these components and that, in doing so, they listen for whispers of their students' previously undetected strengths. Think about your own students, for example. While students in your class who currently struggle with learning mathematics don't often recognize their own strengths, it is in the ways they approach and learn mathematics that we can unearth their points of power. The following chart (Figure 2.1) includes each mathematical proficiency component from *Adding It Up*, its definition, and a brief description of what students look like when they are acting on these strengths.

FIGURE 2.1: Mathematical Proficiencies and Students' Strengths

COMPONENT	DEFINITIONS (NATIONAL RESEARCH COUNCIL & MATHEMATICS LEARNING STUDY COMMITTEE, 2001)	WHAT THIS COMPONENT LOOKS LIKE AS A STUDENT'S STRENGTH
Conceptual Understanding	Comprehension of mathematical concepts, operations, and relationships	Students who demonstrate strength in Conceptual Understanding want to understand the mathematics they are learning and even sometimes demand that the mathematics make sense. They often ask questions: • Why are we learning this? • Why don't we add the numerators *and* the denominators when we add fractions? • When we are dividing fractions using the procedure, why do we change the operation sign in the problem? You've never told me I could change the sign of the operation before when I've been using other operations. • Why do we call some numbers square numbers? Why do we call some numbers cube numbers?

continued >>

COMPONENT	DEFINITIONS (NATIONAL RESEARCH COUNCIL & MATHEMATICS LEARNING STUDY COMMITTEE, 2001)	WHAT THIS COMPONENT LOOKS LIKE AS A STUDENT'S STRENGTH
		When students make a comment when something doesn't make sense to them, that is an indication that they desire mathematics to be a sense-making experience. These students attempt to make spontaneous connections between mathematics content and prior knowledge because they are constantly searching for new connections to support their conceptual understanding. They are Conceptual Understanding seekers!
Procedural Fluency	Skill in carrying out procedures flexibly, accurately, efficiently, and appropriately	Again, this is not just about speed or memorization. Students who demonstrate strength in Procedural Fluency want to record their actions about mathematical problems using procedures, often represented by symbols, sometimes with words, and sometimes with a combination of symbols, sketches, and words. Early on, they construct their own procedures and recording approaches that document their thinking as a way to demonstrate their mathematics learning. Sometimes they use alternative procedures more quickly than standard procedures. These students may want to record equations first and then unpack the process with other kinds of representations such as concrete or semi-concrete or vice versa.
Strategic Competence	Ability to formulate, represent, and solve mathematical problems	Students who demonstrate strength in Strategic Competence thrive when representing their mathematical thinking. They sketch pictures, make graphs from data, and construct and use number lines, hundreds charts, and strip diagrams to solve problems. They may focus on one representation or choose to represent their thinking using multiple representations. These students flourish when they can select their own way to solve a problem or represent their thinking.

	Capacity for logical thought, reflection, explanation, and justification	Students who demonstrate strength in Adaptive Reasoning love to explain their work and hear about the approaches others used. They often remember details about their own work that may seem extraneous to others. For example, they may remember that they first attempted to solve a problem a particular way but changed the approach midstream. They thrive when they are offered opportunities to share their mathematical ideas with peers or other adults. They are typically more engaged when the problem is robust enough to require an explanation of the thinking process. These students also thrive when they apply mathematics they are learning to situations that reflect their interests, culture, or family contexts.
Adaptive Reasoning		
Productive Disposition	Habitual inclination to see mathematics as sensible, useful, and worthwhile, coupled with a belief in diligence and one's own efficacy	Students who demonstrate strength in Productive Disposition express interest and joy when learning mathematics. They are likely to join the after-school math club, even when they believe that mathematics isn't their best subject. They are just curious and fascinated. They work diligently, even when faced with obstacles. They try again when stymied. They understand that learning mathematics can be hard work and they will, therefore, often continue to work well after their peers have given up. They are not dissuaded by confusion. They believe that concentrated effort is the key to learning mathematics. Their motto is "Let me try that another way."

The following Spotlight on Your Practice invites you to contemplate your students' strengths from the perspective of the five National Research Council components for successful mathematics learning.

SPOTLIGHT ON YOUR PRACTICE:
Successful Mathematics Learning Components

Select two or three students in your class who are currently challenged to learn the mathematics your class is studying. Examine each of the five components of Mathematical Proficiency from *Adding It Up*, along with their component definition, and examples. Next, identify each student's mathematics strengths. Imagine how these students engage with mathematics learning to help you determine their corresponding strengths. Finally, provide a description and examples as evidence of this strength. Check out the example for ideas to help you develop your strength-spotting skills in Figure 2.2 and the blank template found online.

FIGURE 2.2: Template With Examples for Strength Spotting the Components of Mathematical Proficiencies

COMPONENT	STUDENT NAME	EVIDENCE
Conceptual Understanding	Hannah (Fractions)	Explains concepts well, uses multiple representations appropriately.
	Elaine	Connects concrete and abstract representations.
Procedural Fluency	Matthew	Develops "shortcuts" for procedures and can explain why he has developed the shortcut.
	Mari	Likes to share equations and steps for other students to record.
Strategic Competence	Jocie	Sketches representations for almost everything. Other students look to her representations to understand.
	Bri	Recognizes operations within word problems by acting out what she reads.

Adaptive Reasoning	Andy	Often notices patterns and summarizes other students' ideas in whole-group discussions. Will say things like, "Michael, Henri, and Maddy all used multiplication to solve the problem."
	Bettina	Is often the first to say, "This is kind of like when we …" Notices how operations are alike and uses mathematical properties to solve.
Productive Disposition	Lanie	Even when challenged, perseveres through problems. Last week, kept going for 25 minutes on one problem!
	Ahmed	Gets excited about every single math problem I introduce! Is ready for action!

online resources For a blank template for Strengths Spotting in the Components of Mathematical Proficiencies, go to resources.corwin.com/teachingturnarounds.

Building Mathematical Practices and Dispositions Through a Strengths-Based Lens

Understanding the National Council of Teachers of Mathematics (NCTM) Process Standards from 2000 supports our understanding of where the Standards for Mathematical Practice (NGA & CCSSO, 2010) and other state or provincial developed practices came from and how to design learning experiences that reflect these documents. The Standards for Mathematical Practices (NGA & CCSSO, 2010) are the behaviors and dispositions that we want students to engage in while doing mathematics. At the core of these practices are the NCTM Process Standards of Problem

Solving, Communication, Reasoning and Proof, and Connections and Representation. The Practices rest on important processes (NCTM, 2000) with long-standing importance in mathematics education. Figure 2.3 illustrates how the NCTM Process Standards support, inform, align, and connect to the Standards for Mathematical Practice.

FIGURE 2.3: Connections Between Mathematical Processes and Practices

NCTM PROCESS STANDARDS	STANDARDS FOR MATHEMATICAL PRACTICE
Problem Solving *(Connects to Standards 1–8)*	1. Make sense of problems and persevere while solving them.
Communication *(Connects to Standards 2, 3, 6)*	2. Reason abstractly and quantitatively. 3. Construct viable arguments and critique the reasoning of others.
Reasoning and Proof *(Connects to Standards 1, 4, 7, 8)*	4. Model with mathematics. 5. Use appropriate tools strategically.
Connections *(Connects to Standards 1, 7, 8)*	6. Attend to precision. 7. Look for and make use of structure.
Representation *(Connects to Standards 1, 4, 5)*	8. Look for and express regularity in repeated reasoning.

Source: NCTM (2000) and NGA & CCSSO (2010).

Building Strengths in Problem Solving

Students are natural problem solvers because the "world is new to them, and they exhibit curiosity, intelligence, and flexibility as they face new situations" (NCTM, 2000, p. 116). If unsure about this claim, take a few moments to watch students play a video game, strategize how to get out of homework, or finagle a few extra minutes of free recess. Students who show strength in problem solving like to solve all kinds of problems, including but not limited to mathematics problems, brainteasers, riddles, and puzzlers. These children cry out in dismay when teachers say that students need to stop their work now and that they will finish solving the task on another day. They may respond with a request to take tasks home to share with their families. They often demonstrate perseverance by persisting through a task even when they are "not there yet." They approach confusion as an opportunity for challenge rather than defeat. They aren't bored as they are busy thinking rather than trying to get attention in other ways. We have noticed that many of our students who struggle with other aspects of mathematics show strengths in problem solving because of their tremendous perseverance skills. Problem solving isn't just about the solution—it is about the process. All students need opportunities to engage in problem solving.

> " We have noticed that many of our students who struggle with other aspects of mathematics show strengths in problem solving because of their tremendous perseverance skills.

In the rush to complete mathematics prompts, some students equate speed with problem solving and often approach every kind of mathematics prompt with the same mindset about how much perseverance they will need and how much time they will need to solve it. As teachers, we casually use the word *problem* to indicate all kinds of mathematics work that we ask students to do. We say, "Please complete the next problem" when the problem looks like this:

- $8 + 5 =$ ___
- $5 \times 6 =$ ___
- $23.4 + 1.9 =$ ___
- Elena picked 14 flowers. She promised to pick 21 for her mother. How many more does she need to pick?
- Ellie and Tia are running a 10K race. Ellie and Tia started out together. Ellie runs every mile faster than Tia. What is happening to the distance between the two runners? Create a graph that represents the story (Williams, Kobett, & Harbin Miles, 2018).

Turnaround Tip

Support students' perseverance with problem solving by cutting out large letter Ps. Some teachers like to make the letter Ps using different kinds of paper, colors, and so on.

Place the Ps in a large jar for the students to see. As students are demonstrating perseverance, hand out a P to the student and describe what you are seeing. They may try to assemble a collection!

Source: Image created by Bob Ronau.

Some of these prompts will cue students to engage at varying levels of problem-solving depth and perseverance. Therefore, it is critical that students recognize different kinds of problems, and tasks will require different ways of engaging with the problem. A true problem involves a question that cannot be immediately answered. What is a problem at one time to one person may be an **exercise** to another person depending on the students' developmental growth. Students truly enjoy opportunities to evaluate whether a mathematics prompt is indeed a problem and then determine what behaviors they will need to solve it. One way to help students differentiate between a problem and a nonproblem is to create a checklist.

> **A true problem involves a question that cannot be immediately answered.**

Exercise: A problem with a known solution path.

SPOTLIGHT ON YOUR PRACTICE:

Spotting Strong Problem-Solving Behaviors

FIGURE 2.4: List of Ways to Spot Students' Strengths in Problem Solving

SPOTTING STRONG PROBLEM-SOLVING BEHAVIORS	
Students—Do They ...	Teachers—Do You ...
• Persevere through problems even when you are confused? • Ask questions such as, "I wonder if I tried ... and I wonder what would happen if I ...?" • Find multiple solution pathways? • Find unique solutions? • Interpret the problem in a different way than you first thought? • Make connections between problems? • Remember another similar problem?	• Encourage students to persevere by calling attention to students who continue to solve the problem amid confusion? • Select tasks for students to showcase their perseverance? • Give students a "walk-back" option by explicitly helping them connect to prior knowledge to break a barrier they are facing? • Engage students in creating different ways to show their solutions through such means as concrete materials, visuals, or verbal presentations?

	• Offer students different kinds of problem-solving options:
	
	  – Alone?
	
	  – Partner?
	
	  – Group?

Teachers can build an environment for students to develop problem-solving strengths by taking these three steps:

1. Look for and recognize when students are showing signs of general problem-solving skills (e.g., "I noticed that you were persevering through the task on your own.").

2. Invite students to help solve a classroom problem or engage in classroom decision making (e.g., "We only have a few minutes of class. What do you think we should do with the math time we have left?").

3. Design tasks that foster and highlight students' problem-solving skills (e.g., "I am so interested in watching you use your problem-solving skills with fractions, so I have designed a special task today for you.").

I know a mathematics prompt is a problem when ...

- I don't know how to solve the problem right away.
- I need patience to solve the problem.
- I need to try a few different strategies.
- I may need to start the problem over or work backward.
- I may need to talk about my idea with a partner.

Remember, at all times you are the official strength spotter in the room! The preceding Spotlight is a chart of what you might see in students and what you need to do to encourage these behaviors. Check out our list (Figure 2.4), and then add your own ideas.

In the following Try It!, students are invited to explore the characteristics that make a problem.

 **Try It!**   **Is It a Problem?**

Use the problem-solving checklist to decide if the following mathematics prompts (Figure 2.5) are problems. DO NOT SOLVE THE PROBLEM! Be prepared to share and explain your group's decisions.

FIGURE 2.5: Possible Problem Examples

I know there are 9 animals in the barnyard. Some are chickens and some are cows. I counted 24 legs in all. How many of the animals are chickens and how many are cows?	34 × 12	Find the area of the room using an object you have with you.

After students have sorted, ask the following questions:

- Which did you select as fitting into the category of a problem? Why?
- If you were going to solve the mathematics prompt, what would you need to do to be able to solve the problem?
- Why is it important to notice the kind of mathematics thinking a problem is asking you to do?
- Are there other ideas you'd like to add to the problem-solving checklist?

 You can find this resource at resources.corwin.com/teachingturnarounds.

Building Strengths in Communication

Communicating about mathematics is a critical part of a positive and productive mathematics environment and includes both listening and speaking. Students' strengths in communication may be revealed in several ways. Some students explain their mathematical ideas orally, while other students organize their thinking and communicate mathematically by using sketches, models, manipulatives, or some combination. Other students listen intently, ask really good questions, or notice small details about a classmate's idea. Teachers should recognize both listening and speaking as separate kinds of communication strengths and leverage those strengths in ways that honor the students. You can nurture communication skills by providing multiple opportunities for students to "share ideas and clarify understandings, construct convincing arguments regarding why and how things work, develop a language for expressing mathematical ideas, and learn to see things from other perspectives" (NCTM, 2014, p. 29). As students begin to share their mathematical ideas, they need teachers and peers to listen attentively and ask good questions that probe reasoning and sense making. We suggest that you plan at least three strategic moments in every lesson for students to communicate their ideas with one another. You might plan strategic mathematics communication moments throughout your lesson. This next Try It! can help you support students in using various communication strengths while contributing to a group presentation.

> " As students begin to share their mathematical ideas, they need teachers and peers to listen attentively and ask good questions that probe reasoning and sense making.

 **Try It!**   Communication Strengths

Arrange students with different communication strengths in a group to prepare a presentation for the rest of the class. Explain to the them that you are placing them in groups based on their different strengths.

ORAL EXPLANATION	LISTENING	USING MODELS
• Organized explanation	• Listens to others speak	• Uses tools strategically
• Explains reasoning	• Does not interrupt	• Explains why tools were selected
• Explains different strategies used	• Asks strategic follow-up questions that connect to the strategy or solution	• Model matches the problem
• Uses precise vocabulary		

Presentation: Design a five-minute presentation of your strategies and solution for the class. All members of the group must participate in the presentation and showcase their strengths.

For more ideas about how to build and leverage students' strengths in communication, please see Chapter 6.

Building Strengths in Reasoning and Proof

Students naturally desire that the mathematics they are learning makes sense. Students reason about mathematics *while* they are learning concepts as they experiment with strategies as they seek solution pathways. Mathematics reasoning must be strategically planned and fostered by teachers because "the ability to reason systematically and carefully develops when students are encouraged to make **conjectures**, are given time to search for evidence to prove or disprove them, and are expected to explain and justify their ideas" (NCTM, 2000, p. 122). The NCTM Reasoning and Proof Standard recommends that mathematics instruction include four components:

> **Conjectures:** Educated guesses about strategies or solutions made from evidence, experience, or information.

- Recognize reasoning and proof as fundamental aspects of mathematics
- Make and investigate mathematical conjectures
- Develop and evaluate mathematical arguments and proofs
- Select and use various types of reasoning and methods of proof

Students who demonstrate strength in reasoning and proof notice patterns and structures in real-world situations and symbolic representations. They ask questions about the patterns that they see and will often want to continue the pattern or rearrange physical objects or numbers to form patterns. They offer up ideas and strategies for solutions and are unfazed when their first idea doesn't work. They enjoy creating mathematical arguments and critiquing the reasoning of others. You can develop students' strengths in reasoning and proof by asking them to offer conjectures, explain, and justify their ideas. You can also buoy students' strengths in reasoning by asking them to analyze student work samples to offer ideas about how the student solved the problem. For example, Justin asked his second graders to analyze how other second graders solved this prompt:

$21 + 18 = \boxed{} + 7$

Justin posed, "Look at how the students solved the problem in these work samples and decide if you agree or disagree with the students and explain why you agree or disagree." The students analyzed two pieces of student work (Figure 2.6) and immediately began a conversation about the meaning of the equal sign.

FIGURE 2.6: Student Work Samples

MARVIN	LEO

Jasmine:	Wait a second! There are four numbers with the equal sign!
Katey:	With an equals sign in the middle!
Jasmine:	I don't think Marvin can cross out stuff. I think he did that because he wasn't sure what to do.
Katey:	I agree. I did that one time.
Jasmine:	Well then Leo must be right, but why is he right? Let's check his math!
Katey:	Well, 21 + 18 = 39. But, why did he subtract the 7 when the problem says plus 7? Wouldn't we add 39 + 7?
Jasmine:	Hmmm. Well let's add that. 39 + 7 = 46. But that doesn't make sense!

Katey:	But why did he subtract?
Jasmine:	Oh I know! The equals sign means they equal each other! So both sides have to equal 39!
Katey:	Oh cool—let's try that on another problem to see if it works.

While the students may not have solved a problem like this before, they used reasoning to make sense of the way the students solved the problem and make a conjecture about how to solve a new problem like this one.

Building Strengths in Connections

Students who demonstrate strengths in conceptual understanding and adaptive reasoning enjoy making connections and thrive when they have opportunities to connect their learning within mathematics and to other content areas. When students learn to make connections between operations, they remember more because they use those connections to retrieve the information. When students learn mathematics as isolated facts, they often struggle to retrieve the learning because it is disconnected. Neuroscience helps us understand what this disconnect looks like for a mathematics learner. Imagine that Leo learns that adding is putting things together. He deposits this memory under adding. Next, the student encounters a missing addend problem such as 2 + ? = 5. Upon seeing the addition sign, Leo attempts to retrieve what he knows about addition. He retrieves the idea of combining things and writes, 2 + 7 = 5 because, as he says, "I saw the plus sign and I know that means I put the other two numbers together to make 7." If Leo had a more flexible conceptual understanding of addition, his understanding would be deeper, and he would be less likely to fall into this common early conception about addition that you just add whatever numbers you have. A memory that has more connections to other memories (aka prior learning) is infinitely easier to retrieve because the student can access the memory from multiple connection points in a mental network of ideas. If Leo understood that addition and subtraction were inversely related, he could use what he knows about addition or subtraction to make sense of the problem. Cognitive scientists Owens and Tanner (2017) explain: "Memories are encoded as synaptic networks and are retrieved when some of the neural connections are reactivated, which prompts the reactivation of the entire network to which they belong. It is logical, then, that a memory that has many connections to other memories would be easier to retrieve than a memory that has only a few entry points, because there would be more ways to reactivate the former" (para. 20). Keeping the importance of building connections between operations in mind, we offer some ways to help students build critical cognitive connections through concept maps and chalk talks. Both of these strategies will highlight students' strengths in making connections and at the same time support other students to seek and develop new connections between mathematical ideas.

 **Try It!** Mathematical Concept Maps

Concept maps offer a way to organize, construct, and connect ideas. Quite flexible in function, students can create concept maps at any point in the learning process, and they are particularly useful as a way to promote metacognition. Students can begin to create a concept map as they are first developing understanding of concepts. These early concept maps may initially show tentative understanding and beginning levels of connections between prior knowledge and new knowledge. At another time, when concepts are better understood, students may develop more sophisticated concept maps that show more robust connections (Ritchhart, Turner, & Hadar, 2009). In both cases, the concept map fosters students' ability to recognize connections and construct new relationships. The open-ended nature of the concept map is perfectly suited to all grade levels as students can show the links that make the most sense to them.

> **Concept Maps:** Visual representations of related ideas.

> **Metacognition:** Awareness and understanding of one's thinking.

Introducing Mathematical Concept Maps

1. Describe your purpose by saying you want to learn more about how the students are thinking about how the mathematics they are learning is connected.

2. Introduce the idea of a concept map by asking the students to brainstorm everything they can think of related to a concept (e.g., addition) and write each idea on a sticky note.

3. Collect the sticky notes from the students and begin reading them aloud, placing them on the chalkboard or whiteboard. As you read the ideas, ask the students if the new idea is similar to one that was already shared. Place those sticky notes together. After you have read all the sticky notes, ask the students to think about how these ideas are connected to each other.

4. Cluster students' ideas that belong together and draw a circle around them. Draw arrows to the main concept (Figure 2.7).

5. Then, ask students to make a concept map to connect ideas between addition and subtraction (Figure 2.8).

6. Display concept maps and discuss with the students.

FIGURE 2.7: A Concept Map About Addition

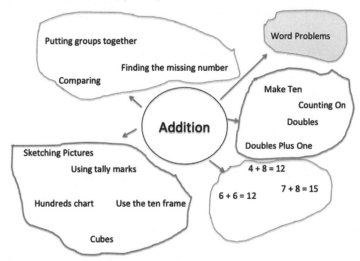

FIGURE 2.8: Connecting Ideas About Addition and Subtraction
With a Concept Map

 Try It!   Chalk Talk

Chalk Talk is a silent brainstorming activity that makes thinking
visible. It is particularly useful for helping students focus on and
seek relationships among mathematical ideas. Teachers conduct
the Chalk Talk in small groups or as a class on a large whiteboard,
chalkboard, or chart paper. For example, Mrs. Monroe stretched
several pieces of chart paper across the front of the classroom
and handed each student a marker. She posed the question,
"How are multiplication and division related?" She then asked
the students to walk to the chart paper and record their ideas in
words, numbers, and sketches. If students see relationships or
connections between their ideas and other students' ideas, then
they can join them with a circle or draw an arrow between them.
Students may also pose questions about an idea on the chart

paper. During Mrs. Monroe's Chalk Talk, there was a period of quiet when no one was writing ideas. Just when she was going to stop the activity, three students moved to the chart paper to write a thought or draw a sketch. As Mrs. Monroe suspected, the wait time provided more time for students to process ideas. As the students recorded their thoughts, the individual and collective thinking in the classroom was revealed. At the conclusion of the visual representation, Mrs. Monroe conducted a discussion:

Mrs. Monroe: What do you notice about our Chalk Talk?

Elena: I didn't even know there were so many ways to think about how multiplication and division are related.

Allison: I like how people drew sketches.

Meha: I like how some people told a multiplication story problem and a division story problem.

Marne: I think the spot where Mimi wrote OPPOSITE is interesting because then someone—I don't know who—wrote "joining equal groups and separating equal groups" and then Alvaro wrote the plus sign above the joining and the minus sign above the separating, which made me think of addition and subtraction.

Michael: Ooooh! I know! The one way multiplication and division are related is because they both have another operation that is connected to them. So I think multiplication is faster than addition and division is faster than subtraction. Can I add that to the Chalk Talk?

Building Strengths in Representations

In the *Principles and Standards for School Mathematics,* the NCTM (2000) explains that "the ways in which mathematical ideas are represented is fundamental to how people can understand and use those ideas" (p. 67). Later, the NCTM developed *Principles to Actions: Ensuring Mathematical Success for All* (2014) and developed a Teaching Practice specifically focused on supporting students through employing representations in instruction:

> *Use and connect mathematical representations. Effective teaching of mathematics engages students in making connections among mathematical representations to deepen understanding of mathematics concepts and procedures and as tools for problem solving. (p. 24)*

Students need many opportunities to represent their thinking about the mathematics they are learning. Students who demonstrate strengths in conceptual understanding, strategic competence, and adaptive reasoning can link representations to the mathematics they are learning. Students may represent their thinking using symbols, words, sketches, manipulatives, and technology tools. Representations "may be visible, such as a number sentence, a display of manipulative materials, or a graph, but it may also be an internal way of seeing and thinking about a mathematical idea. Regardless of their form, representations can enhance students' communication, reasoning, and problem-solving abilities; help them make connections among ideas; and aid them in learning new concepts and procedures" (Annenberg Learner, 2018, para. 1).

Teachers can support students to develop and use representations by doing the following:

- Selecting tasks that allow students to decide which representations to use in making sense of the problems
- Allocating substantial instructional time for students to use, discuss, and make connections among representations
- Introducing forms of representations useful to students
- Asking students to make math drawings or use other visual supports to explain and justify their reasoning
- Focusing students' attention on the structure or essential features of math ideas that appear, regardless of the representation
- Designing ways to elicit and assess students' abilities to use representations meaningfully to solve problems (NCTM, 2014, p. 29)

When students are using representations effectively, they are doing the following:

- Using multiple forms of representations to make sense of and understand mathematics
- Describing and justifying their mathematical understanding and reasoning with drawings, diagrams, and other representations
- Making choices about which forms of representations to use as tools for solving problems
- Sketching diagrams to make sense of problem situations
- Contextualizing mathematical ideas by connecting them to real-world situations
- Considering the advantages or suitability of using various representations when solving problems (NCTM, 2014, p. 29)

Clearly, one way to ensure that students can feature their ability to make and use representations is to focus on *how* and *when* students use effective representations to demonstrate their understanding. The following two Try It! activities support students to develop their strengths in using representations as a daily part of their mathematics learning experience.

 **Try It!**   My Best Representation

One way to highlight the students' strengths as they use representations is to regularly ask students to show and share their best representation. This practice of highlighting good ideas can be done during the lesson closure. You can invite the students to share and explain their representations to a classmate or to the whole class. Many teachers also note that as students begin to represent their mathematical thinking, they emerge as experts in particular representations.

 **Try It!**   Connect the Representation

In this activity, the teacher asks the students to find a classmate who has constructed a representation that is different from the one they created for the same idea. Begin by asking the students to select a representation that they used to solve a task or problem. Next, ask the students to find a partner who has a different representation. Ask the students the following:

- What do you notice about your representations?
- Find something that you like about your partner's representation.
- How can you connect your representations? What are the links?

 **Try It!**   Representation Hot Potato

Like the game hot potato, students take either a representation they created or one provided on a card by the teacher (either they should have the owner's initials or be numbered) and they pass them to the left in a small group or as a whole class. When you call "STOP," they take the representation they currently hold and write a matching word problem/story to go with the problem (putting the initials or number on their work). After a few minutes, they can consult with a neighbor to check their approach. Then they pass only the representations again, and eventually the teacher calls another stop and another word problem is created and marked with matching symbols. At the end, representations are returned to the original owners, and they also get the problems that were created. They compare the results. Great fun and lots of fodder for meaningful mathematical conversations.

The past president of the NCTM, Francis (Skip) Fennell, explains that representations should be included in lesson planning. He notes that teachers must begin the lesson planning process by asking, "What models or materials (representations) will help convey the mathematical focus of today's lesson?" (Fennell, 2006, para. 1). As you are planning, think about how you can also highlight your students' strengths through the representations they create. In this next Spotlight, you have an opportunity to consider how representations can support your lesson planning and implementation.

SPOTLIGHT ON YOUR PRACTICE:
Show Me the Math!

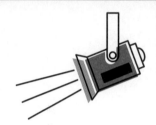

As you plan to build representations into your next lesson, consider the following questions:

Representations and Planning:

1. What models will work best for this lesson topic? Why?
2. When will students have an opportunity to represent their thinking in concrete, pictorial, or symbolic forms?
3. What is the role of representation in this lesson?
4. Will students develop their own representations or use those they have already learned?
5. Will students have a choice of representations? If so, how will you communicate this?
6. How will students communicate their understanding through the use of representations?

Summary

Recognizing and celebrating students' strengths through the mathematical processes they use is strengths finding at its best! As you engage students in mathematical problem solving, communicating about mathematics, representing mathematical ideas, reasoning about mathematics, and seeking and recognizing mathematical connections, celebrate the unique and brilliant ways that your students make sense of the mathematics they are learning.

3

Your Students' Mathematics Content Strengths

If human beings are perceived as potentials rather than problems, as possessing strengths instead of weaknesses, as unlimited rather that dull and unresponsive, then they thrive and grow to their capabilities.

—Barbara Bush

In the second chapter for Teaching Turnaround Two: Discover and Leverage Your Students' Mathematical Strengths, we explore ways to seek, recognize, and celebrate students' content strengths. Now that we have unpacked the many ways that students must understand mathematics through processes, practices, and dispositions, we will take a look at uncovering strengths within particular mathematical content areas. We have selected Meaning of Number and Operations, Fractions, and Geometry as a small representation of the mathematical content understandings that are taught in the elementary grades. This mathematics content is not meant to be exhaustive but a sampling of topics that students learn across the elementary years.

Building Mathematical Content Knowledge Through a Strengths-Based Lens

In Chapter 1, we introduced a list of strengths to jump-start your thinking. As you perused the list, you may have noticed that mathematics knowledge of content was not listed, but instead we included ways of thinking about and interacting with the content. Content strengths are not just academic strengths—they also encompass all the content that students know *and* the dispositions they hold. Throughout this chapter, you will find number of Try It! activities that are meant to reveal and bolster students' strengths as they engage in meaningful tasks that are situated in contexts that are interesting to students, use manipulatives as a tool for promoting understanding, and promote multiple ways of learning and knowing about mathematics.

We have been asked, "How do you see students' strengths in mathematics content when students have misconceptions or show errors in their work?" We ask you to reframe that question to ask, "What does the student know?" What the student *does* know is evidence of strength. Even the notion of a misconception might be considered by some as deficit thinking, and so we are thinking of these instead as early or naive conceptions. For example, let's examine kindergartner Allison, who is learning about grouping objects into groups of ten. When Allison is asked to tell how many groups of ten cubes are on a table (Figure 3.1), she incorrectly says two. Rather than view this as an immediate problem, Allison's teacher asks her to count the cubes (which she does correctly) and then says, "How many groups of ten cubes can you put in this bowl?" Allison responds, "I can put this group of ten in the bowl, but I don't have enough left to put a whole group of ten in another bowl." By asking Allison to physically group the cubes, her teacher was able to capitalize on her strengths of counting to better understand her mathematical content understanding.

In this example, we see the teacher use Allison's strengths to reframe the question. The teacher might also have her use blank ten frames or a hundreds chart.

FIGURE 3.1: How Many Cubes?

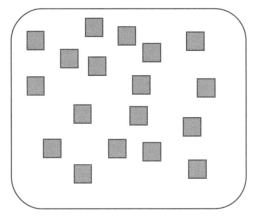

Recently, a preservice teacher we work with discovered that her fourth-grade students were challenged by two-step word problems. Instead of framing it as a student weakness, she asked herself, "What kinds of word problems did they demonstrate strength in solving, and how can I use that knowledge to design problems that will promote access to two-step word problems?" Through careful exploration, she discovered that the students could solve two-step word problems that combined addition and subtraction or addition and multiplication. She shared this discovery with the students and spent time helping them unpack the structure of two-step word problems with subtraction and division operations.

> Even the notion of a misconception might be considered by some as deficit thinking, and so we are thinking of these instead as early or naive conceptions.

Both of these examples reflect how teachers can leverage what students know and can do to help them access the next level of understanding.

Consider how the following content explorations might help you design mathematics learning experiences that at first reveal—and then bolster—your students' strengths.

Building and Recognizing Strengths in the Meaning of Number and Operations and Algebraic Thinking

The topics of number and operations and algebraic thinking are brimming with many opportunities for primary students to form and exercise their strengths. For example, as students develop understanding of number and operations, they can

> Algebraic Thinking: Identifying, analyzing, and extending patterns; determining and representing relationships; and making generalizations.

- Count to show how numbers represent quantity
- Recognize that addition involves combining and joining, and subtraction involves separating and comparing
- Write equations to represent situations
- Develop strategies to add, subtract, multiply, and divide that are different from the standard algorithms
- Recognize the inverse relationship between addition and subtraction and the inverse relationship between multiplication and division

- Make connections between counting and addition and subtraction
- Use multiple representations to solve problems

Let's unpack a few of these areas as examples by sharing with you some activities you can try to identify and build off your students' specific strengths and the mathematics content they do know.

Count to Show How Numbers Represent Quantity

Young students often enter school with a practical understanding of counting and the value of single-digit numbers. They enjoy demonstrating this knowledge by counting objects and reporting how many of their favorite items they have. When we recently entered a kindergarten classroom, a student earnestly reported that he had four dinosaurs at home. Another student overheard this exchange and announced that she had only one teddy bear but that was because her teddy bear was so special. Then, a spontaneous conversation erupted from the two students as they discussed who had more and who had fewer. The owner of the teddy bear exclaimed, "Brandon and I have five things together because one teddy bear plus four dinosaurs equals five things." Brandon then reported, "Five is half of ten you know." It is important to note that we did not invite this particular conversation by asking questions but that the students engaged in this mathematical conversation all on their own, showcasing their ability to make sense of mathematical operations in their own context. We took this opportunity to have the students share their conversation with the whole class, offering an opportunity to honor the students' thinking as they applied mathematical reasoning to their own situation.

> **Teachers can access their students' strengths by situating mathematics learning within contexts that are recognizable and thought provoking to their students.**

As this scenario demonstrates, students often show strength in counting, addition, and subtraction when they are counting, adding, and subtracting objects that are familiar and interesting to them. Teachers can access their students' strengths by situating mathematics learning within contexts that are recognizable and thought provoking to their students. One way that teachers can do this is to feature mathematics-related children's literature books in their lessons that resonate with their students' experiences. For example, teachers might read the counting book, *Feast for 10* (Falwell, 2003), about an African American family that shops for groceries and prepares a meal to eat together. Teachers can pose mathematical questions such as "How many items did the family buy?" Students can sketch representations of the items, write number sentences, and use tally marks to find out how many total food items the family purchased. Then related problems in addition and subtraction can follow. They can read *Guinea Pigs*

Add Up (Cuyler, 2010) and explore the rapid comings and goings of the many baby guinea pigs born to the class pet. Here they can explore the possible ways that 12 guinea pigs can be placed in two cages and to show that they have identified every possible option. It is this exploration and "proof" that they have accounted for all the options that develops their algebraic thinking. Also, there are two stories about the popular character Pete the Cat where he is missing cupcakes (Dean, 2016) or has an adventure with his four groovy buttons (Dean, 2012) that provide entertaining reasons to pose subtraction (and addition) questions. Think of all the authentic and contextually relevant word problems they will think through before some of these young children can even read!

Write Equations to Represent Word Problems

Word problems can often be challenging for students who struggle because the language can be confusing to unpack and students may rush to grab the numbers in the problem and write equations without making sense of the situation. However, you can invite students to develop and display their strengths by asking them to engage in the following Try It! activities.

In this first Try It! activity, students who have conceptual understanding as one of their strengths can take a moment to make sense of the problem without the burden of the values in the problem. You can extend this strategy by writing word problems with contexts that are familiar and interesting for particular students in your class. Ask students to represent the story in pictures, model the story situation using manipulatives, or act the situation out. This active approach is helpful for all students, particularly those developing language and reading comprehension skills.

 **Try It!** **Retell the Problem to a Friend Without Numbers**

The following problem was used with a student who enjoyed playing games on her mother's phone and sharing her results with the teacher every morning.

> Elly played levels of her electronic game. She scored ___ points in first level and ____ points in second level. If the game was over after the second level, how many points did she score?

Elly explained, "Ohhhh! I am going to get points and then add them together to find out how many total points I have! Can I see the numbers please so I can find out?" The absence of the number values helped Elly initially focus on the content of the word problem and that she was combining quantities. How might you incorporate retelling problems in your lesson?

This next Try It! is a sorting activity that supports students who demonstrate strengths in conceptual understanding as well as adaptive reasoning. In this activity, teachers ask students to sort a collection of several problems into two sets and then explain the "rule" that governs why they classified them in those ways. Students will often intuitively understand why particular word problems go together by noticing the structure of the word problem.

 **Try It!**   Sort Before Solving

Micah was asked to sort the following problems (Figure 3.2) into two groups without solving them.

FIGURE 3.2: Sample Word Problems to Sort

Some frogs were sitting on a lily pad. Five more frogs joined them. Now there are 7 frogs on the lily pad. How many frogs were on the lily pad in the beginning?	Lou collected 6 leaves for his leaf collection. Mario collected 3 leaves for his leaf collection. How many fewer leaves did Mario collect than Lou?
Maria has 7 crayons in her pencil box. Allan has 4 crayons in his pencil box. How many more crayons does Maria have than Allan?	The kids were swinging on the swings. Three more kids came to swing with them. Five kids are now on the swings. How many kids were swinging in the beginning?

Micah sorted the problems like this (Figure 3.3):

FIGURE 3.3: Micah's Sorting Decisions

When asked to explain his sort, Micah said, "These top two go together because someone has more than the other person and you have to figure out how many. The other two go together because the beginning is a mystery."

One of Micah's strengths is reasoning. Without the pressure of solving the word problem for a specific answer, he can take a moment to think about what makes sense and notice the structure of the word problems. What is also interesting about the sorting activity is that the first inclination might be for us to worry that the students will become overwhelmed with four problems. However, we have found that students love to sort the problems first without the pressure of solving them. They often take this opportunity to discuss what the problems mean as they interpret the information and share insights about the contexts of the problems. Once the students have sorted them into two groups, we ask them to select one problem to solve. Furthermore, the building of students' understanding of problem types, such as start unknown or change unknown, enhanced their ability to develop a schema for the structure of additive problems. When students recognize the problem structure, they can more easily move to a solution. By the way, these are often structures that still support students for larger numbers or fractions!

Source: Adapted from Caldwell, Kobett, and Karp (2014).

For students who have difficulty to seeing the structure within word problems, you can ask them to look at two word problems and ask the students to explain how the word problems are alike and different. Next, you can show them three cards and ask the students to find two that go together.

Some students who have a strength in procedural fluency are able to quickly represent their thinking using abstract representations. On the other hand, some students may sometimes write equations without reasoning about the problem first. In this activity, students match word problems to the equation first, explain their decision, and then solve the problem. For students who may struggle with language, use pictures in addition to the equations and word problems. This approach supports students in the process of focusing on which equation and operation best match the word problem. In the next Try It! activity, students use reasoning to match equations to word problems, a key component of algebraic thinking.

 **Try It!**   ## Match Equations to Word Problems

Aliyah's teacher presented the following problem and three possible solutions and asked, "Which of the three equations makes the most sense to you as a match for the situation? Why?"

> Aliyah loved running with the girls in the Run Club. Her goal was to run 20 miles this week. She ran 4 miles on Monday, 6 miles on Wednesday, 5 miles on Thursday, and 6 miles on Friday. Did she meet her goal? How close was she?
>
> A. $12 + 9 = 21$
> $21 - 20 = 1$
> B. $4 + 5 + 12 = 21$
> C. $4 + 6 + 5 + 6 = 21$
> $21 - 20 = 1$

Aliyah made sense of each of the equations and then selected the solution she liked the best.

Teacher: Which of the solutions makes the most sense for this problem? Why?

Aliyah: Well, I like that the problem is about me!

Teacher: Yes, these are about your running goals! So, let's read the problem together and then think about which of the solutions you think is most reasonable. Then, you can solve it and see if the solution worked out the way you thought it would.

Aliyah: I can already tell which answer is right! I would pick C because it has all of my miles in there and they are in the same order that I ran!

Teacher: Do you think there are any other solutions that work?

Aliyah: Oh wait! You tried to trick me! I thought there was only one answer! Umm. Well B is wrong because the kid forgot to figure out if I made my goal. Wait, A is right too! Oh, I see what that kid did. He added up the sixes and made a 12! Cool! I still like my way the best because it shows each of my running days.

This conversation reveals how Aliyah was able to leverage her strengths in procedural fluency to make sense of the word problem.

Notice that the teacher gives the student a problem with her name in it and the scenario aligns with a known interest. This practice increases readability of the problem for a student, a practice that is particularly helpful for low–socioeconomic status (SES) and low-proficiency students (Walkington, Clinton, & Shivraj, 2018). What's more is that supplying students with a collection of equations that accurately match a set of given word problems and asking them to find pairs is a perfect accommodation for students who are still learning the connections between a mathematical situation and the corresponding symbolic representations.

Develop Strategies to Add, Subtract, Multiply, and Divide

Students who have one of their strengths related to strategic competence love to visually represent their mathematical thinking and use mathematics organizers like ten frames, hundreds charts, number lines, and place value charts to model their ideas and illustrate their approaches. These students are able to select from a repertoire of strategies at just the right time and flexibly switch strategies as the context warrants (Siegler & Lemaire, 1997). However, we have to carefully consider how these strategies get developed in the first place.

For several reasons, students need multiple opportunities to develop and then select when to apply their own strategies. First, allowing students to construct and/or select their own strategies sends a powerful message that you believe that they are capable doers of mathematics, that their ideas are worthwhile, and that developing and using a repertoire of strategies is a normal and necessary part of learning mathematics. Furthermore, when students are allowed to develop or apply their own strategies, they

- make fewer mistakes,
- develop stronger number sense and the ability to identify reasonable answers,
- develop estimation and strong mental computation skills,
- find these flexible methods are often faster than their use of the standard algorithm, and
- invent a strategy that moves toward or approximates the standard algorithm is *doing mathematics* (adapted from Van de Walle, Karp, & Bay-Williams, 2019, p. 248).

To aid in this approach, students should be introduced to a variety of strategies. But they should not be forced to use particular strategies. Instead, they should be encouraged to use the strategies that make the most sense to them in the circumstances or situations presented.

This use of multiple strategies must be done with caution, however. When we present students with an *overabundance* of strategies, we can sometimes unintentionally overwork their working memory (Bull & Lee, 2014) and actually reduce mathematics success and even create anxiety. We can see evidence of this when students apply a strategy at the wrong time or confuse strategies by combining pieces of not fully digested approaches. In a review of 19 studies examining students' stress, time pressure strategy selection, and math anxiety, Caviola, Carey, Mammarella, and Szucs (2017) found that, overall, time pressure stresses students and causes them to make ill-fated strategy choices. If students feel constrained, they will flounder mentally and respond by selecting the first strategy that they can recall. Given more time, students can gather additional information about the task and select a better-fitting strategy that matches the problem (Heinze, Star, & Verschaffel, 2009).

The bottom line is that the key to helping students make wise decisions about the operations is to allow the students to both develop their own strategies based on their strengths and apply particular strategies that they are learning without the constraints of time and pressure to use specially designated strategies on demand. The following activities carefully summon students to cultivate an awareness of their strongest strategies and approaches to challenges while simultaneously fostering opportunities to deepen their understanding of the meaning of the operations. Think of these tasks as developing a mindfulness for mathematics. With this newfound consciousness, students can then make thoughtful decisions about how and when they use the strategies while at the same time strengthening their understanding of the meaning of these operations. In the next Try It!, students begin to recognize their own strengths as they develop strategies and collect them to use as a reference.

As students work toward becoming proficient with computational strategies, ask them to record the strategy they use and an example in a journal or on a tablet (Figures 3.4 and 3.5). Make sure to set aside a designated time for students to share their strategies with partners, small groups, and the whole class. Also, encourage students to seek out other students to help them find a strategy that works for them.

FIGURE 3.4: Student Work Sample Using Five as an Anchor

Strategy	Example	When I can Use My Strategy
groPing BY five when I add	7+8= 5+2+3+5= 5+5+5=	I will use it alll the time Becuse I like to see the Fives in numBers and add them that wak

This child's developed strategy is also known more formally as Using a 5 as an anchor, which prepares students for the subsequent goal of using 10 as an anchor.

FIGURE 3.5: Student Work Sample Using the Strategy to Add a Group

Strategy	Example	When I can Use My Strategy
dubbling first and then Plussing the leftover group	8 x 9 = 8 x 8 = 64 That leaves a one more group of 8 leftover so I add it to 64 64 + 8 = 72	I noticed that I can use it when the numbers I am timsing are right next to each other like 7x8.

This strategy is also known as Adding or Subtracting a Group, which supports understanding of the distributive property.

> Adding or Subtracting a Group: When students multiply groups and then add or subtract one of the equal groups multiplied.

In this next Try It!, you are invited to conduct a number talk. Number talks often reveal multiple strengths from students as they are stretched to think of new and creative ways to solve and explain computational problems.

 **Try It!**   ## Number Talks

In a number talk (Parrish, 2014), teachers facilitate a short mathematical discourse with students about how to mentally solve a problem or a string of problems. Teachers give students time to think about how to solve the problem and then invite students to share their strategies with a specific focus on the solution pathway rather than an emphasis on one correct answer. Particular care has to be given to provide access to number talks for students who are currently struggling. If only students who are fast at carrying out computations share their ideas, then we fall into the trap of reinforcing the wrong message and at the same time diminishing the possibility for other students' unique contributions. To provide opportunities for more students to shine and showcase their strengths, you can make small tweaks to the typical number talk routine. For example, students can rehearse their ideas with a partner first before sharing with the whole class. Also, some students may want to represent their idea first using a whiteboard before verbally sharing it in front of others. Another way to build on students' strengths is to allow them to conduct a number talk in small groups. When you do this, you shift the authority and the thinking to the students and encourage them to lift up one another's ideas.

In this next Try It!, students can showcase the basic computation facts that they know, make connections between facts, and consider how facts can be related.

 **Try It!**   ## Spin, Circle, and Solve

This activity can be used individually or with any sized group and should be used after students have constructed and learned about a variety of strategies for thinking about basic facts in addition, subtraction, multiplication, or division. The strategies are written on a spinner (spinners can be individualized by strategies that the students should use and favor). Students spin the spinner and then circle all the basic facts that could be solved using that particular strategy. Students must decide which facts to circle and then only solve those. This activity helps reduce the cognitive load on the working memory because students use their ideas about the strategy to decide which facts to select instead of examining the fact and then sifting through all the strategies they know to apply.

Source: Adapted from Caldwell, Kobett, and Karp (2014).

In the following Try It! activity, students explore the strengths in a classmate's solution pathway.

 **Try It!** My Favorite Strategy

Fashioned after the Teaching Channel Video *My Favorite No*, the teacher selects a strategy or strategies that a student used in class and then highlights what she likes about the strategy with the students. This approach can be done as a lesson launch or lesson closure. Here is an example of how to implement this activity:

Mrs. Ramirez begins by saying, "My favorite strategy is . . . Dominique's strategy (Figure 3.6)! Dominique solved the multistep word problems we were working on today by developing her own organizer. Let's take a look at what she did on the first problem."

> Mrs. Sousa is ordering new art supplies! She has 35 paintbrushes left at the end of the school year. She buys packages of paintbrushes that have 8 paintbrushes in each package. Now, she has 99 paintbrushes to start the new school year! How many packages of paintbrushes did she buy?

Mrs. Ramirez says, "Dominique organized her work into three boxes. I can see that she put the first part of the problem in the first box. Then, she put the action in the second box and the total in the third box. What is interesting is how Dominique used an arrow to show what she did after she found out how many paintbrushes Mrs. Sousa bought. This arrow helped me see that Dominique knew she wasn't finished solving the problem. The answer of 64 told her how many brushes, but not how many packages—so she had to go back to that piece of information in the problem to find out that she had 8 packages. The organization here shows me that Dominique is thinking strategically about how to pull apart a two-step word problem!"

FIGURE 3.6: Dominique's Strategy

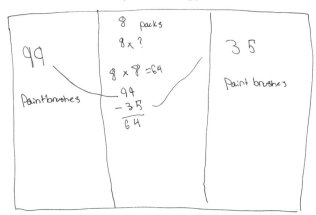

Building and Recognizing Strengths in Understanding Number and Operations: Fractions

Building understanding of fractions begins as early as first grade as students explore the properties of shapes by folding circular and rectangular regions into two or four equal shares and second graders learn how to think about sharing the same shapes with three people. But students need to be aware of the new number system they are learning to fully grasp the shift from thinking about whole numbers to rational numbers. In Ms. Kay's class, she would post a sign on the classroom wall that said "They're coming!" The children took the bait and wanted to know—Who's is coming? But, Ms. Kay was silent, even evasive, and was enjoying the secret she held. The signs became more plentiful over time—even showing up in bathroom stalls—but there was no budging Ms. Kay for the details. Finally, a day came when "they're coming" was announced with an exact date and the children were excited. What was coming was fractions—and although that might not excite you—the children were very excited. Ms. Kay explained that she had to wait until they were sophisticated enough to learn a new set of numbers and they were moving beyond just using whole numbers like their young siblings to a new collection of ideas. The children felt powerful. This approach was also set into motion so Ms. Kay could draw careful boundary lines around how fractions still connected to whole-number thinking and where the systems diverged. Let's look at some models for building understanding of fractions through the following Try It! activities.

This next Try It! helps students learn about the approximate size of fractions using a regional model.

Starting with a regional model is a good place to begin as it aligns with the standards housed in the geometry domain but that support learning about fractions. First, purchase enough of exactly the same-sized party plates of two different solid colors (check out your party storage area first for some you can repurpose—pick a light and dark color). Make a class set. We don't suggest the students make these paper plate models, as precision is very important. On the back of each of the two different-colored plates, put a dot in the center. Using a straightedge, make a line from that dot to the edge of the plate, as a radius. Then link the plates together via the cut lines so one lies flat on top of the other (see Figure 3.7). Have students rotate these plates so that they can show different fractional portions—such as showing the symbols (or calling out the number) one half or one fourth. By holding up their estimated region, you can quickly see their thinking. This activity focuses on the size of fractions. Yes, the fractional number should be linked to the answer in each case, but by focusing on the region, you can see how geometry is related to the development of fractions as suggested in the standards. You can send the plates home for homework and ask families to ask for fractional portions from a supplied sheet that matches what the children have experienced and have the children show them the correct region with the plates. As you might suppose, the same plates can be used for estimating the size of angles (adapted from Reys, 1991).

FIGURE 3.7: Fraction Estimator Plate

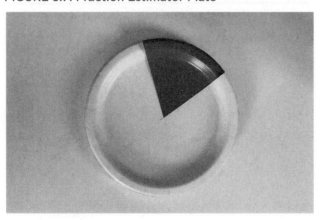

To support students' understanding of multiple representations, the next Try It! uses a length model to estimate the size of a fraction.

Using a long clothesline with clothespins and a set of fractions on cards, you can create a length model (aligns to number lines drawn on paper) to help students think about fraction magnitude. Position one student at the left of the classroom facing the group with a zero positioned in front of them clipped on the string with a clothespin. Then farther down (give as much space as reasonable to keep the clothesline held up), hold the 1 clipped on to show "One whole length." Make sure you say "length" to reinforce the unit. Then put up the benchmark fraction one half by folding the clothesline and finding the halfway point (Figure 3.8). Add the student with the $\frac{1}{2}$ on their card midway. Then move to logical choices for the next fractions by asking $\frac{1}{4}$ or $\frac{3}{4}$ to locate their position on the line. Also, consider fractions greater than 1 with such placements as $\frac{3}{2}$ or $\frac{5}{4}$.

FIGURE 3.8: Visual of the Folding Process to Locate One Half on the Number Line

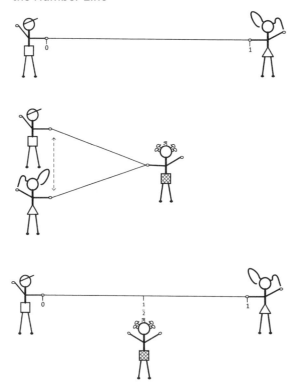

Source: Adapted from Van de Walle, Karp, and Bay-Williams (2019).
Figure created by Bob Ronau.

Using a length model, students explore the magnitude of fractions using estimation and the concrete strategy of folding in this next Try It!

Try It!   The Slowest Race Ever!

Use a piece of cash register tape about 16 inches long for each student or a pair of students working as a team. They should mark a line from top to bottom on the left side of the tape to show the beginning of the race and another similar mark on the far-right side of the tape to show the end of the race. The locations next to the animal show where they are after an hour (Figure 3.9). Now place these "speedy" runners on the track with the beginning of the race representing 0 and the end representing 1 as the whole length of the race.

FIGURE 3.9: Animals and Their Distance in the Race After One Hour

Sloth : $\frac{3}{4}$ Tortoise : $\frac{1}{2}$

Loris : $\frac{7}{8}$

Koala : $\frac{2}{8}$

Snail : $\frac{3}{8}$

Image sources: Sloth: Sudowoodo/iStock.com; Loris: colematt/iStock.com; Snail: FARBAI/iStock.com; Tortoise: rosinka/iStock.com; Koala: MuchMania/iStock.com.

Students can fold the paper to estimate the location of each of the runners. Only if you make the length of the race (the distance between the start and finish lines) the same can students compare their measures to each other. Ask, "Which animal is going twice as fast as another? Half as fast? What other comparisons do you notice?"

Change the fractions to meet the level and needs of your students. Always provide a challenge for all learners.

Source: Adapted from Van de Walle, Karp, and Bay-Williams (2019).

Building and Recognizing Strengths in Geometry

Geometry is rich with opportunities to both recognize and develop students' mathematical strengths. For some students who struggle to learn mathematics concepts and related skills that focus on computation, geometry provides an alternative perspective and a way to showcase other mathematics strengths. Sadly, geometry teaching and learning is often given short shrift during the early childhood and elementary years as "teachers do not teach even the barren geometry curriculum that is available to them" (Clements & Sarama, 2004, p. 151). This deemphasis on geometry is likely the result of an effort to promote number and operations as they are often more prominent on end-of-the-year summative assessments. Therefore, teachers are put in the position of making tough instructional decisions for their students who struggle with computation but could be a "star" in geometry. Geometry, when taught well, is alluring for many students. We are sure that many of you have seen this phenomenon—students who are challenged by computationally focused topics come alive when teachers place buckets of geometric shapes, Geoboards, tangrams, and three-dimensional objects on their desks for exploration. This energy emerges because this is an area of potential strength for them.

Geometry, it turns out, has a rich potential to offer students a sturdy pathway, bolstered by their strengths, to number and operations, fractions, and measurement. Understanding geometric concepts and developing spatial reasoning relies on students' multiple opportunities to use visualization to construct meaning. As students develop visualization skills and understand the purpose for visualization, they strengthen their understanding of geometry and create an entry point to other mathematical topics. Arcavi (2003) notes, "Visualization at the service of problem solving, may play a central role to inspire a whole solution, beyond the merely procedural" (p. 64). Visualization plays a key role in the development of geometric thinking and is highlighted by the van Hieles' (husband and wife team) work to identify the levels that students progress through to understand geometry (van Hiele, 1984). Capitalizing on the concrete nature of geometry and opportunity to stimulate visualization skills, we focus on Level 0 and Level 1 of the five-level van Hiele model to support and promote students' strengths and conceptual understanding as those levels are the focus of the elementary grades:

> **Spatial Reasoning: Capacity to think about objects in three dimensions.**

- Level 0: Visualization
- Level 1: Analysis

Let's unpack each of these levels and share some activities that will help you identify and build upon your students' strengths in geometric thinking.

van Hiele's Geometric Conceptual Understanding Level 0: Visualization

Students demonstrating this level of geometric thought identify shapes by recognizing the visual look of the shapes rather than by their attributes. For example, when they see a triangle, they call out the name. When the shape orientation or position of the triangle changes, they may not recognize it or identify it as a triangle. Let's take a look at how a teacher, Diamond, explores her kindergarten student's understanding of a triangle by placing the following shapes (Figure 3.10) on a table:

FIGURE 3.10: Find the Triangles

Diamond: Find all of the triangles and explain how you know they are triangles.

Jason: That one! (pointing to the second triangle).

Diamond: How do you know the second shape is a triangle?

Jason: Because a triangle always sits on its bottom and points to the sky.

Diamond: Tell me a little more about that.

Jason: Well, you see a triangle sits on its side, not on the pointy part. That's how you know when it is a triangle—it looks like that.

Note how Jason's explanation focuses on the visual of the traditionally shown shape of a triangle. He explains that he knows the shape is a triangle because he can recognize it, much like you might name a person. That person I see is Jennifer. I know that person is Jennifer because that is her name.

Recognizing and naming shapes is an important skill. Much like recognizing a numeral or rote counting, identifying shapes is an entry point for students to develop deeper understanding about attributes and characteristics of shapes. In this case, Diamond practices a strategic strengths-based instructional move:

Diamond: You found a triangle! What would happen if you moved the other shapes around?

Jason:	Hold up! Some of these are triangles, too! (Jason rotates the shapes into new positions with the "bottom" down.)
Diamond:	How do you know?
Jason:	Well look here. I can match them up and turn them all around.
Diamond:	So, is the shape still a triangle when you turn it off its bottom or does it stop being a triangle?
Jason:	That is silly! It is still a triangle!

Instead of telling Jason that it doesn't matter how shapes are placed, Diamond built upon Jason's initially narrow understanding of a triangle by prompting a simple exploration.

Students need many opportunities to flex their visual thinking muscles. Teachers can design concrete activities for students to use a variety of manipulatives and materials and manipulate geometric shapes by combining, folding, and constructing. Throughout the entire process, students should naturally engage in discourse by sorting and classifying shapes, describing the properties of the shapes they see, making connections, and posing new ideas. Students who demonstrate strengths in this area can often predict where the teacher is going next in the lesson and will often pose questions such as "What if we fold the shape?" Or, "Look what happens when I put the triangles together—they make a rectangle." They naturally sort shapes, make connections between shapes, see shapes embedded inside of other shapes (decompose), and combine shapes to make other shapes (compose). It is essential to provide learning experiences that invite students to make discoveries about shapes and engage in discourse and experimentation.

Visualization activities enhance students' visual imagery—an ability that helps students identify shapes from different viewpoints. This next Try It! helps students develop the skill of rapidly recognizing the properties of shapes.

 **Try It!** Geometry Flash

Arrange the students in pairs or small groups. Tell the students that you will flash an image of something related to geometry for a few seconds (Figure 3.11). You will ask them to complete a quick sketch and then compare with a partner. After the students sketch their ideas, ask the students to compare their images with a partner and share the matching geometric term (i.e., trapezoid, perpendicular lines, 90-degree angle). Then reveal the images and ask, "What do you notice?" This flash activity is designed for students to recognize shapes, figures, or concepts in different orientations and also to notice that shapes, when placed together, form new shapes.

FIGURE 3.11: Quick Image Options

Quick Image One

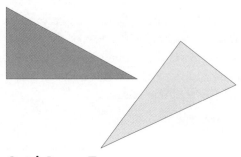

Quick Image Two

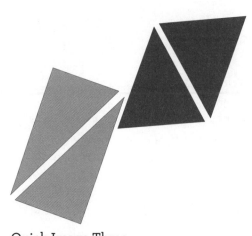

Quick Image Three

Here students use the two-dimensional image of a solid figure to find it at the bottom of a sock using only the sense of touch.

 **Try It!** Search the Sock

Find several knee socks and fill each with five to six different three-dimensional solid shapes. Then create a set of cards with the two-dimensional representations of the three-dimensional solids in each sock. Have students flip a card over and then reach in the sock without peeking and search for the matching shape in the sock. Once they've found it, they replace the shape and another card is selected. Children can do this activity independently or with a teammate. Ask, "What was the clue that you had the right shape in your hand? What property did the solid have that helped you locate it? Did you touch any shapes and eliminate them— why?" This activity is an enjoyable one to share with families as a take-home activity. The children can have the adults at home or a sibling pick the card and then they find the shape, or they can reverse the roles. More challenging solids can always be added to the collection. You can also include a card that has no match and see if the students recognize the shape is missing.

Source: Adapted from Van de Walle, Karp, and Bay-Williams (2019).

In the next Try It!, students build their imagery skills as they try to create an image from verbal directions given by the teacher.

 **Try It!** Visualize It!

In this activity, the directions are imprecise, and therefore, students are likely to vary the representations. Distribute a collection of pattern block shapes to the students and a blank piece of paper. Say, "I am going to describe some shapes and I want you to first visualize what I describe." Wait one minute and then say, "Next, I want you to make what I describe." Then read one of the visualizations below. Ask students to share their visualizations with a partner. Ask, "What do you notice? How are your images alike? How are they different?"

Visualize It One

(Adapt for your students by including grade-level appropriate vocabulary.)

Visualize two squares the same size, side by side, with sides touching.

Visualize It Two

Visualize two triangles and two squares. One of each of the triangle's sides matches up to one of each of the square's sides.

Visualize It Three

Visualize a hexagon and a triangle. One of the sides of the triangle is matched up to the hexagon.

Visualize It Four

Visualize three triangles. One side of each triangle is matched up to another side of another triangle.

This next Try It!—Zoom (Ritchhart, Church, & Morrison, 2011)—for the Harvard Zero Project helps students create mental images of shapes, thinking about how they look from different viewpoints.

 **Try It!**   Zoom

The idea of Zoom is to show only a small portion of a figure slowly revealing an additional portion until the whole figure is revealed (Figure 3.12). With each successive reveal, the teacher asks the following:

- What do you notice?
- What do you think you will see next?
- Have any of your previous ideas changed?

Learners play close attention to detail and make inferences.

FIGURE 3.12: Revealing a Figure Through Multiple Zoom Images

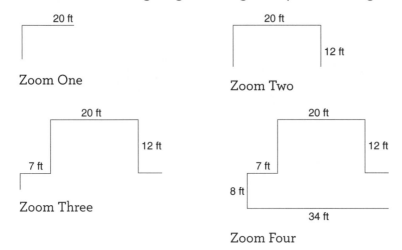

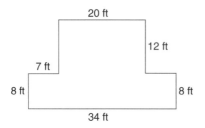

Zoom Five

What is the perimeter of this shape?

What is the area? How many different ways can you find the area?

Source: Adapted from Ritchhart, Turner, and Hadar (2009).

The following Try It! helps students make unique images of two-dimensional shapes in multiple orientations given particular constraints. In addition, this activity helps students develop visualization skills by using a net (a two-dimensional drawing of a three-dimensional shape) to bridge between the two dimensions.

 **Try It!** **From Pentomino to Box**

Give students one-inch tiles and have them identify the 12 (don't tell them—let them find them) existing pentominoes. A pentomino is a two-dimensional shape created from five tiles so that the tiles touch only on a full side (no corner-to-corner touches and no partial sides [only half a side]) without any repeats (Figure 3.13). A rotation of a pentomino is NOT a new pentomino. For each one they find, they should use grid paper to outline the shape as a way to record their discoveries.

FIGURE 3.13: Example and Nonexample of a Pentomino

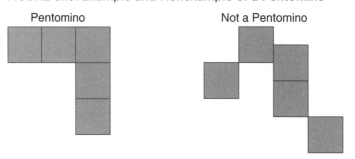

Once they've recorded all 12 pentominoes, the activity continues to a new task. Using the pentominoes as a net (a two-dimensional version of a three-dimensional shape), how many of these pentomino nets can be folded so that they make a three-dimensional box without a cover (Figure 3.14)?

FIGURE 3.14: Example and Nonexample of a Pentomino That Folds Into a Box Without a Top

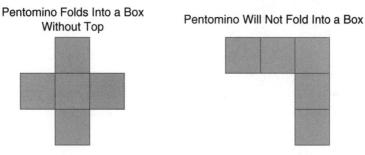

Pentomino Folds Into a Box Without Top

Pentomino Will Not Fold Into a Box

Source: Adapted from Van de Walle, Karp, and Bay-Williams (2019). Figures created by Bob Ronau.

Constructing two- and three-dimensional shapes enhances students' identification of the properties of shapes and their defining attributes. This building experience can also be extended to have students consider the volume of the constructions.

 **Try It!**   Skeleton Shapes

Students need to begin by making building materials for use with this task. Collect a lot of newspapers over time. Have students use a pencil or a wooden dowel and place it diagonally at the corner of two pieces of paper aligned together and roll a rod (remove the pencil/ dowel by tipping it out). Use tape to secure the thin newspaper rod in place. Have students make as many of these rods as needed. Children in the primary grades can make a representation of two-dimensional shapes such as triangles, squares, and trapezoids. They need to put the rods in place and use masking tape or duct tape to wrap the two rods together at a vertex. Ask, "How do you know you have a triangle? How did you decide how to make the trapezoid?" Slightly older children can measure the perimeter and tag the angles with their measures. For upper elementary students, they should venture into creating three-dimensional shapes such as tetrahedrons (Figure 3.15), pyramids, cubes, and prisms. As students build them, they should label important elements with tags or sticky notes to note the edges and vertices. For the right rectangular prisms, they can try to create a layer of one-inch cubes across the bottom of the smallest surface and estimate how many it would take to fill the shape. Then they can move to identifying the measures of the edges and calculate the volume only once they realize the formula is merely figuring how many layers times the number of cubes in a single layer. The main question after this activity is over is always, "Can I be the one to take the tetrahedron home?" Children will vie for the privilege—and that's what makes this a most memorable mathematical adventure. This activity is ideal for a Family Math Night where parents can get into the action of building these not-so-scary skeleton figures and experiencing how we teach about volume now (actually thinking about filling this big prism) versus how they likely learned about volume (a formula).

FIGURE 3.15: Tetrahedron Skeleton

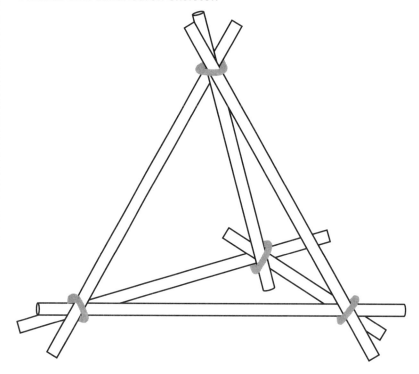

Source: Adapted from Van de Walle, Karp, and Bay-Williams (2019). Figure created by Bob Ronau.

As students develop their visualization skills, you may see some students' strengths in this area take off as they incorporate their newly developed visualization process into their mathematics work. Teachers should enrich their geometry lessons by building multiple opportunities for students to visualize and describe what they see and feel as they manipulate two-dimensional and three-dimensional shapes. The following Spotlight helps to structure these experiences to enhance students' development of mental images—an essential skill in geometry.

SPOTLIGHT ON YOUR PRACTICE:
Opportunities for Visualization

In the first column, list the geometry topics you teach at your grade level. In the second column, consider ways you could integrate visualization into each of your topics.

GRADE-LEVEL GEOMETRY TOPICS	INTEGRATE VISUALIZATION

Reflect: How do you think visualization enhances students' mathematics understanding? In what ways does visualization play a role in topics outside of geometry such as word problems, fractions, place value, or understanding the meaning of the equal sign?

van Hiele's Geometric Conceptual Understanding Level 1: Analysis

Students at this level have moved past naming individual shapes ("That's a rectangle!") to recognizing that a group of shapes are rectangles based on specific properties they share. They begin to understand that if a shape is a rectangle, it also has all the properties associated with that shape. As students advance, their vocabulary and ability to classify shapes become more sophisticated and precise.

Students who demonstrate strength at van Hiele's analysis level can sort, classify, and discriminate shapes based on their attributes. It is important to note that students at this level are just beginning to notice the properties of the shape and will likely demonstrate tentative language and uneven vocabulary use. Elise asked her students to find which shapes go together from the following collection (Figure 3.16):

FIGURE 3.16: Which Shapes Go Together?

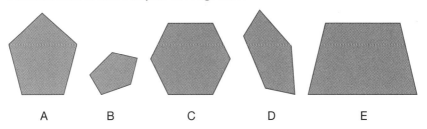

| A | B | C | D | E |

Maria and Evan picked A, B, and D and explained, "We picked these shapes because they are all pentagons, which means they have five sides and five angles. The five sides do not have to be equal. We almost picked C because if you are just looking and not paying attention, you might think C belongs, but it doesn't because it has six sides." Elise pushed the students a bit and asked them if they could change their "rule" to include the hexagon. What could they add? Students need numerous opportunities to sort, classify, and find relationships among shapes. These experiences are essential in helping them develop understanding about the relationships among and between geometric concepts. van Hiele suggested that the way students advance through the levels of geometric thought is via intensive involvement with geometric experiences. Students who demonstrate strength at the analysis level will ask questions that help refine newly developed informal definitions. For example, these students initially notice that the quadrilaterals have four sides but progress to developing definitions for particular kinds of quadrilaterals.

The following activities help students develop and build analysis skills.

Try It!   Some of These Things . . .

Display the following image of shapes (Figure 3.17) to students and say, "Some of these things are different and some are the same. Decide which are like each other and which ones are the same and why." Encourage students to share ideas with one another in pairs, and then have pairs share. Record their ideas on chart paper. Make sure that students have access to vocabulary on a math word wall with pictures and names. This approach will support all students, particularly English learners.

FIGURE 3.17: Which Shapes Are the Same, and Why?

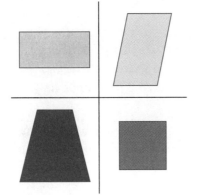

Try It!   Shapes Inside of Shapes

Use masking tape on the floor or large sheets of chart paper to draw the outlines of following figures (Figure 3.18):

FIGURE 3.18: Finding Embedded Shapes

Pose the following question to the students: "How many shapes can you find in these shapes? Use materials to find the shapes and record the shapes that you find." For example, the students might break the quadrilateral in the following ways (Figure 3.19):

FIGURE 3.19: Decomposing Shapes

 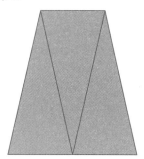

Ask students to keep track of and organize the ways they decomposed the shapes. Ask students to share their ideas. Ask, "What do you notice when you decompose a shape in different ways?"

Reflect: What do you notice about the classroom environment that involves shapes? How do students respond to the use of the large shapes?

Summary

In Chapter 3, we've moved from providing opportunities for students to showcase their processes and practices to adding the importance of mathematics content to the mixture. By combining a blend of topics that receive consistent attention such as number and operations and fractions to that of geometry—an area of study that so often reveals different strengths from students—we expand options for all to shine.

Students' content strengths extend well beyond just knowing mathematics content knowledge for particular topics. Certainly, knowledge of mathematics concepts is one way to recognize the strengths that students exhibit while they are learning mathematics. However, as this chapter illustrates, students' content strengths are best discovered and built through mathematics instruction that fosters multiple perspectives and approaches for learning the content. All students hold mathematics content strengths, and all students deserve an opportunity to thrive in mathematics classrooms that celebrate their individual strengths within mathematics content rather than in comparison to what other students know.

Notes

_____

_____

_____

_____

_____

_____

_____

_____

_____

_____

_____

_____

_____

_____

_____

_____

_____

_____

_____

_____

_____

_____

_____

_____

PART THREE

Teaching Turnaround Three
Design Instruction From a Strengths-Based Perspective

Teaching Turnaround Three: Design Instruction From a Strengths-Based Perspective is the first of three chapters about the ways teachers can implement mathematics lessons that promote their students' mathematics learning and their mathematics strengths. As a gentle reminder, we revisit our definition of strengths. When we think about our lessons and the structures that we use to deliver instruction, we may naturally equate mathematical strengths with mastery of mathematical content. However, we ask that you continually jostle prior notions of what it traditionally meant to be strong in mathematics and expand upon it to demonstrate other strengths in the mathematics classroom. In the last few chapters, we explored how students demonstrate strengths in developing and using representations, working with others, persevering, making connections, explaining their ideas, listening to others' ideas, setting goals, reflecting on learning, and more. As we design instruction, we must keep in mind the comprehensive array of students' learning strengths in addition to their content strengths. When we do this work, the possibilities for supporting our students' mathematical learning are truly infinite!

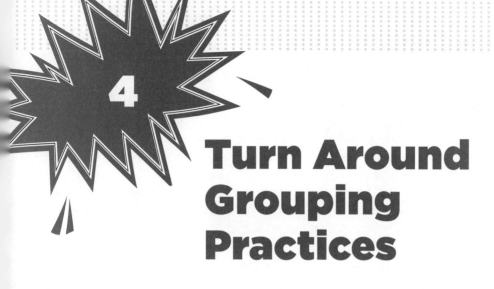

Turn Around Grouping Practices

It is the long history of humankind (and animal kind, too) that those who learned to collaborate and improvise most effectively have prevailed.

—Charles Darwin

This chapter is about the most effective instructional practices—with a special focus on grouping practices—for a strengths-based approach to mathematics teaching and learning. Throughout this chapter, we are focusing primarily on the instruction that all students should receive in heterogeneous, or mixed, groups with grade-level content. The goal for educators of mathematics should be to facilitate a consistent and coherent high-quality mathematics learning environment for each and every student. Achieving this goal means that teachers must design and facilitate learning in a way that

> Heterogeneous Groups: Mixed academic strengths and challenges within a learning group.

- provides multiple access points to the grade-level standards-based content,
- addresses all students' learning needs, and
- maintains high expectations for all learners.

This vision of mathematics education is best realized when, during instruction, teachers provide a safe, welcoming, and warm environment for students to take risks and share ideas with peers. It means that students and teachers are actively engaged in meaningful and relevant learning activities that support students in developing conceptual understanding, procedural fluency, and application of mathematics. It means there is an emphasis on providing all students with *daily access* to this very rich, high-quality mathematics instruction.

> " The goal for educators of mathematics should be to facilitate a consistent and coherent high-quality mathematics learning environment for each and every student.

Planning Effective Strengths-Based Instruction

When we design effective mathematics instruction within heterogenous classrooms, we promote strengths-based beliefs about our students and provide opportunities for all our students to engage in meaningful mathematics learning. Students can and do learn during heterogeneous instruction, particularly when that instruction is high quality and evidence based (Burris, Heubert, & Levin, 2006). The National Council of Teachers of Mathematics' (NCTM, 2014) *Principles to Actions* outlines eight research-based teaching practices (Figure 4.1) that need to be present in every mathematics lesson for each and every student to learn meaningfully.

FIGURE 4.1: Effective Mathematics Teaching Practices

EFFECTIVE MATHEMATICS TEACHING PRACTICES *PRINCIPLES TO ACTIONS: ENSURING MATHEMATICAL SUCCESS FOR ALL* (NCTM, 2014)	
Establish mathematics goals to focus learning.	Effective teaching of mathematics establishes clear goals for the mathematics that students are learning, situates goals within learning progressions, and uses the goals to guide instructional decisions.
Implement tasks that promote reasoning and problem solving.	Effective teaching of mathematics engages students in solving and discussing tasks that promote mathematical reasoning and problem solving and allow multiple entry points and varied solution strategies.
Use and connect mathematical representations.	Effective teaching of mathematics engages students in making connections among mathematical representations to deepen understanding of mathematics concepts and procedures and as tools for problem solving.
Facilitate meaningful mathematical discourse.	Effective teaching of mathematics facilitates discourse among students to build shared understanding of mathematical ideas by analyzing and comparing student approaches and arguments.
Pose purposeful questions.	Effective teaching of mathematics uses purposeful questions to assess and advance students' reasoning and sense making about important mathematical ideas and relationships.
Build procedural fluency from conceptual understanding.	Effective teaching of mathematics builds fluency with procedures on a foundation of conceptual understanding so that students, over time, become skillful in using procedures flexibly as they solve contextual and mathematical problems.

Support productive struggle in learning mathematics.	Effective teaching of mathematics consistently provides students, individually and collectively, with opportunities and supports to engage them in productive struggle as they grapple with mathematical ideas and relationships.
Elicit and use evidence of student thinking.	Effective teaching of mathematics uses evidence of student thinking to assess progress toward mathematical understanding and to adjust instruction continually in ways that support and extend learning.

As you read the descriptions about these teaching practices, the tendency might be to check off particular parts of your lesson as evidence of the practice. However, the key is to *plan* deliberately and mindfully for how each lesson will incorporate the teaching practices. As you consider the practices from a strengths-based approach, imagine what this emphasis might look like in a lesson (Figure 4.2).

FIGURE 4.2: Strengths-Based Approach to the Effective Teaching Practices

EFFECTIVE TEACHING PRACTICES (NCTM, 2014)	WHAT A TEACHER IN A STRENGTHS-BASED CLASSROOM DOES	WHAT A STUDENT IN A STRENGTHS-BASED CLASSROOM HEARS	WHAT A STUDENT IN A STRENGTHS-BASED CLASSROOM FEELS
Establish mathematics goals to focus learning.	Teachers let students know that they can achieve the goal and makes references to this goal throughout the lesson.	"Yesterday we learned about _____. Today, we are going to build on what you learned."	"I understand what I am supposed to do and why I am learning this material."
Implement tasks that promote reasoning and problem solving.	Teachers ensure that all students have opportunities to solve problems and hear other students' reasoning.	"Both of you thought of unique and different ways to approach the problem. It is valuable to hear one another's ideas about solving problems. Let's have you both share your thinking with the class."	"I am working on a task with other students. We are not expected to know the answer right away, but we are expected to persevere. I explain my reasoning. I can ask questions, use manipulatives, and sketch representations to explain my ideas."

continued >>

EFFECTIVE TEACHING PRACTICES (NCTM, 2014)	WHAT A TEACHER IN A STRENGTHS-BASED CLASSROOM DOES	WHAT A STUDENT IN A STRENGTHS-BASED CLASSROOM HEARS	WHAT A STUDENT IN A STRENGTHS-BASED CLASSROOM FEELS
Use and connect mathematical representations.	Teachers encourage students to identify and use representations that make sense to them. They leverage the students' strengths by bridging each strength to new learning.	"You are really great at using the base ten blocks to show your thinking. Let's use your representation to connect it to the place value mat. Let's place your representation right on the mat so we can show your thinking to the class."	"There are many different kinds of manipulatives and materials that I can pick from and use when I am working on a problem."
Facilitate meaningful mathematical discourse.	Teachers are explicit about how they want students to communicate with one another. They vary the ways that students share their strengths and vary their opportunities to identify strengths.	"I am noticing each of the groups thought of completely different ways to solve the task. I would like us to engage in a group-to-group share. I will match your group up with another group to share your ideas. After both groups have shared, I want you to point out a strength you heard from the other group and explain why it is a strength."	"I can talk to my classmates at different points throughout the lesson. I am expected to share my ideas, listen to my peers, and ask good questions."
Pose purposeful questions.	Teachers plan for and ask questions that showcase all students' thinking. They prompt students to share how others' ideas promote understanding.	"What about _____'s explanation and representation helps you understand their approach?" "How did your thinking change as a result of someone else's explanation?"	"My teacher asks lots of questions. She listens to what we say and then asks more questions. She also encourages us to ask each other questions."

Build procedural fluency from conceptual understanding.	Teachers recognize that fluency is built over time and facilitate opportunities for students to reflect on how they use flexible thinking.	"Which strategy is easiest for you to use? Why?"	"I don't feel rushed. I am expected to explain my strategy and know why I am using a particular strategy."
Support productive struggle in learning mathematics.	Teachers recognize that students have different tolerance levels for productive struggle. They consistently tell students they appreciate their hard effort.	"I am noticing that many of us are struggling productively. I see a lot of students trying different ways to solve the problem! Let's take a moment to share with a partner how you are working toward solving the problem."	"I am expected to try my hardest and let my teacher know if I get too frustrated. My teacher believes in me. I am ready to try another way when I seem to get stuck."
Elicit and use evidence of student thinking.	Teachers ask for evidence of students' thinking from correct, novel, and creative thinking.	"Please tell me more about your strategy here. This is very interesting thinking."	"My teacher likes to hear what I am thinking. Even if I am not sure how to explain my ideas, I am encouraged to explain what I can."

Effective instruction for all students is a critical component of strengths-based teaching. As we design mathematics lessons, we consider the learning strengths and needs of our students and construct learning opportunities for students to engage productively with one another in rigorous mathematics learning. This instructional approach doesn't occur magically in the moment but becomes habit over time as you institute new strengths-based practices through mindful planning.

 Turnaround Tip

Turn a mathematics teaching practice into a personal area of strength! Select a mathematics teaching practice or two to strategically target during your lesson planning. After implementing the practices, record how students responded. Ask yourself, "How did the shift to focus on the Effective Teaching Practices help me to attend to the students' strengths during this lesson?"

The following two Spotlights on Your Practice activities invite you to take a close look at your mathematics instruction from the lens of the Effective Teaching Practices (Figure 4.1). Of course, our instruction varies from day to day, but a self-appraisal often can help us examine our own strengths and opportunities for growth.

SPOTLIGHT ON YOUR PRACTICE:
Mathematics Teaching Practices

For this spotlight activity, examine each of the Effective Teaching Practices and reflect where you feel your teaching generally falls on the continuum, and then provide an example from your teaching (Figure 4.3).

FIGURE 4.3: Effective Teaching Practice Self-Analysis

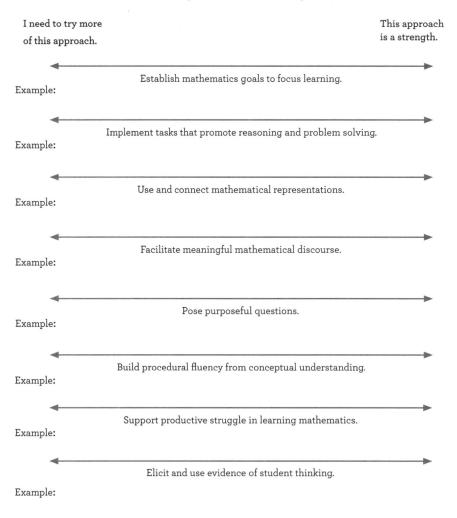

I need to try more
of this approach.

This approach
is a strength.

←——————————————————————————————————————→
Establish mathematics goals to focus learning.

Example:

←——————————————————————————————————————→
Implement tasks that promote reasoning and problem solving.

Example:

←——————————————————————————————————————→
Use and connect mathematical representations.

Example:

←——————————————————————————————————————→
Facilitate meaningful mathematical discourse.

Example:

←——————————————————————————————————————→
Pose purposeful questions.

Example:

←——————————————————————————————————————→
Build procedural fluency from conceptual understanding.

Example:

←——————————————————————————————————————→
Support productive struggle in learning mathematics.

Example:

←——————————————————————————————————————→
Elicit and use evidence of student thinking.

Example:

Reflect: Which Mathematics Teaching Practices did you describe as your strengths? Which practices do you want to further develop?

 You can download this activity at resources.corwin.com/teachingturnarounds.

In the next Spotlight, we invite you to examine a lesson from the perspective of the Mathematics Teaching Practices.

SPOTLIGHT ON YOUR PRACTICE:
Collecting Evidence for Mathematics Teaching Practices

For this Spotlight activity, identify a specific lesson you have already planned to teach. Examine your lesson for evidence of one or more of the Effective Teaching Practices. If there is no or little evidence of any of the teaching practices, write how you might incorporate one or more practice into your teaching. If there is a lot of evidence, write how you will grow this practice even more (Figure 4.4).

FIGURE 4.4: Evidence of Effective Teaching Practices in My Lesson

MATHEMATICS TEACHING PRACTICE (NCTM, 2014)	EVIDENCE	INCORPORATE THE PRACTICE
Establish mathematics goals to focus learning.		
Implement tasks that promote reasoning and problem solving.		

continued >>

>> continued

MATHEMATICS TEACHING PRACTICE (NCTM, 2014)	EVIDENCE	INCORPORATE THE PRACTICE
Use and connect mathematical representations.		
Facilitate meaningful mathematical discourse.		
Pose purposeful questions.		
Build procedural fluency from conceptual understanding.		
Support productive struggle in learning mathematics.		
Elicit and use evidence of student thinking.		

Reflect: Which practice most helps you attend to your students' strengths? Why?

online resources 🔍 You can download this activity at resources.corwin.com/teachingturnarounds.

Fixed Versus Flexible Grouping Practices

How and when students are grouped may vary widely within a school and across a school district. Sometimes, beliefs about our students' deficits interfere with their access to mathematical ideas. While often well intentioned, when we decide ahead of time that students will likely struggle, we often prevent them from engaging in high-quality instruction. We may do this because we do not want the students to become frustrated or because we worry that the students won't understand the concept, so we put them in a homogeneous group that targets their learning level but doesn't give them opportunities to strive. In fact, this practice, also known as ability grouping, or tracking, may be suggested or even required by school district policies, administrators, and teachers. Generally, this happens in one of two ways:

> **Homogeneous Grouping:** The placement or grouping of students with similar academic abilities into one classroom or group.

> **Ability Grouping:** Also known as tracking, the grouping of students by ability for the majority of the instruction over a long time; this is considered a form of fixed grouping.

1. Long-term whole-class ability grouping
2. Small-group in-class ability grouping

Both of these are considered fixed-grouping practices, and both come with similar drawbacks.

Long-Term Whole-Class Ability Grouping

In long-term whole-class ability grouping, students are perceived to have a particular level of ability to do mathematics and are placed into a designated and sustained fixed whole-class grouping. Often, we hear teachers, students, and parents refer to these groups as "low," "middle," and "high" classes. Students in each of these groups typically receive a substantially different kind of learning experience. The students in the lowest track can experience instruction characterized by teaching that emphasizes rote skills and procedures from typically less qualified teachers (Heubert & Hauser, 1999) while students in the highest track experience instruction that probes their thinking through problem solving (Flores, 2007). Student placements into these classes may be formalized through school district exams, teacher recommendations, and even IQ tests. Tracking may begin before students even enter elementary school through activities such as kindergarten screening. Oakes and Lipton (1999) describe how placement into these groups influences students' beliefs about themselves and contributes to their identity formation:

> *Both students and adults mistake labels such as "gifted," "honors student," "average," "remedial," "LD" and "MMR" for certification of overall ability or worth. These labels teach students that if the school*

does not identify them as capable in earlier grades, they should not expect to do well later. Everyone without the "gifted" label has the de facto label of "not gifted." The resource classroom is a low-status place and students who go there are low-status students. The result of all this is that most students have needlessly low self-concepts and schools have low expectations. Few students or teachers can defy those identities and expectations. These labeling effects permeate the entire school and social culture. (p. 171)

Students of color are disproportionately placed in lower-ability groups and lower-track courses as early as the first grade (Entwisle, Alexander, & Olson, 1997; Kelly, 2009) and are more likely to be placed in the lowest-track mathematics courses by the 10th grade (Kelly, 2009). Furthermore, multiple research studies have determined that students of color and students representing low income with a variety of academic abilities, including the highest, are often placed in the lowest tracks (Ascher, 1992; Burris & Welner, 2005; Wyner, Bridgeland, & Dilulio, 2007).

> **Sometimes, beliefs about our students' deficits interfere with their access to mathematical ideas.**

Remarkably, ability tracking practices don't match the levels of the assessment data results. Welner (2001) analyzed the San Jose, California, public schools' tracking practices and discovered that students with the highest assessment performance existed in all tracks. In other words, many students in different tracks performed in similar ways. The Rockland School District in New York launched an ambitious detracking program for all middle school students and dramatically reduced the achievement gap for all students, including students identified as in need of special education, students in all socioeconomic groups, and students of color (Burris & Welner, 2005).

Buoyed by the research evidence of the harmful effects of tracking, national organizations are now calling for detracking. The NCTM's (2018) newest publication, *Catalyzing Change in High School Mathematics*, offers four key recommendations, one of which specifically addresses tracking:

High school mathematics should discontinue the practice of tracking teachers as well as the practice of tracking students into qualitatively different or dead-end course pathways. (p. 23)

On the other side of the argument, proponents of tracking cite three main reasons for maintaining this practice.

- Parent pressure
  - Parents of students in the higher tracks may believe that the curriculum will be watered down if detracking occurs.

- Parents of students in the higher tracks may believe that students who struggle will slow/weigh down other students.
- Special educator access
  - Location of special educators to provide services can be challenging when the students are integrated in heterogeneous groups across many classrooms.
- Class size
  - Teachers believe that students who struggle need to be in smaller classes.
  - Teachers may be challenged to meet everyone's needs when students with varying abilities are placed together.

As we review this list, we note that the reasons for grouping students by ability is complex yet may not demonstrate flexible thinking about *students'* strengths and learning needs.

Small-Group In-Class Ability Grouping

Similar to tracking, students may be homogeneously grouped *within* a classroom—again for an extended time and based on similar criteria as when tracking occurs. In this scenario, even when the overall makeup of the classroom 's heterogeneous, students still receive long-term instruction in their small homogeneous or heterogeneous group.

That is why this is also considered an example of fixed-ability grouping. Once students are sorted into these groups, teachers design instruction to target the students' learning needs. At first glance, this makes sense to most teachers because they can differentiate their lessons for each ability group. However, the problem is the same as when the students are tracked—they still don't have the same access to high-quality mathematics tasks, peer and teacher feedback, and opportunities to talk with one another. They simply don't get to do the same kinds of mathematics. Sadly, rigid grouping practices within the classroom also promote or reinforce students' fixed mindsets about their own mathematical abilities (Boaler, 1997).

> Heterogeneous: Grouping of students with varying strengths and learning needs.

Research evidence demonstrates that the practice of fixed-ability grouping—either in whole classrooms or in small groups—is not associated with increased achievement (Hattie, 2009) and that students arranged into heterogeneous learning groups actually learn more and achieve at higher rates (Boaler, 2007). Therefore, the educational community needs to consider alternatives to fixed-ability grouping that will help students' strengths become more evident and flourish.

> The educational community needs to consider alternatives to fixed-ability grouping that will help students' strengths become more evident and flourish.

Flexible Grouping Strategies

After reading some of the effects of ability grouping and tracking, you may be wondering if the only way to proceed is to randomly group the students! While random grouping certainly has a place during instruction, we also encourage you to use flexible grouping strategies. Flexible grouping strategies allow you to purposely construct groups of students to stimulate a variety of mathematics learning opportunities, build an interconnected mathematics community, and highlight your students' individual and group strengths. By considering our grouping decisions with this more fluid lens, we have the opportunity to let students shine in a variety of grouping possibilities. Much more pliable and responsive, flexible grouping positions you to consider how the mathematics content, lesson purpose, and students' learning strengths and needs point toward a specific instructional grouping strategy. The rest of this chapter will share some flexible grouping strategies that you can implement in your own classroom.

> Flexible Grouping:
> Students learn in different groups and are assigned in a fluid manner.

The Spotlight on the next page offers an opportunity for you to discover interesting and, perhaps, revealing patterns about your grouping practices.

Strengths-Based Flexible Grouping Practices

In the next section, we explore two flexible grouping strategies that will support teachers to recognize, bolster, and strategically use students' strengths as they plan and facilitate mathematical learning experiences:

- Mixed-strength whole-group instruction
- Homogeneous-strength small-group instruction

Mixed-Strength Whole-Group Instruction

We have noticed that in some school communities, whole-group instruction is considered by some as subpar, or when it is used, they suggest it is not designed with the effective teaching practices in mind. In fact, teachers have told us that they are not allowed by their administration to teach students as a whole group because the leadership suggests it is impossible to meet the needs of each and every student using that approach. We would agree that traditional whole-group instruction where the teacher stands at the front of the room and presents a "same-size-fits-all" lesson to all the students for an hour is not likely to meet the needs of the students.

SPOTLIGHT ON YOUR PRACTICE:
Grouping Decisions

For this spotlight, examine the variety and kinds of grouping decisions that you make during your instruction.

1. How often do your students have an opportunity to work with others who share their strengths?

   Seldom   *Once Every Few Weeks*   *Daily*

   1   2   3   4   5

   When they do, what does this look like?

2. How often do students have an opportunity to work in mixed-ability groups?

   Seldom   *Once Every Few Weeks*   *Daily*

   1   2   3   4   5

   When they do, what does this look like?

3. How do/might flexible grouping opportunities support your students to demonstrate their strengths in your classroom?

4. What particular mathematics content areas at your grade level invite flexible grouping strategies?

When we use the term *whole group*, we mean that the entire group of students will engage in the same mathematics lesson. However, this does not mean that students will receive and interact with the mathematics as a whole group during the entire mathematics class period. Students will have an opportunity to engage with partners or small groups throughout the lesson. Understanding what this form of whole-group instruction would look like from a strengths-based perspective can help you meet your learners' needs and build a strong, strengths-based mathematical community. For this reason, we call this kind of instruction mixed-strength whole-group instruction, meaning that the students are situated in a variety of small groups within the whole group and are instructed to complete the same or similar task or series of tasks at the same time while the teacher circulates the room, facilitates thinking, and advances learning through probing questions. The tasks can appear to be the same, but often differentiation is taking place because the teacher is available to facilitate questions, provide clarification, and collect formative assessment data as she interacts with each group. While students are still working in groups, this model is different from what may be the common alternative to whole-group instruction—which would be more akin to workstations or a station rotation model.

> **Mixed-Strength Whole-Group Instruction:** All students in the whole class work on the same task (i.e., whole group) but collaborate in smaller mixed-strength groups.

First, let's unpack what mixed-strength whole-group instruction might look like in a classroom. Casey, a first-grade teacher, wants to begin her place value unit with an open-ended place value task that will encourage her students to use a variety of strategies to find out how many groups of ten are in the counting collection. Casey begins the lesson by arranging the students in their small heterogeneous-strengths groups. She displays eight one-gallon transparent bags (one for each group) filled with a variety of materials (e.g., toothpicks, googly eyes, rubber bands, paperclips) to the whole class. She then asks the students to gather in their mixed-strength groups, which she refers to as students' *Strong* groups to discuss what they notice and wonder about the bags. She then records what the students notice and wonder.

I NOTICE . . .	I WONDER . . .
There are a lot of things in the bags.	Where did you get the stuff?
There are more toothpicks!	How many toothpicks?
They look like craft things.	Are we going to make something?
There are eight bags.	How many things in all the bags?
They are colorful.	If we could organize them?
	Can we skip count the objects to find out how many there are?
	Are there the same number of things in each bag?

Casey notes that one of the students who sometimes struggles with tasks such as this one posed an advanced question about the skip counting, so she decides to connect his wonder to the task. She says,

> *I really like when we work in our Strong groups because you are able to hear some really powerful thinking. Jem asked, "Can we skip count the objects to find out how many there are?" which is an excellent mathematics question because he is wondering if he can use mathematics that we have been learning to find out how many objects are in the bag. Also, Mariela asked, "Are there the same number of things in each bag?" Both of these questions are excellent questions because we can use mathematics to answer them. We are actually going to use Jem's and Mariela's wonders for our task today!*

Next, Casey poses the task: How can we arrange our objects to find out how many are in each bag? What would be a useful amount we should group the items into? Then, how could we use what we know about counting or skip counting to count the number of items in the bag? She distributes a bag to each group, chart paper, and markers for each group. She then states, "I have ten frames, place value mats, and hundreds charts on the table if your group would like to use them." While the students work in their Strong groups, Casey travels around and collects formative assessment information about student thinking on her clipboard.

Casey chose to use the mixed-strength whole-group instruction for several reasons:

1. *Mathematics Content:* Place value understanding of numbers up to 100 is well suited for this grouping model because students can use a variety of strategies to build conceptual understanding for the unit of ten and groups of ten.

2. *Lesson Purpose:* Students first build conceptual understanding of using ten as a unit by using their own strategies about efficient ways to group and count large numbers of objects.

3. *Students' Learning Strengths and Needs:* Students possess varying strengths in developing models for place value. Some students excel at building representations using place value materials while others draw representations or use tallies on place value charts. Casey wants the students to have an opportunity for students to share their unique perspectives.

Figure 4.5 visually depicts the lesson. Students engage in the launch as a whole group, break into their *Strong* groups to solve the task, and come back together as a whole class to unpack the task.

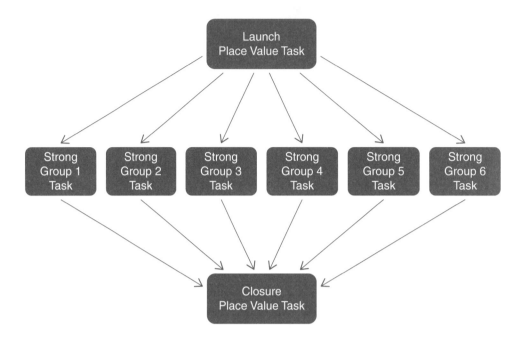

Casey closes this lesson by highlighting the students' place value representations, specifically using strengths language. She asks the students to conduct a gallery walk to identify the strengths of the representations made by the different groups and then calls on students to lift up each other's strengths before she highlights the students' work.

Casey: What were some of the strengths of your classmates' place value work that you saw during the gallery walk?

Louella: I saw that Kendra was organized.

Marta: I saw that Michael put his cubes in ten frames, so I could easily count by tens.

Eli: I saw that Bernie used color to draw his tens and ones. His colors matched the blocks!

Henri: I saw that lots of people organized their bags into tens so I didn't have to count them one by one.

Casey noted, as she often does, that the students' work and their noticings about their peers' work are very powerful and thoughtful.

Setting Up Your Classroom for Mixed-Strength Whole-Group Instruction

As described in the preceding example, we suggest that you arrange the classroom to reflect the variety of strengths that students possess. Here's an example of this process you may use in your classroom:

Step 1: Organize the students' desks in clusters of four (Figure 4.6) and assign each student to a cluster with a particular strength in mind. The purpose of mixing the students is to provide opportunities for the students to support and learn from one another. Students benefit from contributing and hearing different ideas from classmates. It is important to also let the students know why and how you have grouped them so they can acknowledge their own strengths as well as their classmates' strengths. However, it is important that students are not pigeonholed as identifying with particular strengths but rather celebrated for contributing various strengths. For example, a teacher may say, "I have organized your groups so that each of you can contribute your strengths to solving the problem."

FIGURE 4.6: Sample Student Work Cluster

Source: Created by Bob Ronau.

Step 2: Consider the types of mathematics content and lesson purpose that invite whole-group instruction. For example, when first introducing a new topic using an open-ended task that the whole class engages in, students can explore ideas and strategies within their mixed-strengths groups, capturing different ideas and perspectives. You may first decide to use the mixed-strength whole-group instruction because you want students to contribute to the problem-solving process using their strengths, build off one another's ideas, and engage in lively discourse.

Step 3: Let's look at another example. A third-grade teacher, Marlo, began her fraction unit by asking students to find all the ways they could show $\frac{1}{2}$ using pattern blocks using the yellow hexagon as the whole. Students then recorded these representations on chart paper and shared their thinking with the whole class. After a brief large-group lesson launch, the students worked in smaller mixed-strengths groups to find and record all their ideas. The teacher circulated while the students were working, asking questions such as the following:

- How many ways to show one half have you found?
- What are you noticing about your halves?
- How are you using your strengths to work together?
- What are some of the good ideas that your group members have shared?
- How does the representation that _____ constructed help you?
- Is there another way to record your idea?
- How can you prove that [pointing to the yellow hexagon] is a whole?
- How are you using your mathematics strengths to help your group solve this task?
- How is _____ using her strengths to help the group?

As the teacher walked around to the groups, she put sticky notes on the children's desks with a 1, 2, or 3 on it as a way to signal the teams the order they would come to the document camera to explain their strategy to the class during the discussion. By asking mathematics content questions and by calling on students to identify their contributions using strengths language, the teacher is capitalizing on large-group instructional opportunities. She is able to move about the room to observe all the students' thinking, collect formative assessment data, question students, and probe student thinking and strategy use. On the flip side, the students are able to communicate mathematically and work together to showcase their strengths, recognize others' strengths, and support one another's mathematical thinking.

Marlo is also observing how the students are using their strengths to contribute to the group's efforts. As she observes, she shares her observation with the students making the mathematics visible and connecting the students' strengths. For example, when she observes the group work illustrated in Figure 4.7, she notices that the students have used the three sheets of paper to show $\frac{1}{2}$ in multiple ways, with different-sized wholes.

FIGURE 4.7: Student Representations

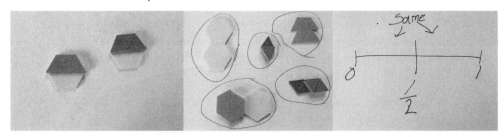

Marlo probes, "This is very interesting to see how you have organized your work to show many different ways to make $\frac{1}{2}$. Can you tell me about your work?"

Cara shares, "Well I made the $\frac{1}{2}$ like we did last year using the hexagon as the whole, but Kia made all these other halves I never thought of and Treasure made a numberline!"

Marlo asks, "What are the strengths that each of you brought to this work?"

Kia explains, "Well Cara always remembers stuff and Treasure likes the numberlines. I thought of new ways to make a half. So what we did is good."

Marlo says, "The different models bring up a very interesting idea! Are all of the halves that you made equal to each other?"

The students exclaim, "Yes!" in unison.

Marlo waits while they look at their models. Then, Kia exclaims, "Wait a minute! They are all $\frac{1}{2}$ but they are different sizes! Can they still be $\frac{1}{2}$?"

Marlo smiles and says, "Let's bring that spectacular question up for the whole group. I want you to present your work and your observations and then pose that question to the class for a discussion."

 Turnaround Tip

A critical part of whole-group instruction is trying out different types of grouping strategies. Some students work best alone or in pairs, while other students thrive in slightly larger groups of three or four students. Experiment with different grouping strategies within the large group. Observe student discourse and student engagement to determine the grouping strategy that works best for you.

Homogeneous-Strength Small Groups

This type of flexible grouping strategy is likely more familiar to you, but the key is that this is one of several grouping strategies you should use to support student learning. With this strategy, first, the teacher launches the lesson by grouping the students in mixed-ability groups to explore ideas and strategies within a particular content standard. Next, the teacher assigns students into two or three small homogeneous groups to develop further students' mathematical understanding. Take the example of Casey you read about earlier in the chapter. Following Casey's lesson on place value, she notes that some students have discovered the place value patterns and can connect the place value base ten materials to the corresponding digits, while other students still need to count objects by ones to find out how many groups of ten are in a set and then assign the numeral. Therefore, Casey launches her place value lesson but displays the following (Figure 4.8).

FIGURE 4.8: Which One Does Not Belong?

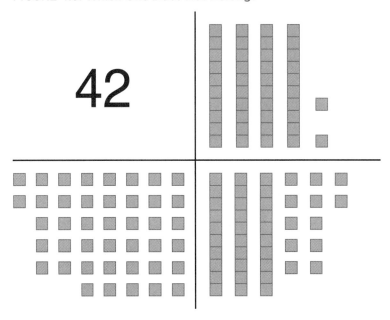

She says, "Which one of the four parts does not belong?" While all of the examples represent 42, Casey is interested in how the students explain their selection. Some students might notice that all of the amounts equal 42, but the representations are different. Some of the representations show pictures of three ways to represent 42 using place value models—unitary (count by ones), base ten (groups of ten), and equivalent (nonstandard modeling of the number)—while one does not. Casey believes the whole-group launch will engage students in a lively discussion in which all students will benefit from participating, hearing, and explaining. Next, Casey arranges the students in two homogeneous groups for additional targeted instruction. For this particular lesson, one group will continue to count to find out how many tens in a group of cubes, arrange the cubes into units of ten (group into a rod or collect in a cup), and then write the corresponding digits on a place value chart. The other group will draw two-digit cards from a bag, create the largest number, and then identify the number of groups of tens and ones each number has. While the students are working on the task, Casey will be walking around observing student performance and asking questions such as "What pattern do you notice about your place value representation and the digits in the number?"

This visual represents the lesson structure for the strengths in a small-group lesson (Figure 4.9). Students engage in the launch as a whole group, break into two smaller strengths groups to work on separate tasks, and come back together in the whole group to share strategies. While students are working on the task, Casey is circulating, observing, asking questions, collecting formative assessment data, and highlighting students' mathematical strategies and ideas.

FIGURE 4.9: Model of a Homogeneous-Strength Small-Group Lesson

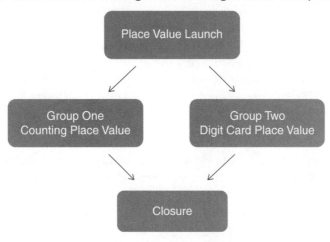

During the closure, Casey will ask a few students from each group to share their work with the rest of the class. In this way, she can recognize the strengths of individual students and highlight place value vocabulary. The differences between this kind of homogeneous small groups and that described earlier as fixed groups are very nuanced. This example illustrates the kind of flexible grouping strategy that teachers can use to target students' conceptual understanding that is responsive and fluid. Students are not placed in these rigid groups to complete the task for the entire topic but are selected and moved as students' needs arise in the moment. In this model, each group is working on different but related tasks while the teacher is circulating between both groups (see Chapter 5 parallel tasks). As the teacher circulates, she observes, asks questions, and probes student thinking. In the next chapter, we discuss a parallel task, which pairs nicely with this model. This grouping strategy often occurs after teachers have provided students time to develop mathematical concepts. Some teachers provide students an opportunity to self-assess their understanding of the concepts, and then the students select the group they would like to participate in. The whole-group discussions that students engage in allow all students to continue to make connections and contribute to the discussion, which champions mathematical authority for all.

Targeted Small-Group Instruction Through a Strengths-Based Lens

Different from the previous organizational strategies, this strategy is for when students receive targeted instruction in small groups. Typically, small-group instruction is conducted with students' abilities in mind. Students are grouped by ability and rotate through a series of activities. Versions of this include the workshop model, the guided math model, and station rotation model. These activities typically include time for students to receive instruction; work on a computer, iPad, or other technology device; and complete an independent activity. While the teacher is monitoring the entire class, she is generally also focusing on providing strategic instruction for a small group of students who possess the same mathematics learning need while the other students are working independently. The philosophy behind this kind of grouping practice is that students' needs can sometimes best be addressed in same-need groups. The key is that the students should not be placed in fixed groups but rather be assigned fluidly to the groups as students' learning needs are revealed.

A common and concerning characteristic of this grouping practice is the extended time that students spend working independently. In a typical one-hour mathematics instructional period, students may spend up to 45 minutes working independently with little to no interaction from the teacher or peers. Therefore, not only must the teacher-led small-group instruction be strategically planned and implemented, but teachers must also plan the independent activities to address the students' mathematics learning strengths and needs. Sometimes we can be persuaded to think that all of our students' needs are being met because they are rotating through a series of activities, but Nanci Smith (2017), author of *Every Math Learner, Grades 6–12: A Doable Approach to Teaching With Learning Differences in Mind*, advises that we need to ensure that students are engaged in activities that are not generic but, instead, appropriate and differentiated for the students' particular learning needs.

The targeted small-group format can buoy students' strengths in very strategic ways. For example, all students rotate through the teacher-led stations and complete activities as a small group or in pairs that help them leverage their strengths to develop both conceptual understanding and fluency. In this example, students work with the teacher on the same learning need. After students complete this strategic learning activity, they choose to complete one of the other activities independently or in pairs. In the following example, the teacher has created an activity to address a student or group of students' learning needs by leveraging a strength. The teacher can assign one or more students to the activity. In this case, the teacher is very purposeful in setting the learning intention for the activity through a strengths-based lens. In Figure 4.10, the teacher has determined the learning needs and strengths of her students and then designed a learning activity to meet those needs.

Once again, the teacher closes the lesson by highlighting mathematics strengths that she noted as she worked with each group. She asks the students to demonstrate their mathematical understanding for the entire class while also emphasizing the students' strengths.

Flexible grouping is so powerful! You are able to nimbly group your students by considering the mathematics content, lesson purpose, and students' strengths and learning needs.

FIGURE 4.10: Setting Learning Activities Through Students' Needs and Strengths

Student Names:		
Standard: Place value understanding of tens and ones.		
LEARNING NEED	STRENGTH	ACTIVITY
Conceptual understanding of the value of the tens and the position of the digit in the tens place.	Visual Mathematics Drawing	***Roll and Draw*** Students roll a red die to represent the number of tens and a green die to represent the number of ones. Then they draw a picture (i.e., lines and dots) to record the values. Students continue to roll five times, each time drawing a picture to represent the values. Finally, students order their pictures from least to greatest and explain how they know particular values are greater.
Symbolic representations to the models.	Perseverance	***Mixed-Up Digit Challenge*** Students are given digit cards and a clue. They must read the clue and make the matching two-digit number using the digit cards. Digits: 8 and 3 The digit in the tens place is an odd number. What is the number? Digits: 2 and 4 The digit in the ones column is two less than the digit in the tens column. What is the number?

 Turnaround Tip

Develop an environment for sharing how classmates helped one another while you were teaching a small-group lesson. As you close a lesson, ask students to share who and how someone else helped them.

In the following Spotlight, consider when and how you might use these strengths-based grouping strategies.

SPOTLIGHT ON YOUR PRACTICES:
Mathematics Topic, Standard, and Lesson Purpose

In this Spotlight, consider how the mathematics topic, mathematics standard, and lesson purpose point toward a specific instructional grouping decision (Figure 4.11). An example has been provided for you.

FIGURE 4.11: Collection Sheet for Data That Supports Grouping Decisions

MATHEMATICS TOPICS OR STANDARD(S)	LESSON PURPOSE (CONCEPTUAL UNDERSTANDING, PROCEDURAL FLUENCY, OR APPLICATION?)	GROUP SIZE (HOW MIGHT STUDENTS BE GROUPED?)	AT WHAT TIME DURING THE TOPIC? (DURING THE MATHEMATICS CLASSROOM, WHEN DO STUDENTS WORK WITH OTHERS?)	WHO (RECORD THE NAMES OF THE STUDENTS.)
Geometry Defining attributes of 2D shapes	Conceptual understanding	Whole-group exploration in strong groups	Launch	All students

The following Try It! activities suggest a way to organize students in their strengths groups. You can use the list of strengths suggested in the introduction or develop your own list.

Try It! Strengths-Based Compass

Introduce the compass wheel (see Figure 4.12) to your students to establish new grouping strategies around their strengths. For each compass point, students are assigned to a different student and grouping arrangement. Prior to using the compass, predetermine the groups below. Explain to students that you have grouped them so they can feature their strengths to support one another. For example, you might say, "For this task, you will work with your East group because each of you have different strengths that you can contribute."

Compass Partners

North: Partner (same strengths)

South: Triad (multiple strengths: group of three with different strengths)

East: Quad (multiple strengths: group of four with different strengths)

West: Partner (different strengths)

Example:

North: Partners—Sammy (sketching) and Micah (visual representation)

South: Triad—Carlo (procedural thinking), Bettina (persevering through a task), Max (using manipulatives)

East: Quad—Patricia (mathematical communication), Henry (visual representation), Mimi (making connections), Jacob (sketching)

West: Partner—JayLynn (mathematical communication), Markus (persevering through a task)

(Continued)

FIGURE 4.12: Compass Partners

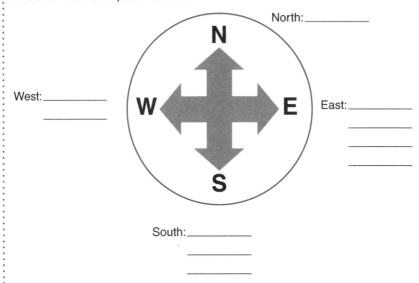

North: _____

West: _____
_____

East: _____
_____
_____
_____

South: _____
_____
_____

Reflect: How do students respond to this grouping strategy? How do you feel it was successful? What do you notice about the students' engagement?

 This planning tool can be downloaded for use at resources.corwin.com/teachingturnarounds.

In the preceding Try It!, the teacher makes the grouping decisions about the students. In the following Try It!, students are invited to strategically select partners.

 **Try It!** Choose a Partner

You can empower your students to select partners who can support their learning and productivity by asking them to identify classmates to help them work within a variety of grouping structures. You can collect this information through a survey or by conducting a short interview, using a template such as Figure 4.13.

FIGURE 4.13: Identifying Classmates Who Can Support Learning Interview Protocol

PROMPT	NOTES
I work well with _____.	
_____ and I listen to each other's ideas.	
I work harder when I am partnered with _____.	
_____ tells me how smart I am doing in math.	
_____ encourages me.	
_____ learns from my math strategies.	

Reflect: How does this information support your instructional decision making? How do students respond?

online resources 🔎 This activity can be downloaded for use at resources.corwin.com/teachingturnarounds.

Summary

This chapter explores the variety of options that highlight the power of using strengths as a variable for student group placement rather than the traditional grouping by weakness. As you will note in the summary table shown in Figure 4.14, important similarities and differences can steer you to one choice over another given the combination of learners' needs, mathematics content, children's strengths, and materials needed.

FIGURE 4.14: Characteristics of Four Grouping Approaches for Instruction

	WHOLE-CLASS ABILITY GROUPING (TRACKING)	ABILITY-RANKED SMALL GROUP (WITHIN CLASS)	MIXED-STRENGTH WHOLE GROUP	HOMOGENEOUS-STRENGTH SMALL GROUP
Fixed	✓	✓		
Flexible			✓	✓
Long term	✓	✓		
Short term			✓	✓
Based on perceptions or occasional performance assessments	✓	✓		
Based on daily formative assessment with a strengths focus			✓	✓

Turn Around Tasks

Every day, my daddy told me the same thing. "Once a task is just begun, never leave it till it's done. Be the labour great or small, do it well or not at all."

—Quincy Jones

The mathematical tasks teachers choose to use in their instruction hold the potential to captivate students' attention, recognize and appreciate their strengths, and build a bridge to areas where the work may become more difficult. Problems that ignite students' interests and, frankly, their motivation are problems *worth* solving. Consider, for example, the infamous Peanuts cartoon strip when Sally ponders a word problem and says, "Only in word problems can you buy 60 cantaloupes and no one asks what the [heck] is wrong with you" (Schulz, 1963). Sally's sentiment resonates with many students who also wonder what interest does this subject hold when they see tasks that are outside their daily experiences during mathematics instruction. Beyond student interest, tasks that are cognitively rich challenge students to think creatively, explore multiple solution pathways, connect mathematical ideas, apply prior or develop new understandings, and regulate and moderate cognitive processes and dispositions (i.e., perseverance, positive attitudes) (National Council of Teachers of Mathematics [NCTM], 2014). This chapter explores various ways to use what we call turnaround tasks to promote students' strengths and thereby build their mathematical success.

> Over time, as the students engage in a variety of tasks, they also begin to develop overarching ideas about themselves as learners and doers of mathematics.

High Cognitive Tasks

Task: A segment of a classroom activity that is devoted to the development of a particular mathematical idea (Stein & Smith, 1998, p. 269).

Teachers construct, choose, and implement many different kinds of tasks in the mathematics classroom. These tasks provide varying opportunities to influence student thinking and learning; some tasks push students to think more deeply while others require minimal thought and perseverance (Hiebert, 1997; Stein, Smith, Henningsen, & Silver, 2009).

As students see a pattern of task types, they begin to develop ideas about what it means to learn mathematics. Over time, as the students engage in a variety of tasks, they also begin to develop overarching ideas about themselves as learners and doers of mathematics. Stein and Smith (1998) explain, "The day-in and day-out cumulative effect of classroom based tasks leads to the development of students' implicit ideas about the nature of mathematics—about whether mathematics is something about which they can personally make sense and about how long and how hard they should have to work to do so" (p. 269). These tasks may vary in depth, richness, and cognitive demand. The four levels of cognitive demand (NCTM, 2014) adapted from Smith and Stein (1998) describe the characteristics of these mathematics tasks in terms of their cognitive demand (Figure 5.1).

Cognitive Demand: Level of cognitive effort that a student must exert while engaging in a task.

FIGURE 5.1: Levels of Cognitive Demand With Task Types

LOWER-LEVEL DEMANDS	HIGHER-LEVEL DEMANDS
Memorization Tasks	*Procedures With Connections Tasks*
• Involves either reproducing previously learned facts, rules, formulae, or definitions or committing facts, rules, formulae, or definitions to memory.	• Focus students' attention on the use of procedures for the purpose of developing deeper levels of understanding of mathematical concepts and ideas.
• Cannot be solved using procedures because a procedure does not exist or because the time frame in which the task is being completed is too short to use a procedure.	• Suggest pathways to follow (explicitly or implicitly) that are broad general procedures that have close connections to underlying conceptual ideas as opposed to narrow algorithms that are opaque with respect to underlying concepts.
• Are not ambiguous—such tasks involve exact reproduction of previously seen material and what is to be reproduced is clearly and directly stated.	• Usually are represented in multiple ways (e.g., visual diagrams, manipulatives, symbols, problem situations). Making connections among multiple representations helps to develop meaning.

• Have no connection to the concepts or meaning that underlies the facts, rules, formulae, or definitions being learned or reproduced.	• Require some degree of cognitive effort. Although general procedures may be followed, they cannot be followed mindlessly. Students need to engage with the conceptual ideas that underlie the procedures in order to successfully complete the task and develop understanding.
LOWER-LEVEL DEMANDS	**HIGHER-LEVEL DEMANDS**
Procedures Without Connections Tasks	*Doing Mathematics Tasks*
• Are algorithmic. Use of the procedure is either specifically called for or its use is evident based on prior instruction, experience, or placement of the task. • Require limited cognitive demand for successful completion. There is little ambiguity about what needs to be done and how to do it. • Have no connection to the concepts or meaning that underlie the procedure being used. • Are focused on producing correct answers rather than developing mathematical understanding. • Require no explanations, or explanations that focus solely on describing the procedure that was used.	• Requires complex and nonalgorithmic thinking (i.e., there is not a predictable, well-rehearsed approach or pathway explicitly suggested by the task, task instructions, or a worked-out example). • Requires students to explore and to understand the nature of mathematical concepts, processes, or relationships. • Demands self-monitoring or self-regulation of one's own cognitive processes. • Requires students to access relevant knowledge and experiences and make appropriate use of them in working through the task. • Requires students to analyze the task and actively examine task constraints that may limit possible solution strategies and solutions. • Requires considerable cognitive effort and may involve some level of anxiety for the student due to the unpredictable nature of the solution process required.

Source: These characteristics are derived from the work of Doyle (1988) on academic tasks and Resnick (1987) on high-level thinking skills, the Professional Standards for Teaching Mathematics (NCTM, 1991), and the examination and categorization of hundreds of tasks used in the QUASAR classrooms (Stein, Grover, & Henningsen, 1996; Stein, Lane, & Silver, 1996). Republished with permission of the National Council of Teachers of Mathematics, from Smith and Stein (1998); permission conveyed through Copyright Clearance Center, Inc.

High cognitive tasks are those that push students to think outside the boundaries of the traditional mathematics that you were likely taught when you were in elementary school. Instead, the tasks invite students to identify subtle patterns, make generalizations, and, in some cases, ask students to have a disposition to be ready for anything—even "ready to be wrong." When you are incorporating tasks that are developed to unearth students' mathematical thinking rather than focusing on the one right answer using one correct approach, you are moving rapidly toward the use of high cognitive tasks. After students carry out these tasks over time, they become more ready and able to tackle a challenge. They know that in giving them such tasks, you as their teacher have a high regard for their ability, which in turn increases their self-efficacy. They learn to be unafraid of cognitive dissonance, they begin to love puzzles and counterintuitive situations, and they begin to trust themselves to persevere. They feel more confident leveraging their own strengths, even when the pathway to success may not be clear. For all of these reasons, rigorous mathematics using high-cognitive tasks is not just for some—it is for all. Over time, working with these high cognitive tasks, students then say—Bring it on!

To illustrate the sometimes subtle differences between the levels of cognitive demand, take a look at the tasks in this Try It!

 **Try It!**   **Task Matching Cards**

Look at the task descriptions in Figure 5.2 and match the tasks types to the cards.

FIGURE 5.2: Task Matching Cards

Paulo's grandpapa is 63 years old. His mother is 36 years old. How old was his grandpapa when his mother was born? How could you explain your strategy and solution to someone else using manipulatives or math tools?	Solve. 415 + _____ = 900
Think of a real-life situation that describes the following problem. Solve it and then write a word problem that matches your situation. $\frac{2}{6} + \frac{1}{2} =$	Solve. 5 × 5 = 4 × 6 =

| Solve.

6 + 6 =

7 + 7 = | Think of a real-life situation to go with this problem. Write the word problem and solve.

☐ + ☐ = ☐ |

Reflect: What do you notice about the tasks? Which task type was easiest to identify? Which task type was most difficult to identify? How might this activity help you consider the kinds of tasks you use in your classroom?

Next, we give you an opportunity to analyze the tasks you use in your classroom!

The following Spotlight provides teachers with an opportunity to explore the tasks they use.

SPOTLIGHT ON YOUR PRACTICE:
Analyzing Your Tasks

Collect and analyze at least a week's worth of already taught mathematics instructional tasks.

1. Using Figure 5.2 as a guide, what do you notice about the cognitive level of the tasks?

2. What did you notice about the types of questions you asked?

3. How did students respond to each of the tasks?

4. Where did you notice the most student engagement?

5. Where did you notice the strongest evidence of students' use of strategies?

6. Where do you notice their best descriptions of their thinking?

7. What were the characteristics of the most successful tasks for students' learning? How can you make more of the same happen next time?

Once teachers have successfully navigated task selection by developing or identifying a rich task to use, they can strategically plan how they implement their turnaround tasks. In other words, they think about those seemingly endless but critical daily teaching decisions that influence how they facilitate learning within the task with intentional questions and prompts. The tasks that teachers construct, select, and facilitate make a substantial difference to students' learning! The combined effort of the teacher to select and implement the task matters. Students actually learn the most when they routinely engage in high-level tasks, with a high level of implementation that requires students to think and reason about the mathematics they are learning (Boaler & Staples, 2008). On the flip side, students learn the least when the tasks are at a low level and are largely procedural, even when the implementation is at a high level (Boaler & Staples, 2008; Figure 5.3).

> " The tasks that teachers construct, select, and facilitate make a substantial difference to students' learning!

FIGURE 5.3: Looking at the Learning Results of Different Levels of Task Quality and Implementation

TASK QUALITY	IMPLEMENTATION	RESULTS
Low	High or low	Low
High	Low	Moderate
High	High	High

Source: Adapted from Stein and Lane (1996).

When teachers are implementing tasks at a high level, they ask high-level questions, promote student-to-student discourse, arrange students to work together to develop and compare strategies and solutions, and make the mathematics visible by using students' mathematical ideas to promote understanding. Well-intentioned teachers may reduce the cognitive demand of the task by overexplaining or focusing on procedures without meaning, modeling before students have opportunities to interact with the problem, or breaking down the task into small chunks that make the larger task unrecognizable (Stein, Grover, & Henningsen, 1996). Positioning students' strengths as a focus of the task design and setting students as "thinkers" rather than simply "doers" during lesson implementation create an environment that promotes success. The following discussion explores ways to design turnaround tasks that will engage and promote your students' mathematical strengths.

Turn Around a Task: Designing a Personalized, Strengths-Based Instructional Task

Several years ago, we began asking teacher candidates and teachers to first identify their students' strengths and learning challenges and then design targeted instructional mathematics tasks for the students to solve. The results were empowering for both the elementary students and the preservice teachers. The students basked in the attention and performed beyond our wildest imaginations. The novice teachers were equally empowered as they discovered opportunities to authentically connect with students by leveraging their strengths. The teachers learned that the tasks could be designed to be completed by individual students or in small cooperative groups. In this chapter, we explore several ways to design, adapt, and implement mathematics turnaround tasks from a strengths-based approach.

First, let's examine how, by way of practice, a team of teachers cooperatively planned a strengths-based instructional task for a student. We acknowledge that this process is time-consuming, and we are not suggesting that teachers prepare these tasks for every student. However, this is a worthy exercise to help you become accustomed to and see the potential in adapting and designing tasks through a strengths-based lens. In this example to start, one teacher selected a student who was mystifying in some way. Perhaps the student faced learning challenges or some other obstacles that seem to interfere with success. Or, perhaps the teacher was challenged to develop a deeper relationship with the student. The team used a strengths-based task design protocol to set the stage for their discussion (Figure 5.4).

FIGURE 5.4: Strengths-Based Task Discussion Protocol

1. Appoint a recorder and agree that the discussion will include observable student behaviors or evidence via student work samples.
2. Distribute the student's work samples and other evidence of performance.

Based on the work samples and the teachers' descriptions of the student:

3. Discuss, identify, and record the student's strengths.
4. Discuss, identify, and record the student's challenges.
5. Discuss, identify, and record the student's interests.
6. Develop a preliminary theory for the student's current struggle.
7. Develop a new task for the student and collect data on the student's performance.
8. What differences do you notice? What might be the key to a more effective task for this student?

The teacher participants analyzed the samples of student work and classroom anecdotes and recorded their conjectures (Figure 5.5). By establishing a protocol, the teachers were able to keep their focus on using evidence to describe each student's strengths and challenges.

FIGURE 5.5: Strengths-Based Analysis

STRENGTHS-BASED ANALYSIS

NAME _____   GRADE _____

COMPONENT	EVIDENCE OF STRENGTHS	EVIDENCE OF CHALLENGES
Mathematics concepts		
Communication		
Representation		
Disposition toward mathematics		
Working memory		
Attention		
Socio-emotional		
Organizational		
Perseverance		
Clarity of ideas		
Ability to take a risk		
Connections to other mathematical ideas		

online resources ➤ This template can be downloaded for use at resources.corwin.com/teachingturnarounds.

Let's look at Marco, a student who has documented learning disabilities. The team, consisting of the mathematics teacher, paraeducator, and reading teacher, discussed Marco's strengths and challenges and recorded the following information (see Figure 5.6).

FIGURE 5.6: Strengths-Based Analysis of a Student's Work

STRENGTHS-BASED ANALYSIS

NAME __Marco__ GRADE __4__

COMPONENT	EVIDENCE OF STRENGTHS	EVIDENCE OF CHALLENGES
Mathematics concepts	Addition facts Knows most multiplication facts Uses "think addition" to subtract whenever possible.	Struggles with multidigit subtraction with an internal zero. Fraction understanding including equal parts, comparing fractions, and ordering fractions. Overgeneralizes understanding from whole numbers to fractions. He said, "Eighths are always bigger than thirds because 8 is bigger than 3." When he then uses manipulatives to compare, he says, "But that doesn't make sense!" as he trusts his whole-number comparisons. He relies on rote understanding or rules when confronted with challenges to his conceptual understanding.
Communication	Enjoys talking with peers and adults. Seeks out adults to tell stories about weekend activities.	When frustrated, will stop talking, sit back, and become unresponsive. It is critical to intervene or redirect before he gets to this point. Struggles to articulate needs. Sometimes struggles to listen to peers when he has an idea to share. Can lose the idea if he has to wait too long.

continued >>

>> continued

COMPONENT	EVIDENCE OF STRENGTHS	EVIDENCE OF CHALLENGES
Representation	Prefers to initiate problem solving with manipulatives, particularly regional models for fractions. Regularly uses the place value chart. Enjoys drawing and will often draw elaborate interpretations of the manipulatives.	Struggles to use the numberline (continuous model) for fractions. Sometimes struggles to select the appropriate manipulative to use for a given context. Can become too focused on drawing rather than the sketch's connections to other mathematical representations (i.e., equation).
Disposition toward mathematics	Consistently responds positively to group tasks. Productively struggles well when other students are teaming with him.	If unsure, will stop working on a task when working alone. Seeks teacher's early feedback before starting a task by asking, "Am I doing this right?"
Memory	Remembers particular previous learning experiences that interest him such as the carnival task.	Inconsistent working memory. Can lose track of ideas if they are not recorded. Remembers more toward the end of the week (Wednesday to Friday).
Attention	Attends to tasks that interest him and/or those that involve working with a partner or small group. Particularly attends well when working with Sammy and Jerome.	Rapidly loses attention when working solo, particularly when the task is routine. Can exhibit learned helplessness when he stops working and waits for teacher attention.
Socio-emotional	Prefers working with boys to girls but enjoys working with Soha. They are a good pair and complement each other well.	In the afternoon, sometimes struggles to regulate emotions and will on occasion call out about his feelings.
Organizational	Often chooses large blank paper over lined paper. Likes using grid paper when recording equations.	Uses space on a paper in nonconventional ways. Will often start at the bottom of the paper and work up.

Next, the team looked at the interest interview that Petra, the math teacher, conducted with Marco.

Petra had asked the following:

1. If you could do any activity right now, what would you like to do?

2. What is your favorite way to spend your time on the weekend?

3. What do you like to do most in math class? Why?

4. Do you like to work alone or with a partner? Why?

While the teachers knew that Marco loved to play video games, they learned something new from the interview. Marco loves to bake with his grandmother. His mother and father work two jobs and do not have time to bake, but his grandparents just moved in with the family and have been teaching him how to make special Greek cakes from old family recipes. Marco shared, "We made a Greek honey cake that the whole family gobbled up so we are going to make two cakes next weekend. My grandpa even said it was the best cake Ya-Ya [Grandmother] ever made!"

The team was thrilled with this illuminating information and decided to design a task using Marco's new interest in baking cakes and strength in drawing or sketching representations to address his current struggle to conceptually understand fractions. They wrote the following task:

Marco and his grandmother are baking honey cakes for the family to eat. Marco's whole family is excited to eat the cakes. Here is a list of how much of a cake each family member plans to eat:

Andrew: $\frac{1}{8}$

Alexander: $\frac{1}{2}$

Grandpa: $\frac{1}{3}$

Yaya: $\frac{1}{6}$

Marco: $\frac{1}{4}$

Which is the largest amount of cake a family member wants? Smallest amount? What is the order of the family's requests from largest to smallest cake amounts? How many cakes should Marco and his grandmother make? Prove your idea with representations of the family's different portions.

Petra launched the lesson by showing a photograph of Marco and his grandmother baking a cake. Then, she introduced the task to the students and distributed chart paper and same-sized cake templates to the student groups. Students excitedly worked on the task. Petra noticed that other students asked Marco to look at their cake sketches, on which he either approved or made suggestions. Petra overheard him saying to Sammy, "Yes, but you should make sure your drawing is clear so you can compare the fractions."

We understand that designing a task with an individual student in mind is, perhaps, unrealistic. However, teachers can collect information about their students' interests and then alter or adapt tasks using contexts that are meaningful to their students. The tasks can be filed electronically and be adapted to meet the needs of particular students. Designing tasks using students' interests is sometimes called personalization and can increase students' achievement in both the short and long term (Bernacki & Walkington, 2018). Remarkably, personalization can increase students' initial engagement with a mathematics task, improve achievement on personalized mathematics tasks, and increase achievement on the nonpersonalized mathematics tasks students complete after engaging with personalized tasks (Walkington, 2013). The tasks are also easier to read and understand when they relate directly to students' names and interests. Teachers can design generalized tasks using surface details with positive results (Bernacki & Walkington, 2014), but deep, individualized personalization is more important for students who demonstrate low overall interest in mathematics (Bernacki & Walkington, 2018). Teachers can use interest surveys to collect information about surface interests (e.g., music, sports, food) or conduct interviews to learn more about students' funds of knowledge, which support individualized personalization. In the example above, the teachers knew that Marco liked to play video games (generalized knowledge) but learned through the interview that Marco and his grandmother bake Greek cakes together on Saturdays (individualized knowledge). The teachers designed this individualized knowledge task focused on comparing fractions that was situated within Marco's family context and built upon his knowledge and experience with baking cakes and possibly reading recipes with fractional amounts using and celebrating Marco's funds of knowledge.

> **Funds of knowledge:** The essential bodies of knowledge and information that households use to survive, to get ahead, or to thrive (Moll, Vélez-Ibañez, & Greenberg, 1990, p. 2).

Individualized Personalization

Individualized personalization supports students' strengths because their interests are often tied to their assets. Teachers can design or alter the context of the tasks they find in their curriculum to reflect the interests of their students. Interest inventories and surveys should be conducted at the beginning of the year and repeated quarterly throughout the year as students' interests may change rapidly. For examples of ways to engage and learn about students' interests, please see the following Try It! activities.

Try It! Time Capsule

Select a collection that is appropriate for your students from the following prompts and develop them into a survey format to give to the students.

> Time Capsule: What I think on this day _____ (date)
>
> 1. Favorite mathematics topic
>
> 2. The person or animal I like to be with most
>
> 3. Favorite weekend pastime
>
> 4. Favorite sport to play or watch
>
> 5. Favorite book
>
> 6. Favorite place to go in my neighborhood
>
> 7. Favorite person or thing that makes me laugh the most
>
> 8. If I had a wish about something, I could change during my school day, it would be _____.
>
> 9. If I had a wish about math class, it would be _____.
>
> 10. I love it when my teacher _____.
>
> 11. If I could go to the past, I would _____.
>
> 12. If I could go to the future, I would _____.
>
> 13. If I could change into another person or an animal, I would change into _____.
>
> 14. I feel happiest when _____.
>
> 15. The day last year when I did my best mathematics was when _____.
>
> 16. *Allow space for a drawing and ask students to draw a picture of themselves doing mathematics.*

Then use empty toilet paper rolls or paper towel rolls with the student's name on each to roll and store the survey (peek at them before they get put in a box and stored in the back of the room). At the end of the year, ask students to fill out the same information and then open the time capsule to compare.

 This template can be downloaded for use at resources.corwin.com/teachingturnarounds.

To connect our goals in mathematics to poetry, use this eight-line formulaic template (Figure 5.7) for a poem that focuses on students' math strengths. Find the formula in this next Try It!

FIGURE 5.7: Sample Math Strengths Poem

Janie
Determined, Dillegent, Persistent, Helpful
Math Stations, Cubes, Graphs
Geometry, Decmils
Understanding fractions, More confident
My teacher, My friends, My Mom
Protractor, Ruler, Geoboard, Calculator
Greene

Try It! Math Strengths Poem

Line 1—First name

Line 2—Four adjectives that describe your math strengths

Line 3—Three math activities we have done in class that you love

Line 4—Two of your favorite mathematics topics

Line 5—Two ways you have grown as a math student this year

Line 6—Three people who you like to ask for math help

Line 7—Four math tools you are an expert in using

Line 8—Last name

 This template can be downloaded for use at resources.corwin.com/teachingturnarounds.

Funds of Knowledge

Using students' funds of knowledge connects so nicely to the strengths-based approach because the focus is on the rich background knowledge that students bring to the classroom from their families and communities. This knowledge is viewed as an asset to be celebrated rather than a deficit to be changed, altered, assimilated, or erased in the school setting. Examples of funds of knowledge include school and personal background knowledge; life experiences, skills, and knowledge used to navigate family and social experiences; and historical, religious, and political perspectives (Rodriguez, 2013). Designing tasks around students' deeper interests requires a commitment to gathering information from students in a respectful and thoughtful manner that honors the know-hows, culture, and lived experiences of the students and their families. Many teachers conduct home visits, family surveys, or phone interviews at the beginning of the year and attend community events throughout the year to learn more about their students' lives. Once teachers gather this information, they can consider ways to design tasks that reflect the students' funds of knowledge. The following Try It! is a great way to connect to the students' communities in a positive, respectful, and thoughtful way that is demonstrated by the research to mitigate deficit thinking (McKenzie & Scheurich, 2004).

> Using students' funds of knowledge connects so nicely to the strengths-based approach because the focus is on the rich background knowledge that students bring to the classroom from their families and communities.

 **Try It!**   **Eyes! Camera! Action! Adventure**

Image source: rustemgurler/iStock.com

Drive through the neighborhoods where your students live with your camera and your best observational skills at the ready. Use the following suggestions to guide your adventure and then use your findings to take action in your mathematics lessons by linking mathematics instruction to students' everyday environment. Look for and photograph the following as you consider contexts for problems, words, and places to use in problems and tasks and resources you may need to adapt from the curriculum you are using to better align with your students' funds of knowledge:

- Historical sites or buildings
- Parks or nature areas
- Restaurants, shops, haircutters, and so on
- Busy intersections or main street names
- Places of worship and transportation options
- Places children would like to go
- Interesting attractions that others would like to see
- A beautiful view
- Other features of the area

When captured, use the names of restaurants and shops in the problems you share, create questions about creating a playground in the local park with a particular perimeter, and so on.

Three Perspectives for Adapting a Task to Support Students' Strengths

In addition to designing personalized tasks for students, teachers can adapt and facilitate tasks found in textbooks and curriculum guides to leverage students' strengths by considering three perspectives:

1. Access and equity
2. Mathematical goals
3. Formative assessment

Rather than starting from scratch, teachers can collect a series of tasks from their curriculum guides or texts and consider small ways that they could adapt the task to recognize their students' strengths and needs.

Evaluating the task from an access and equity position helps teachers determine how they are meeting their students' developmental, cognitive, and social-emotional needs. Consider the following task that second-grade teacher Emma found in her textbook, and then let's look at how it could be adapted through each of the three lenses mentioned earlier:

> Farmer Becky collected eggs every day from her henhouse. On Monday, she collected 23 eggs. On Tuesday, she collected 12 eggs. On Wednesday, she collected 18 eggs. On Thursday, she collected 15 eggs. Farmer Becky's total egg collection for Monday through Friday was 81 eggs. How many did she collect on Friday?

Access and Equity

Emma thought about how her students, who lived in an urban environment, would respond to the task. Later in the year, the students would be taking a field trip to a farm where they would watch a farmer milk a cow and collect eggs from hens. She thought that after the trip to the farm, a problem with this context would be ideal. However, for now, Emma decided to change the context of the word problem to focus on a context that the students would enjoy and immediately connect to. Lately, her students were obsessed with Fire Hot Corn Chips, so she developed the Fire Hot Corn Chip Challenge Task (Figure 5.8).

FIGURE 5.8: The Fire Hot Corn Chip Challenge Task

Diego challenged Michael to a Fire Hot Corn Chip Challenge. He challenged Michael to eat as many corn chips as he could during the school week (Monday through Friday). On Monday, Michael ate 23 hot corn chips. On Tuesday, he ate 12 hot corn chips. On Wednesday, he ate 18 hot corn chips. On Thursday, he ate 15 hot corn chips. If, Michael ate a total of 81 hot corn chips, how many did he eat on Friday?

This task attends to access and equity because the students are familiar with and interested in the content and can focus on the mathematics content. The following student work sample highlights a student's understanding (Figure 5.9).

FIGURE 5.9: Fire Hot Corn Chips Student Work

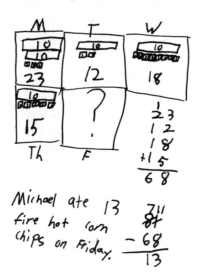

Mathematical Goals

Once Emma selected a relatable context that the students would enjoy, she focused next on the mathematical goal. Emma anticipated that her students might be challenged with this word problem because they had struggled in the past when they encountered two-step word problems. So her goals were for students to learn how to break a problem into two components and also to consider which operations they would need to employ in each component to solve the word problem.

Formative Assessment

> **Pair-to-Pair Share:** When the teacher arranges two pairs so that each pair shares ideas and strategies with one another.

While the students were working, she moved throughout the room and asked the students to prove their ideas and share their thinking. She also verbally recognized the students' perseverance while working on the problem. While observing, she noticed that some students started immediately adding all the numbers together. She asked, "Does your solution make sense?" "Does that approach answer the question?" "You are good at imagining the situation. How did you imagine this problem in your head?" After students had been working, Emma organized a strategic pair-to-pair share so students could explain their strategies. Pairs then had an opportunity to refine their ideas and solutions before Emma conducted a whole-class discussion. As students were sharing in the pair-to-pair share, Emma asked, "What are the strengths of the strategies that your pair shared?" and "How might their ideas make your solution stronger?"

Emma made several powerful strengths-based moves. First, she grouped the students in strategic pairs and provided an opportunity for them to share their ideas. Next, she asked students to highlight their peers' good ideas, creating a positive, affirming mathematics learning environment. Finally, as a whole class in the final lesson closure, she asked each group to share a strength they used, which ranged from sketching diagrams, making lists, and trying three approaches and selecting the best two.

Emma adapted the task design and facilitation of this textbook task to better meet her students' interests and strengths while also maintaining the mathematical goal (and challenge) of the task. Keeping the initial goal of the mathematics is essential as there are multiple ways that a task can be adapted for the mathematics classroom. Check out the following Try It! for more ideas.

Try It! Adapt a Mathematical Task Tool

Select a task from your curriculum guide, textbook, or online resource that is not quite targeted for your students. Use the following tool (Figure 5.10, on the next page) to adapt the task to meet your students' needs. Then reflect on the following:

• What do you notice about how the students responded to the revised task?

• What other adaptations might you make to the task?

Promoting Strengths Through Parallel Tasks

Teachers can also promote students' strengths by allowing them to choose from similar but parallel tasks. Teachers design a set of two or three tasks within the same content area that targets the varying needs of students. Although teachers may be tempted to assign students to a particular task that they feel is most appropriate for them, we encourage you to allow students to select the task they will solve. Much like selecting a book to read, students appreciate opportunities to make choices whenever possible, and they may surprise you. Enabling choice supports student empowerment, critical thinking, and motivation (Brooks & Young, 2011; Flowerday & Schraw, 2000; Simmons & Page, 2010). We recommend the following steps and implementation suggestions for using parallel tasks within a lesson (Figure 5.11).

> Parallel Tasks: Two or more tasks that are similar in context and mathematical topic but vary in developmental level presented to students at the same time.

To look more deeply into a lesson using parallel tasks, let's visit a third-grade classroom. Mabelle decided to offer two parallel tasks to her students on the topic of subtraction of multidigit numbers with regrouping. She had several goals in mind for designing and implementing the following parallel tasks (Figure 5.12) in her classroom. First, she wanted to address the grade-level standard by maintaining rigor and high expectations. Second, she wanted to know how students with various strengths and challenges approached the task. She was interested in observing the following:

• Which task the students selected to solve

• Strategies students used to solve the task

• Discourse among students about their thinking

• Similarities and differences students noted between the tasks

Adapt-a-Mathematical TASK Tool

Do you have a task that is not quite right? Use this guide to adapt the task to meet your needs!

How does the task meet your STUDENTS' needs?

ACCESS and EQUITY: Ensure that the task is "responsive to students' backgrounds, experiences, cultural perspectives, traditions, and knowledge" (NCTM, 2014, para. 1, https://www.nctm.org/uploadedFiles/Standards_and_Positions/Position_Statements/Access_and_Equity.pdf). Consider students' language readiness, including access to mathematical vocabulary.

- How can you differentiate the context of the task to support the students' backgrounds, experiences, and cultural needs?
- How can you group students to engage the students' socio-emotional and developmental needs?
- How can you "open up" the task to encourage access to the task for all learners?
- How can you connect the task to the mathematics the students have learned and students' interests?

Notes

How do you PLAN for students to learn from the task?

MATHEMATICAL GOAL: The task should provide students opportunities to access new mathematical knowledge and to solidify, consolidate, or extend knowledge. Tasks can be changed to highlight multiple learning needs and content standards. Ensure that you strategically connect the learning goal to the task.

- What do your students know how to do right now?
- What do you expect your students to understand as a result of this task?
- What do you anticipate students will do? What changes might you make as a result of your anticipation?

FACILITATE: Task facilitation is critical to student success. Consider how you will organize students and **design** purposeful questions to help them discover and connect mathematics concepts and procedures.

- What **questions** are you going to ask? What tools will you provide? How will students be grouped?
- How and when will you provide opportunities for student **discourse**?

Notes

How do you move learning FORWARD?

FORMATIVE ASSESSMENT: Collecting information about student understanding will help you adjust instruction as you conduct the task.

- How will you listen, observe, and identify students' strategies?
- How will you respond to students' understanding?
- How will you provide feedback to students?
- How will you provide opportunities for students to provide feedback to one another?
- How will you provide opportunities for students to persevere and productively struggle through problems?
- How will you make the mathematics visible for your students?

Notes

Source: Rich Mathematical Tasks, Adapt-a-Mathematical TASK Tool, created by Beth McCord Kobett, Greta W. Richard, and Megan Gitterman. Copyright © 2019 by Corwin. All rights reserved.

[online resources] This template can be downloaded for use at resources.corwin.com/teachingturnarounds.

FIGURE 5.11: Steps for Lesson Implementation for Parallel Tasks

STEPS	IMPLEMENTATION SUGGESTIONS
1. Display both tasks to the students and let them discuss with a partner.	Cover up the numbers and/or question so that the students focus on the context and the structure of the problem.
2. Have students select the problem they want to solve.	Arrange students who chose the same task in pairs to solve together.
3. Once pairs have solved the problem, organize the students in a pair-to-pair share.	Ask the pair-to-pair groups to share their strategies and solutions. Ask: • What do you notice about your strategies and solutions? • What is similar about your strategies? • What is different about your solutions?
4. Bring the class together for a whole-class discussion.	Have two pairs share their thinking for each parallel task. Ask: • What do you notice about the strategies and solutions? • What is the same about the mathematics that the other groups used? Different from what you tried? • Why does the same strategy work for both problems? • If you were going to solve the other problem now, what would you do first?

FIGURE 5.12: Parallel Tasks

BLUE TASK	RED TASK
Ms. Mosely recorded the school attendance as 487 students in the morning. After the announcements, 98 students left for the field trip to the museum. How many students are left in the school?	There are 71 students in third grade at Central Elementary. There are 29 third graders in the library. How many third graders are left in the classrooms?

Mabelle was thrilled that the students self-selected the task that they felt was most appropriate for them. As she moved about the classroom, she asked the students why they selected the blue or red task. Some students chose the blue task because they thought it was more challenging and they wanted "harder problems," yet others chose the red task because the context was about third graders. She was quite surprised and pleased to note that most of the

> **"**
>
> Much like selecting a book to read, students appreciate opportunities to make choices whenever possible, and they may surprise you.

students asked if they could solve both tasks! Mabelle was also heartened to hear powerful conversations during the pair-to-pair share when she asked, "What do you notice about the two tasks?" The pairs realized that both tasks required regrouping but that many students used other strategies from the one they used to find the difference. One of the students, Missy, who sometimes has to put in great effort to get started on a task, shared, "I saw that I was probably supposed to subtract, but I like to add it up instead. Lena wanted to try out my idea so she added up, too." During the whole-class discussion, Mabelle asked the following:

- How are the red and blue tasks alike?
- How are the red and blue tasks different?
- What do you notice about the strategies everyone used to solve the red and blue tasks?
- What strategy did you learn that you might try?
- Who had an idea that surprised you because you didn't think of the task that way?

She was able to engage the students in an exciting conversation about subtraction with base ten materials and empty numberlines, as well as highlight students' use of "think addition" strategies.

To design your own parallel tasks, explore the following Try It!

 **Try It!**   Design Parallel Tasks

Select a task from your curriculum guide, textbook, or online resource. Then consider the following questions to develop parallel tasks:

1. What are the learning needs of your students?
2. What do you want students to notice and discuss?
3. How will you support students to discuss the two tasks? What questions will you ask before they start working?
4. What contexts will you use for this task?
5. What types of learners (i.e., student strengths, interests) do you anticipate will select each task?
6. What kinds of strategies do you anticipate students will use?
7. What questions will you ask while students are solving the tasks?

8. Record your tasks.

BLUE TASK	RED TASK
_____	_____
_____	_____
_____	_____
_____	_____
_____	_____
_____	_____
_____	_____
_____	_____
_____	_____
_____	_____
_____	_____
_____	_____
_____	_____

Reflect: What did you notice about how students responded to the choice of tasks? What did you notice about how students responded to the parallel tasks?

online resources — This template can be downloaded for use at resources.corwin.com/teachingturnarounds.

Exploratory Discourse About Tasks

As students explore their initial, often partially formed understanding of tasks, they may be reticent to share tentative thinking or ideas about their strategies and solutions for the problems they encounter. This tension between emerging understanding and the movement to more complete understanding is complex. Barnes (2008) describes this tension:

> Our culture offers to young learners powerful ways of understanding and influencing the world, so that much learning is a matter of 'getting inside' an adult view of the world in order to use it for thinking and acting. School learning is at once social and individual. Schools provide for pupils the opportunity of partially sharing the teacher's perspective, for successful lessons build up cumulatively a set of meanings that it is the task of each pupil to make his or her own. Each must deal with new experiences that challenge existing schemes and pictures of the world, for only he or she has access to the particular preconceptions and misunderstandings which need to be reflected on and modified. (p. 7)

As students challenge prior schemes and preconceptions, they need extensive time, opportunities to collaborate with peers, and freedom to explore their ideas through exploratory discourse (Barnes, 2008), also known as **rough draft talk** (Jansen, Cooper, Vascellaro, & Wandless, 2016). Teachers first describe their own rough draft talk to students and thereby create safe spaces for students to model this example and discuss their tentative ideas when they first approach the problem (Jansen, 2020). Through thoughtful discourse, students shape their ideas and make connections to their strengths and prior knowledge. After students have solved the problem, the teacher asks students to reflect on how the rough draft talk opportunity supported their thinking and sense making. This strategy is a strengths-based practice because students' fledgling ideas are honored and celebrated from the very beginning. Students also are surprised to realize that other students do not always know exactly how to solve the problem, and this sense of not knowing what to do at first is a normal part of solving problems. By finding out that everyone doesn't know the answer immediately, they see a new side to the problem-solving process and a more realistic reason to persevere. Let's listen in on a conversation between two students discussing their ideas for determining which fraction is greater, $\frac{2}{3}$ or $\frac{5}{6}$.

> Rough Draft Talk: "Talking to learn. Rough-draft talk looks like false starts, expressions of uncertainty, and incomplete or imperfect sentences" (Jansen, Cooper, Vascellaro, & Wandless, 2016, p. 304).

Sarita: Are we looking at the numerator or the denominator?

Jordy: I think I remember the teacher saying she thinks about the whole fraction when comparing fractions. Do you remember how she talked about it?

Sarita: Right, she said she thinks about the benchmark fractions. Should we try that?

Jordy: I'm doing $\frac{5}{6}$ first because it is close to 1 as it is only one piece (sixth) away from the whole. What about $\frac{2}{3}$, though?

Sarita: Two thirds is also one piece away from a whole, but it is a bigger piece—so I think it is less than $\frac{5}{6}$. Let's check with pattern blocks.

Jordy: I'll get the green sixths and you can get the blue thirds.

Sarita: Putting my two blue pieces on top of your six green ones makes this easy!

Jordy: That makes sense to me now too.

Here's an early conversation from another pair about the same fraction comparison problem.

Lince: Uhmmmm, I was thinking that I would make a numberline.

Marissa: Okay, you make a numberline for $\frac{2}{3}$ and I will make one for $\frac{5}{6}$?

Students make numberlines and show them to each other.

Marissa: Well, it looks like $\frac{2}{3}$ is bigger!

Lince: I don't know. Your numberline is really small and mine is really big.

Marissa: What should we do?

Lince: What if we made our numberlines the same?

The following Try It! can help you get started on facilitating early conversations about the task.

Try It! Planning and Implementing
Rough Draft Talk Opportunities

1. Select a task and record it here:

2. Anticipate students' initial ideas.

3. When and how will students engage in early conversations about the tasks? Why are you selecting this particular cooperative arrangement?
   - Pairs
   - Pair-to-pair share
   - Small groups

4. How and when will you recognize and value students' early contributions?

5. How and when will you give students an opportunity to reflect on how the early conversations about the task were helpful in planning a path to a solution?

Math Amendments: Revising the Task Solution

When students begin learning to write, they come to understand that revising is a critical part of that process. They typically engage in several revision stages where they examine the writing piece from different perspectives. Like solving a math task, when students are writing, they may draft a solution by exploring strategies, asking questions, organizing their solution(s), collecting feedback, and applying precise vocabulary. In the typical writing scenario, students create, solve, and perhaps share an early draft with peers. However, sometimes teachers find it useful to have students revise or amend their drafts after soliciting and hearing peers' ideas and solutions. Similar to revising writing pieces, students may select a completed mathematics task and solution and alter or add ideas to improve the presentation of the solution or their explanation. Teachers can encourage students to develop *math amendments* by asking the following questions:

- What representations will enhance your solution?
- How can you use more mathematics vocabulary to communicate your idea?
- What can you add to your explanation to communicate your understanding of the task and the reason you picked a particular solution strategy?

Summary

Turnaround tasks are those we create as well as those we adapt from existing curriculum materials that can highlight students' strengths. Using an asset-oriented approach, we bring the child into the mathematics by bringing the mathematics into the child's life. Instead of purchasing an unrealistically large number of cantaloupes as in the *Peanuts* cartoon described in the beginning of this chapter, we use students' names, the names of streets near where they live, places in their neighborhoods, and the familiar things, people, and experiences in their world as components of the tasks we present. Our attempts are not merely to capture their interest but also to make the connection to a future life that is filled with problem solving related to mathematical situations a REALITY. Adapting a metaphor by Strayton and Lawton (2019), we agree that not only do these shifts to relatable tasks improve individual students' growth like a seedling toward mathematical proficiency but they also enhance the entire garden.

Turn Around Feedback

We all need people who will give us feedback.
That's how we improve.

—Bill Gates

After exploring grouping practices and tasks in the previous chapters designated to Turnaround Three: Design Instruction From a Strengths-Based Perspective, we turn to our last topic for this Turnaround as we examine the power of giving, collecting, receiving, and facilitating feedback in the mathematics classroom as a critical and powerful strengths-based practice.

Our society has become rich with opportunities to receive and give feedback. Did you love your hotel stay? Answer our online survey and give it a five-star rating. Were your sandwiches from our sandwich shop delicious? Drop a feedback card in the box on your way out the door. Unhappy with your last-minute flight cancellation? You can let our airline know by tweeting about it. Of course, companies that encourage and provide such services seek feedback because their businesses depend on the information to improve and expand their effectiveness.

We wonder, have you ever been asked, "Would you like some feedback on . . . ?" when you had not solicited the feedback? How did such a request make you feel? What kind of feedback did you receive? Did you outstretch your arms wide to openly receive the information? Or did you brace yourself for what you imagined could be the impending doom? Requesting or providing feedback can be tricky because the purpose, timing, quality, and esteem for the person doing the assessing matter—a lot in how the information is interpreted and acted upon. The words we choose and the nonverbal communication we display when we provide feedback also matter to our students and have an impact on whether that feedback will actually be acted upon in meaningful and productive ways.

The Importance of Feedback in a Strengths-Based Classroom

Feedback is an integral element of a larger formative assessment process. When teachers use a systematic and thoughtful assessment plan, students who are at diverse levels of learning can experience significant learning gains (Black & Wiliam, 1998; Wiliam, Lee, Harrison, & Black, 2004). Students who are striving to improve have even more to gain by teachers' formative assessment practices. Black and Wiliam (1998) reported that intentional formative assessment practices are particularly helpful to students who are struggling when teachers are "concentrating on specific problems with their work and giving them [students] a clear understanding of what is wrong and how to put it right" (p. 14).

> **Formative Assessment:** An iterative process for collecting evidence of student understanding to adjust instruction.

The potential for **feedback** to support and increase student learning is powerful. The purpose of feedback in the mathematics classroom is to advance students' mathematical understanding, support students to reason mathematically, and promote students' strengths and positive dispositions toward mathematics. Studies that resulted in the greatest learning gains involved students receiving specific feedback about how to accomplish a task more effectively. However, in another study, students learned less when feedback was delivered as praise or criticism (Hattie & Timperley, 2007). Hattie shared the following statement in an *Education Week* interview (Sparks, 2018): "The key questions is, does the feedback help someone understand what they don't know, what they do know, and where they go? That's when and why feedback is so powerful, but a lot of feedback doesn't— and doesn't have any effect" (para. 3). Let's explore the type of feedback Hattie encourages in three major categories: teacher-to-student feedback, student-to-teacher feedback, and student-to-student feedback, all from a strengths-based perspective.

> **Feedback:** Information provided by an agent (e.g., teacher, peer, book, parent, self, experience) regarding aspects of one's performance or understanding (Hattie & Timperley, 2007).

Teacher-to-Student Feedback From a Strengths Perspective

Teacher-to-student feedback is a powerful and necessary strengths-based move for both the teacher and the student. When teachers ask students to explain students' ideas, the teacher carefully determines the students' strengths and needs and then strategically provides feedback that highlights the students' strengths while moving their learning forward. Teachers provide feedback that is strengths based when they note what strategies students know and how they can use what they understand to advance their thinking. The power is in the way teachers acknowledge the brilliant ideas that students have and in the ways they encourage students to take risks and test new ideas from a point of strength.

Let's take a look at some classroom examples of teacher-to-student feedback. Think about how you would sort and then classify the following examples.

 **Try It!** Classifying Feedback

Without thinking about preestablished categories, do the following card sort activity. How would you sort, classify, and name the feedback samples on these cards (Figure 6.1)? You can group them in any way that makes sense to you.

FIGURE 6.1: Cards for Classifying Feedback

You used a numberline and the fraction circles to represent $\frac{1}{2}$. Is there another way to show $\frac{1}{2}$?	I can see some of your thinking by looking at your diagram, Ashley. How could you explain your thinking in words?	I can see that you used tallying to add. Is there another strategy you could use that would be more efficient?	The presentation would be more effective, Cooper, if your visuals were more polished.
You taught us about angles, Bryce? I LOVE geometry!	Next time, Chase, you'll want to make the discussion you provided of your solution path clearer to the reader.	You did an amazing job on this problem task! I am so impressed with your strategies.	You used partial products to solve this multiplication problem. Your solution is clear and easy to understand.
I noticed a lot of perseverance during this task. Rosa, you tried at least three different strategies and never gave up.	Marion, you have a correct answer, but I cannot tell how you solved this problem. Can you explain your answer?	Mansoor, your table and equation show me that you understand linear functions. Your next step is to represent the data in a graph.	Timmy, you used the halving and doubling strategy to multiply. Would this strategy also work for 23 × 14?
Nice job on the exit task!	That is a great idea, Janel!	I love your thinking, Alejandro!	That solution is correct, Karlo.

Source: Adapted from Fennell, Kobett, and Wray (2018).

Reflect: On what basis did you initially group the feedback examples provided? How did you classify the feedback? What do you notice about your classification categories? Which kinds of feedback have the potential to further student understanding? Why do you think so? Which kinds of feedback have the potential to hinder or not advance student understanding? Why do you think so?

online resources ↖ You can find this card sort activity at resources.corwin.com/teachingturnarounds.

We have conducted this activity with many groups of preservice and inservice teachers and appreciate the clever ways they approach the complexity of thinking about different kinds of feedback. Notice how these preservice teachers classified this feedback (Figure 6.2). How does your sort and classification compare?

FIGURE 6.2: Results of Sorting and Classifying Feedback

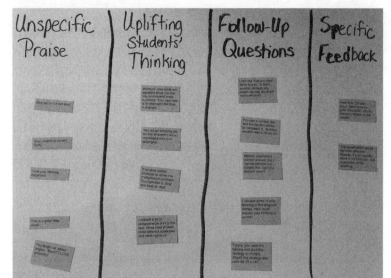

When comparing the resulting groupings, the category of uplifting student thinking seemed to us to be particularly strengths based and powerful. When asked for clarification, the preservice teachers commented, "Well, we really liked this feedback example, 'Mansoor, your table and equation show me that you understand linear functions. Your next step is to represent the data in a graph,' because the teacher said what she liked, why she liked it, and the next step to move forward." Others described the unspecific praise such as "Nice job on the exit task" as not that helpful yet the kind of praise they had often offered in the past.

Teacher-to-Student Feedback Loop

Providing feedback that is thoughtful, equitable, and strengths based can be a daunting task. Hattie and Timperley (2007) propose that effective feedback must answer three kinds of questions posed by teachers and students: (1) Feed Up, (2) Feed Back and Forth, and (3) Feed Forward. Our three-stage Strengths-Based Feedback Loop model (Figure 6.3), adapted from Hattie and Timperley's (2007) research analysis of numerous studies of teachers' feedback, demonstrates a comprehensive feedback cycle as students become aware of the purpose for their learning (Feed Up), receive and respond to strengths-based responses to their learning (Feed Back and Forth), and then act on the feedback (Feed Forward).

FIGURE 6.3: Strengths-Based Feedback Loop Model

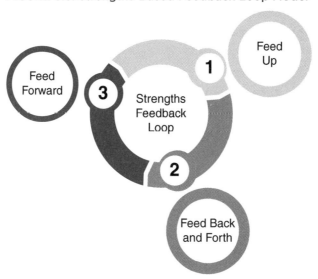

Source: Adapted from Hattie and Timperley (2007).

Each of the three stages of the Strengths-Based Feedback Loop model represents different actions that are part of the feedback process, from the onset of goal setting (Figure 6.4) to the receipt and initial reaction to the feedback (Figure 6.5) to the important follow through of related actions (Figure 6.6). In the Feed Up stage (Figure 6.4), we ask, "What are the goals for today's learning activity?" and imagine what this feedback looks like in the mathematics classroom as a critical part of the strengths-based loop.

FIGURE 6.4: Stage 1: Feed Up

DESCRIPTION	WHAT DOES IT LOOK LIKE?	STRENGTHS-BASED LOOP
When students know the goals for the learning activity, they are more likely to work toward the goal because they understand the purpose of the learning. Students are more likely to demonstrate persistence, even in the face of frustration, when they can identify the goal (Bargh, Gollwitzer, Lee-Chai, Barndollar, & Trötschel, 2001). Students also respond to challenging goals with more commitment, particularly when the goals are connected to success criteria (see Chapter 2).	What will students be learning versus what will students be doing? Example: *Learning Intention* We will be learning to compare fractions with different denominators using both pattern blocks and a numberline. *Success Criteria:* I know I am successful at comparing fractions when I can use manipulatives and a numberline to demonstrate how one fraction is greater than another fraction.	Revisiting prior goals and the success of those goals. Example: Last week, you divided different fraction regions to make sure they had equal-sized parts. I really appreciate how precise you were in dividing the regions. Precision is important to mathematicians, particularly when they are proving that one fraction is greater than another fraction. Today we are going to build on what you learned last week about comparing fractions. I want you to use those skills again today!

In the Feed Back and Forth stage (Figure 6.5), we ask, "What kinds of feedback are teachers and students giving and receiving in the mathematics classroom?"

FIGURE 6.5: Stage 2: Feed Back and Forth

DESCRIPTION	WHAT DOES IT LOOK LIKE?	STRENGTHS-BASED LOOP
Feedback is most effective when it is specific to the learning process. Feedback that attends to the student's use of a particular strategy is effective because the student then knows that the strategy is effective or ineffective.	Example: "You used base ten blocks to compare the number 145 to 154. This is an effective strategy because you were able to compare the hundreds, tens, and ones represented in your model. I like that you chose to model the numbers with materials. Can you tell me more about why you decided to use base ten blocks to represent the values?"	This example is considered strengths based because it is so specific and attends to the solution pathway that the student pursued. The question acknowledges the student's strategy and asks for more information that can provide clarity for both the student and teacher. *Note that the feedback is specific and focuses on what the student did, not on the person.

In the Feed Forward stage (Figure 6.6), we ask, "Where do I go next?"

FIGURE 6.6: Stage 3: Feed Forward

DESCRIPTION	WHAT DOES IT LOOK LIKE?	STRENGTHS-BASED LOOP
After attending to the student's strategy, process, or solution pathway, the teacher identifies the next moves to advance the student's mathematical understanding. This step can be formed in several ways.	What might you do next? _____ What would happen in _____? I wonder if _____ would work the same way? Examples: "Next, find a way to record the value by sketching the base ten blocks (square, line, and dot) and noting the answer on the place value chart." Or "I wonder if this same strategy would work for larger values? Why don't you compare 465 and 456 and see what you think about the strategy. I am wondering, do you think it is an efficient strategy as you move to larger quantities? Why or why not? I will be back to hear your thoughts."	The teacher leverages the student's prior strategy use to build new understanding. In this example, the teacher poses the feedback as a question, sets up a new task, and positions the student as the mathematical authority.

> " ....
>
> Feedback is most effective when it is specific to what students are learning.

Feedback is most effective when it is specific to what students are learning. Looking back at our classification activity, we see that explicit feedback that attends to the student's use of a particular strategy is effective because the student now knows that the particular strategy used for that situation is appropriate. As we consider ways to facilitate the Strengths-Based Feedback Loop, we must ensure that our feedback acknowledges the student's process and strategies used rather than just reward task completion (e.g., you finished the worksheet), leverages what the student has accomplished toward future potential use, and moves the learning forward in a positive and actionable way. The following Spotlight activity (starting on page 156) provides an opportunity for you to reflect on your current practices for facilitating student feedback using the Strengths-Based Feedback Loop model.

Elements of Teacher-to-Student Feedback

Next, let's dive into some specific strategies that can enhance and support the Strengths-Based Feedback Loop process. These strategies, when implemented, will make a difference in the quality of feedback that you facilitate in your mathematics classroom and promote a positive, strengths-based environment. These strategies include wait time, questioning, and listening.

Wait Time

More than 40 years ago, Mary Budd Rowe (1974) reported that teachers, on average, wait 1.5 seconds after asking an initial question of one student before moving to get a response from another student and less than a second when responding to a comment from a student. This time in between the asking and the answering of questions is called wait time. Importantly, she also noted that when teachers extended their wait time to 3 to 5 seconds, wonderful things began to happen for both students and teachers (Figure 6.7).

> **Wait Time:** The amount of time that a teacher give students to think before calling on another student to answer a question.

FIGURE 6.7: Benefits of Increased Wait Time for Students and Teachers

STUDENTS	TEACHERS
• Increased the depth and length of their responses	• Showed an increased flexibility in responses to students
• Showed increased confidence	• Varied questioning patterns
• Asked more of their own questions	• Changed perceptions of students who felt they were struggling to believing they could be successful
• Offered ideas and conjectures	

Source: Rowe (1986).

Wait time is important within the context of learning. Mary Budd Rowe (1974) explains, "Exploration and inquiry require students to put together ideas in new ways, to try out new thoughts, to take risks. For that, they not only need time, but they need a sense of being safe" (p. 4). Wait time is think time (Stahl, 1994). This opportunity to stop and think needs to be strategically used so students can process tasks, behaviors, teacher's and classmates' responses, and actions. You can enhance this think time for students who struggle

SPOTLIGHT ON YOUR PRACTICE:
Reflecting on Your Feedback

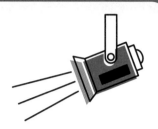

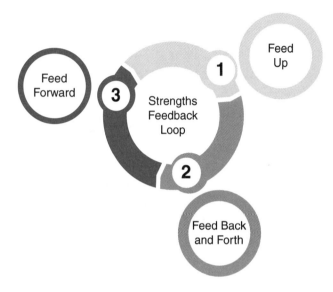

Source: Adapted from Hattie and Timperley (2007).

Video or audio record a portion of one of your mathematics lessons or a full lesson. Listen or watch the recording and capture the feedback that you communicated to the students in each of the following three feedback categories.

Feed Up	Feed Back and Forth	Feed Forward

Next, reflect on your feedback groupings. What do you notice?

Feed Up

- How do you establish learning goals with your students?

- How might you acknowledge student strengths within these goals?

Feed Back and Forth

- How do you provide explicit feedback to the students?

- How might you acknowledge student strengths as you provide this feedback?

- Do you mostly provide feedback as statements or questions?

Feed Forward

- How do you provide feedback that moves students forward?

- How might you acknowledge student strengths as you provide this feedback?

Next Steps

Using the information you have gathered from your data collection and reflection, what's your next step?

online resources This activity can be downloaded for use at
resources.corwin.com/teachingturnarounds.

Turnaround Tip

Consider ways to increase your wait time:

- Plan for strategic points in your lesson to implement extended wait time opportunities for students.

- Post large Think Time posters around the room as a reminder to provide sufficient wait time. Position them so that they are within your line of vision and can be regularly seen as you are teaching. Note how they gently nudge you to give students more time to think.

- Ask a colleague to observe you teach for 10 or 20 minutes and record your wait time.

by being transparent about what you are doing. Let your students know that you are trying to give them "think time" so you can help them process information and provide them with ample time to think about the question. Letting students know that you are working on this behavior and want feedback from them can be very empowering.

Questioning Practices

Beyond providing time for students to understand and respond to questions, we also want to examine our questioning patterns from a strengths-based perspective. We can support or discourage student thinking by engaging in particular questioning patterns with our students. Teachers tend to use two main questioning patterns as they facilitate lessons: funneling and focusing.

The funneling questioning pattern occurs when the teacher asks a series of questions that point the student in a specific direction (Herbel-Eisenmann & Breyfogle, 2005). For example,

Teacher: What is a rectangle?

Student: A shape with four sides.

Teacher: And four?

Student: Angles.

Teacher: Is it three-dimensional or two-dimensional?

Student: Two.

When students are engaged in such funneling patterns, they often focus on generating one correct answer and are not invited to express original thoughts, describe multiple possible ideas, or make connections among ideas. They're essentially filling in the blank that the teacher offers. When teachers and students interact in a funneling pattern, the teacher is doing the heavy lifting by asking questions that lead the students to the answer. In effect, the teacher is doing the thinking.

In contrast, a focusing pattern of questioning encourages students to participate in robust discussions to explain their thinking (Wood, 1998). Students feel valued for their ideas because the teacher is listening carefully to them and responding to what they say rather than a fixed answer he or she has in mind.

Teacher: I am looking at how you grouped these shapes. Why did you put these shapes together (points to rectangles) and these shapes in a different pile (points to squares)?

Student: Well, they all have four sides, but this pile has shapes with equal sides because they are squares and this pile doesn't so they aren't squares.

Teacher: Hmm—can you tell me more about your thinking?

Student: Well, these are rectangles because they have two short sides and two long sides, see?

Teacher: Ahhhh. So, you have sorted them by side length and named these piles squares and rectangles. So, I am wondering, what are all the properties that these two groups share?

Notice how the teacher invited the student to share more ideas. This moment is critical because the teacher is still moving the students toward the learning goal and as such uses the student's explanation to formulate the next question (Herbel-Eisenmann & Breyfogle, 2005). The focusing questioning pattern is strengths based because the teacher is highlighting the student's best thinking in a very strategic way toward the learning goal.

 **Try It!** **Strengths-Based Questioning**

You can incorporate particular questions into a focusing questioning pattern to cultivate strengths building in students. Try to integrate these questions into your regular routine to help your students discover and share their mathematical strengths.

1. What approach is working well for you?
2. What strategies have your tried? Which of those strategies was most helpful?
3. What small thing could you try that might make a difference in your solution approach?
4. What is a challenge you faced while solving the problem?
5. You are so good a persevering! Why did you keep trying to find different approaches? How do you think up new approaches?
6. How could you use your strategy or idea to help someone else?
7. Who would you like to share your strategy with?
8. How do you think this strategy will help you tomorrow?

Listening

We have one surefire way for teachers to become better listeners. Yes, this strategy works every time! Talk less. Hattie (2012) reports that the proportion of teacher talk to listening needs to shift to far less talk and much more listening (p. 80). Other findings include the following:

- Students who struggle engage more when teachers talk less.
- Only 5% to 10% of teacher talk actually triggers more student discourse.

Taking the time to lean in and hear our students among the many noises, interruptions, and general hubbub of the classroom can be extremely challenging. Attentive listening offers a special opportunity to nurture strengths in our students. Arcavi and Isoda (2007) identify several challenges of teacher listening that interfere with our ability to hear student thinking. Figure 6.8 offers descriptions of those listening challenges along with ways that you can address them—creating opportunities for students to speak and be heard.

Figure 6.8: Listening Challenges With Tips to Build Strengths

LISTENING CHALLENGE	STRENGTHS BUILDER TIP
"Packaged" Knowledge: *"I have always understood place value."* We tend to view our knowledge as it is in the present, complete and whole, as if we always knew and understood it that way. We have erased our memories of how we developed that knowledge. The challenge for listening is that we often just listen for a correct response rather than the natural development of understanding.	*Unpacking Knowledge:* *"What was it like to learn . . . ?"* *Unpack* a concept from the developmental trajectory. What do students believe and know about the concept when they enter your classroom? For example, students who are learning multiplication may skip count to find the product but not realize that each skip count represents the addition of an equal-sized group. They begin skip counting in kindergarten as a rote method or chant but don't attach meaning and connection to the count until they have more experience thinking about how the count and the quantities are connected. Thinking about the ways students develop understanding is helpful in breaking this listening challenge.

Pinpointed Listening:	*Perceptive Listening:*
"I am listening for students to use particular vocabulary while they describe their understanding."	*"I hear students use the word* timesing *to explain that they used multiplication to solve a problem. Why do they call it that when I have never used that word?"*
Children (and adults) are often awkward in the ways they describe their mathematical thinking. Their logic, language, and mental map may differ from ours, and we may have a habit of rushing to judgment and make assumptions about what we are hearing. For example, we may listen for what we want to hear or even push students to use the language we want them to use without first hearing what they have to say.	This approach involves removing yourself and your ideas from the center of your listening. We need to step outside of our own perspectives and try to adopt the students' perspective as we listen. To prepare for this, practice describing the scenario in a way that a student would. Identify the vocabulary and representations they might use to explain their thinking. Consider the language, representations, and explanations that will make sense to another student of the same age. While encouraging precise mathematical language is important, we can't prioritize the correctness of language over our ability to evaluate if students understand what they're saying, regardless of the terminology they use.
Selective Listening:	*Open Listening:*
"Yes, that is correct, you multiply the numerators and denominators."	*"How do you know when you have a reasonable answer after you multiply fractions?"*
Teachers sometimes listen only for correct or incorrect answers or for specifically anticipated errors. They may move in rapidly with a quick fix, sometimes telling students what to do but without attending enough to hearing student thinking.	Conduct a brief formative assessment interview (Fennell, Kobett, & Wray, 2017; Kobett & Karp, 2018) to learn more broadly about a student's thinking. The goal here is to listen and learn about how the student sees the mathematics or works through a problem-solving process, rather than correct or change student thinking or focus simply on the correctness of the answer.

continued >>

LISTENING CHALLENGE	STRENGTHS BUILDER TIP
Biased Listening: *"I need you to use all English words in your explanation."* Our lived experiences provide a lens for the way we look at and perceive the world. Arcavi and Isoda (2007) named this concept *unavoidable bias.* It is naturally there, but is it productive? Teachers' prior lives and community experiences may vary greatly from those of their students. These biases influence our listening when we censor and judge what we are hearing.	*Suppressing Biased Listening:* *"Please tell me more about your thoughts. Your ideas help me understand your thinking."* Recognizing your possible bias is the first step in listening for the strengths of your students. For example, when a student has not completed homework and attempts to explain to you why the homework is not done, suppress thoughts like, "Well, I always had my homework done as a child." Or, "Why can't this child's parents help him?" Another example might be when a student says, "I don't know what to do." Resist the urge to think or say, "Why weren't you listening?" Instead, say, "Tell me more about that."
Distracted Listening: *"I see you . . . yes you can go to the bathroom . . . what does your denominator . . . one sec, so what's going on with your denominator here?"* Listening can be difficult in a classroom full of students with different needs and challenges. Probing student thinking and at the same time understanding a student's perspective can be very demanding and at times nearly impossible to do in real time, often without immediate results.	*Focused Listening:* *"Logan, can you share with Cherise what your denominator represents? . . . Cherise, how does Logan's thinking compare to your own representation? . . . Here's what I'm hearing; help me make sure I understand correctly."* Help the students understand that they have an important role in the classroom to teach, support, and provide feedback to one another. Ask students to share an idea, strategy, or question with one another. Observe students as they collaborate by walking around with your only intent to listen. Then, share the things you heard to honor your students' listening to one another. You can also ask students to note their ideas and schedule some time just for students to share ideas.

Student-to-Teacher Feedback From a Strengths Perspective

Students need to be able to give teachers feedback about their own understanding in a safe environment. As students ask questions or explain an idea or solution, they are, in essence, giving feedback to teachers. You can intentionally build in three timeframes for students to give you explicit feedback: prior to the lesson, during the lesson, and as you close the lesson. However, if you are going to collect feedback, then you need to ensure that you are in a positive place to receive the feedback, communicate your appreciation for the feedback, and explain how you will use the feedback to help in your planning and instruction.

> **As students ask questions or explain an idea or solution, they are, in essence, giving feedback to teachers.**

Prior to the Lesson

As teachers and in our work with our colleagues, we like to ask the students for feedback when we are planning lessons for future units. We find that the students love to know that their ideas are part of our planning process. Some questions we ask include "Would you like to work in pairs or small groups next time?" and "What are your interests so I can create some problems that are related to what you enjoy? And what manipulatives would you like to use to support your thinking?"

During the Lesson

Students need opportunities to communicate with you about their learning. In many cases, you can ask a direct question. However, students can use signals to let you know if they need more time to think, work, or talk with a partner (Figure 6.9).

FIGURE 6.9: Communication Paddles

Students can also communicate to you where they are in the learning process using a red, yellow, and green cup at their desk or table. Students signal to the teacher if they need help (red cup), still working (yellow cup), and ready to share (green cup) by placing the appropriate cup on the outside of the nested collection.

Closing the Lesson

As you close the lesson, consider ways you can collect feedback from the students on their perspective of the lesson. Also, use such feedback to influence your planning and instruction for the next day, week, and what you might do in the future, related to that topic. The following Try It! offers opportunities for teachers to solicit feedback from students during a lesson closure.

 **Try It!**   Strengths-Based Closing Questions

You can collect feedback from students by asking students questions orally or in writing as a possible exit ticket:

- What are the strengths of today's lesson?
- What made you interested in the lesson?
- What questions made you think?
- What could I have done in this lesson to help you learn more about adding decimals?
- What do you think would best help you get started with the task?
- What are you still confused about?
- What can we do better tomorrow?

If teachers are going to gather student feedback, then they need to ensure that they are in a positive place to receive and respond to the feedback. Creating a safe and inviting environment for the feedback is critical. Receive the feedback with appreciation and let students know how you will act on their information.

Once you receive students' feedback, consider ways that you can respond to your students' ideas with a strengths-based approach.

Try It! Strengths-Based Responses to Feedback

Try these suggestions of strengths-based responses or one of your own after eliciting feedback from your students.

1. I know it can be hard to let me know that you are having trouble understanding what we are learning, so thank you so much for letting me know what you find challenging. I am going to think about what we can do tomorrow to help you learn _____ (e.g., adding fractions with different denominators) in a different way.

2. I appreciate your ideas for planning our next lesson. I will try to use as many of your suggestions as I can. Let's keep a list of these ideas for the tasks we are working on.

3. Thank you for sharing your understanding with me. I really enjoy hearing how you think about the mathematics we are learning. When you share your understanding with me, I can do a better job planning lessons for you and sharing other activities that you might enjoy trying.

Reflect: What do you notice about your students' responses? How might your planning and instruction for future lessons (i.e., tomorrow, next week, with a class next year) be influenced by the student responses (feedback)?

Student-to-Student Feedback From a Strengths Perspective

Peer-to-peer feedback is likely already happening in your classroom. Hattie (2012) reports that more than half of the verbal feedback students receive comes from classmates, which expands the prospect for students to give and get positive and frequent feedback. Peer feedback is the perfect opportunity to illuminate your students' strengths. First, make sure that the classroom environment is safe. We suggest that you build your own classroom protocol with the students about how they want to experience feedback with one another. You can use these agreed-upon protocols to make a poster to display prominently. Here is a model (Figure 6.10) to get you started.

FIGURE 6.10: Listening to Peers Classroom Poster

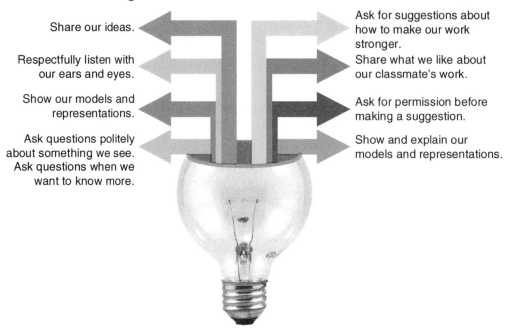

Share our ideas.

Respectfully listen with our ears and eyes.

Show our models and representations.

Ask questions politely about something we see. Ask questions when we want to know more.

Ask for suggestions about how to make our work stronger.

Share what we like about our classmate's work.

Ask for permission before making a suggestion.

Show and explain our models and representations.

Source: Created by Bob Ronau.

 This poster can be downloaded for use at resources.corwin.com/teachingturnarounds.

When we share our ideas with classmates about **our** work, we

- share what we understand about our work. We show and explain our models and representations.
- listen respectfully by paying attention, giving eye contact, and nodding our heads.
- ask questions politely about something we see or something we want to know more about.
- ask for questions from our classmates about ideas we presented.
- ask for suggestions about how to make our work stronger.

When we share our ideas with classmates about **their** work, we

- share what we like (strengths) about their work.
- listen respectfully by paying attention, giving eye contact, and nodding our heads.
- ask a question about their work or an explanation of something we would like to know more about.
- ask for permission to make a suggestion to make their work stronger.

Nurturing courteous relationships among the students as they give and receive feedback develops all students' strengths as future community members and workplace colleagues. They become more confident at unpacking their own understanding, publicly sharing their work, and developing their questioning and critiquing skills.

Students need to practice giving feedback using strengths-based sentence starters before you set them to work on their own in the classroom (Figure 6.11). Begin by setting up a role-play modeling exercise for students to see a positive example for giving and receiving feedback. Also ask them what not to do so they can understand counterexamples. Next, ask students to practice this approach. As the students are practicing, walk around, listen, and collect data on the great examples that you hear. If you identify a particularly powerful example, ask the students to reenact the feedback session for the whole class.

> Nurturing courteous relationships among the students as they give and receive feedback develops all students' strengths as future community members and workplace colleagues.

FIGURE 6.11: Strengths-Based Statement and Question Starters (with blank lines to add your own)

STRENGTHS-BASED STATEMENT STARTERS	QUESTION STARTERS
My work shows . . .	I wonder if . . .
The best part of my work is . . .	I wonder how . . .
I am good at . . .	What would happen if you tried . . . ?
The strongest part of my work is . . .	Can you show me how you thought of this strategy?
The part of my work that helps me understand the math the most is . . .	Can you explain your ideas?
_____	What are some of the strategies you tried before you settled on this strategy?
_____	
_____	_____
	_____

Classroom-Based Formative Assessment and Feedback

Situating student feedback within a targeted formative assessment process gives teachers the opportunity to notice and use students' strengths to advance their mathematical understanding. Selecting, planning for, implementing, and documenting responses from a carefully chosen collection of formative assessment techniques at just the right time is what makes formative assessment powerful. When teachers carefully and mindfully tuck formative assessment techniques into their lessons, they heighten opportunities to provide students with rich feedback that is timely, appropriate, and strengths based. Before we move on, take a moment to reflect on the formative assessment techniques you are currently using in the following Spotlight on Your Practice. Your teaching will reflect the formative assessment techniques you had planned to use to monitor student progress and the lesson's overall effectiveness. The following questions may help guide your planning and teaching as related to your use of formative assessment:

- What tasks and questions will be used to engage students in the lesson?
- How will learning trajectories of the mathematics content focus of the lesson be considered to ensure the developmental appropriateness and student prerequisite background for this lesson?
- How might you be prepared to further challenge a student who quickly finishes?
- How will you communicate student learning expectations for this lesson?
- When and how will students receive feedback for their contributions during the lesson?
- What responsibilities do your students have for assessing their learning in this lesson?
- How will formative assessment be used to monitor student progress in this lesson?
- Will students be assessed individually, in groups, or both individually and within a group?
- How will formative assessment be used to determine the effectiveness of the lesson? (Adapted from Fennell et al., 2017, pp. 11–12)

SPOTLIGHT ON YOUR PRACTICE:
Reflecting on Formative Assessment

1. How does your lesson planning account for classroom-based formative assessment?

2. What formative assessment techniques are you regularly using? When do you use them in a lesson?

3. How do you monitor and document student proficiency and understanding?

4. As you plan, how do you regularly anticipate how students will respond to particular formative assessment prompts (e.g., an interview)?

5. How do you typically respond to observed misconceptions? Strengths?

6. What are the particular benefits of regularly planning for and implementing formative assessment in a strengths-based approach?

7. What challenges you most about your use of formative assessment?

Let's take a look at how the Formative 5 assessment techniques (Fennell et al., 2017) can be used to leverage those strengths. These classroom-based formative assessment techniques include observations, interviews, Show Me exercises, hinge questions, and exit tasks. A brief description of each of the Formative 5 techniques, when the technique might be used, and how the technique can be used to support students' strengths is provided in the following. It should be noted that for every technique, the teacher must anticipate how the students might respond, plan for ways to adjust instruction, and consider the feedback that will be provided.

Observation

Observation is something teachers naturally do every day and all day long. When observation is used as a formative assessment technique, teachers plan for different ways students will respond to a mathematics prompt, carefully document what they are observing, and adjust instruction in the moment.

When: Observations can be conducted at any point in a lesson and in any classroom setting—whole class, small group, or when working with an individual student.

Opportunities for Strength Building: Observation is a particularly effective technique for students who struggle because teachers often see things they might not notice if they were not focused on observing. Alaine reflected after designing and implementing a strategic formative observation in her classroom:

> I am shocked. I am shocked because if I hadn't conducted this observation, I would never know about Maya. I thought that Maya did not understand anything about what we were doing with decimals. Everything I had collected from her in paper form was completely wrong. After I conducted an observation of her group ordering decimals, I realized that Maya **did** understand the values when the group was using the base ten blocks to model the decimal values. When she recorded the values on the paper, she completely switched them around. I started to intervene when I realized that where she was sitting at the table was confusing her. Her group was ordering them, and she was on the opposite side of the student who was recording the order. Maya was looking at the decimal values upside down! I noticed that this frequently happens because her group members have strong personalities and take over the recording.

Alaine used what she saw happening to build upon Maya's strength with the base ten blocks. Instead of telling the group to stop doing what they were doing, she used a lovely strength-building feedback move. She asked the group to change places and see what they noticed when they looked upside down. Immediately the students understood that what they were doing could be confusing and made sure that Maya was able to take the lead in some of the recording. Later in the lesson, Maya noticed that the students had moved all their chairs to face the chart paper. As a result of the observation, Alaine's feedback move was far more powerful and impactful for her students' mathematical understanding.

Interview

The interview technique is a brief investigative probe that is used with an individual student or small group of students. Anticipating responses and documentation is also important to the successful implementation of this technique.

When: Interviews can be conducted at any time during a lesson.

Opportunities for Strength Building: Students enjoy being interviewed, particularly when the interview focuses on their best thinking instead of their perceived weaknesses. To build your students' strengths, particularly for those who struggle, look for students who are demonstrating an interesting technique or initial understanding of a concept. Ask the student:

- What ideas do you have for solving?
- What are you thinking about doing next?

Next, record what you heard the students say and decide on the next instructional step by using information from the interview. For example, "You mentioned that you thought you should multiply to solve this word problem. Mathematicians try out ideas to make sure they make sense. Why don't you try out your idea and then let me know if multiplication makes sense for solving this word problem."

Show Me

The Show Me technique is when teachers ask individuals, small groups, or large groups of students to respond to a performance-based question (Fennell et al., 2017). Students may use manipulatives, small whiteboards for sketching solutions, digit cards, and/or response cards to demonstrate their understanding.

When: The Show Me technique can be implemented at any time during the lesson. Most teachers like to use the Show Me technique as it engages students to do the mathematics within a lesson.

Opportunities for Strength Building: When teachers pose a Show Me, they offer students an opportunity to showcase their ideas, highlight particular strategies individually and publicly, and then make strategic planning and teaching decisions that support student learning. For example, Melissa posed the following Show Me prompt to her students: "Show me a decimal value between 4.5 and 5.0. Make sure that you use a representation." As she looked around the room, she saw that some students used base ten blocks, some represented the value using a sketch, and others positioned a point on a numberline. She noticed that Alice, one of her struggling students, used base ten blocks to show the value. She asked Alice to explain how she knew her base ten representation was between 4.5 and 5.0. Alice, responded, "Well, I know that 4 is the whole number so I grabbed four wholes. Next, I grabbed the five tenths to make the 4.5. I wasn't sure what to do next, so I decided to get another tenth, which makes 4.6. Then I realized that I was between 4.5 and 5 because it was one-tenth more than 4.5 and four tenths away from 5.0!" Melissa stated, "This is a great way to show a concrete representation of 4.6. I would like the class to show Alice and me where 4.6 is placed on a numberline with the two endpoints 4.5 and 5.0. Alice, will you walk around the room with me and tell me what you notice about the other students' representations on the numberline?" After walking around, Melissa asked, "Alice, what did you notice?" Alice responded, "I noticed that decimals are like fractions because Janie and Meha both divided their numberlines up by tenths to make sure they have equal parts." By using Alice's representation to initiate another Show Me, Melissa leverages Alice's strength, which is concrete representation, and supports Alice and other students to make connections from the concrete regional model to the length model shown with the numberline.

Hinge Question

A hinge question is a question that provides a check for understanding or proficiency at a particular hinge point in a lesson. Responses to these questions provide information to the teacher about the direction to go within a lesson and/or next instructional steps (Wiliam, 2011). These questions can be formatted as open-ended responses or in a multiple-choice format. Fennell et al. (2017) suggest that the questions should be designed for students to respond within two minutes and invite an array of responses that can inform the teacher's next steps.

When: The hinge question can be posed at the beginning or middle of the lesson to help the teacher decide how to group the students for instruction or at the end of the lesson to determine instructional steps for the next day.

Opportunities for Strength Building: Hinge questions can be implemented to answer the teacher's question, "Are they ready to move on?" They can also be used to match students who have different understandings to provide student-to-student feedback.

Figure 6.12 shows a pinch card. Pinch cards can be used to collect information from many students at once. To use them, students pinch the part of the card that has the letter that matches the answer they select, and then they hold the card up. Jerome asked his students to use ABCD pinch cards to answer the following hinge question:

A	B
C	D

Ms. Ramos has 28 students in her class. She currently has 6 tables in her room, which seat 4 students per table. Mrs. Ramos asked the students to sit down and some children did not have a seat. How many students didn't have a seat? How many additional tables will she need to seat all the students?

A: 2 students, 2 tables

B: 4 students, 2 tables

C. 4 students, 1 table

D. 2 students, 1 table

As she looked around the room, Jerome noticed that there was an even distribution among the B, C, and D answer choices. He very quickly decided to use his analysis of the student responses instructionally, saying, "I want you to find someone who has a different answer from you. Then work together to find the solution. You have five minutes!" As students worked on their solutions, Jerome could hear students exclaiming, "Ooooh, it is C! Looks like we got confused with the leftovers!" This self-correcting through collaboration is often the kind of outcome revealed by the use of hinge questions.

Exit Task

An exit task is a "capstone problem or task that captures the major focus of the lesson for that day, or perhaps the last several days" (Fennell et al., 2017, p. 109). More robust than an exit ticket, students will need time to showcase their thinking and demonstrate their understanding.

When: The exit task is typically conducted toward the end of a class period. However, plenty of time should be allotted for students to show their understanding.

Opportunities for Strengths Building: The exit task is suited for strengths building because teachers can design the task to include multiple parts or scaffold the task to highlight students' conceptual understanding. Keith designed an exit task (Figure 6.13) for his students as a three-part scaffolded task (see Chapter 5). After students complete Part One, they can move to Part Two, then Part Three. Keith knew that not all students would have time to complete all three parts. However, he knew that Parts One and Two would give him the assessment information he needed to determine whether students understand the concepts of perimeter and area.

FIGURE 6.13: Three-Part Exit Task

PART ONE	PART TWO	PART THREE
Emilio wants to build a table that has a perimeter of 20 feet. What are the dimensions of three possible options he could build? Sketch all the representations and label their dimensions.	Emilio wants to make the table with the largest area. Which table of the ones you sketched has the largest area? Prove your answer.	Are there any other tables with a perimeter of 20 feet that could have a larger area than the ones that you drew? Yes or no? Prove your answer.

Note: For more information about the Formative 5 (Fennell et al., 2017), check out https://us.corwin.com/en-us/nam/the-formative-5/book250542.

 **Try It!**   Formative 5 Techniques

Select one of the Formative 5 techniques to test out in your classroom. Complete the planning organizer (Figure 6.14) to consider how and when you will use the technique.

FIGURE 6.14: Formative 5 Planning Organizer

TECHNIQUE	ANTICIPATION	WHEN	STRENGTHS BUILDING
What technique will you try? *Describe your use of the technique. Include questions and prompts if appropriate.*	*What are the different ways students might respond?*	*When will you implement the technique?*	*How will you leverage your students' strengths? Think about how you will acknowledge students' ideas and provide feedback.*

Reflect: What did you notice about students' engagement? What did the formative assessment reveal about your students' strengths? What were the strengths of your implementation? What were the challenges of your implementation? What Formative 5 technique will you try next time?

When teachers design and implement classroom-based formative assessment techniques to assess student learning from a strengths-based perspective, they identify and nurture students' strengths by building on the strategies they use and the mathematics content they know. The goal of the formative assessment process and the feedback provided within is always to help learners progress. This idea resonates with the approach of using assessment *for* learning rather than assessment *of* learning. Instead of just capturing a snapshot of a student's understanding at a given moment on a test, the everyday use of classroom-based formative assessment combined with targeted feedback improves learning over time.

Summary

Strengths-based feedback is clearly complex. In this chapter, we explored the importance of feedback: teacher-to-student feedback within the Strengths-Based Feedback Loop as well as strategic use of wait time, questioning practices, and listening from a strengths-based perspective. We looked at opportunities for student-to-teacher feedback and student-to-student feedback, and we shared five targeted formative assessment techniques. The ways that we respond to students and collect information about their mathematical understanding is critical to creating a positive, strengths-infused classroom.

PART FOUR

Teaching Turnaround Four
Help Students Develop Their Points of Power

Teaching Turnaround Four: Help Students Develop Their Points of Power is the central emphasis of Chapter 7, particularly as we continue to support students to develop positive mathematical identities. Students' collective in-school and out-of-school experiences of learning mathematics contribute to their beliefs about their ability to be doers of mathematics. In this chapter, we focus on helping you identify the students' strengths through the identification of their Points of Power by designing strategic activities that reveal students' mathematical brilliance. Although this chapter is positioned later in the book, enhancing students' Points of Power is one of the most significant components in building strengths-based instruction.

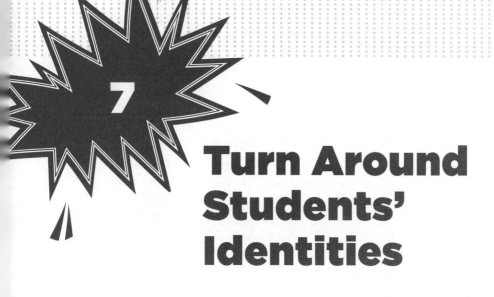

Turn Around Students' Identities

If you want to lift yourself up, lift up someone else.
—Booker T. Washington

All students need to see themselves as mathematicians in the same way they see themselves as readers. Without a disposition that exudes confidence, it is harder to persevere and take on puzzling problems and challenges with vigor. This confidence is built through finding elements that we can think of as bricks that build a framework of their strengths. One by one, as they are told they are creative, logical, hardworking, resourceful, flexible, innovative, collaborative, supportive, a good explainer, an independent thinker, and organized, the bricks assemble not into roadblocks but instead into interconnected structures that reinforce their continued growth and interest in the subject. All children should leave school being able to articulate what they do well in the activity of learning mathematics. Can all students do that? Their strengths need to be visible to them through obvious recognition and attention; then and only then can these carefully communicated strengths be translated into Points of Power. A Point of Power (POP) is that "something" the students do well in mathematics, which they can not only state but rely upon when they face a novel challenge or problem. Teachers must seek out and acknowledge these POPs while giving students opportunities to both practice and showcase their POPs—not unlike a talent show.

> A Point of Power (POP) is that "something" the students do well in mathematics, which they can not only state but rely upon when they face a novel challenge or problem.

Such talent showings should be embedded into daily lessons. What is the best format for that opportunity? Rather than the traditional language arts–based I do, We do, You do approach, Lampert (as cited in Green, 2014) flips that sequence to

- YOU—the students start the problem on their own.
- Y'ALL—the students share ideas with a peer.
- WE—students share strategies, ideas, drawings, or manipulatives on the document camera or chart paper with the whole class. Those whole-class components include sharing strengths and possible misunderstandings. Let's not wait for a test to find out what students do not know!

The following Try It! allows a different format for having students share their mathematical strengths—a performance!

 **Try It!**   Talent Showcase

Have students create a short video or audio with a QR code to explain their approach to a mathematical problem to another student. This mini student-to-student tutorial gives all students the opportunity to be the teacher. Here are a variety of phone and computer apps that will be helpful as your students first create storyboards and then put their ideas into a brief lesson. Because they select their topic, they can begin to pinpoint their content area strengths in mathematics. Use Figure 7.1 as a planning tool to ensure a variety of topics are being discussed.

FIGURE 7.1: Planning Tool for a Talent Showcase

VIDEO TOPIC	STUDENT

Here are some sample talent showcase performance topics:

- Mental math—Multiplication and Memory
- Guessing a number between 1 and 15 using number cards—Addition and Patterns
- Magic Squares—Addition and Problem Solving

- Creating 3-D Shape Skeletons—Geometry and Volume Measurement
- Stories to go with Graph Images—Communication and Data Interpretation
- Sharing a community math problem (i.e., recycling problem)—Data Gathering and Interpretation
- Social justice and math problem (i.e., homeless, foodbank collections)—Problem Solving and Reasoning

Windows and Mirrors

As we build students' mathematical identities, we can use the metaphor of windows and mirrors (Style, 1988) to both open vistas to children and also reflect their own selves in becoming mathematical thinkers. Students use the windows to explore the way others see mathematics and mirrors to reflect their experience as in the following Try It!

> **Windows:** Looking through a window to notice how other see and do mathematics.
>
> **Mirrors:** Looking at a mirror to reflect on the way one thinks about and engages with mathematics.

 **Try It!** **What's Outside Your Window and What's in Your Mirror?**

Use this template to structure students' thinking about ways to expand their horizons and links to their own world as they think about their Points of Power.

Windows

Identify some Points of Power for a person you have read about or a person you have met who has strengths in mathematics. What did they do to show you they had this strength?

Image source: dyeekc/iStock.com

Mirrors

Draw a picture of yourself of a time when you demonstrated perseverance. Then explain how you showed that Point of Power!

Image source: duleloncar_ns/iStock.com

Another way to explore new outlooks as a window into other's thinking is to either learn about a mathematician from outside resources or invite people (start with family members of your students) who do mathematics on the job to the classroom. Highlight that people who do mathematics in the workplace are not working on who is fastest but who has the wisdom and perseverance to strategize and work through problems. For example, Figure 7.2 shows a list that students developed to document former mathematics work habits or behaviors that may have demonstrated limited success and then invite them to add new and different habits they acquire as they engage in new ways of learning mathematics (Figure 7.2).

FIGURE 7.2: Students' Past and Current Learning Habits

WHEN LEARNING MATH, I USED TO . . .	WHEN LEARNING MATH NOW, I CAN ALSO . . .
List my steps.	Explain my thinking.
Copy the teacher's approach.	Try my own strategy for solving the problem.
Work independently and quietly.	Work with others and share ideas with partners and the whole class.
Try to be the first one done.	Realize that it's okay to take my time and celebrate my thinking.
Believe the algorithm is the most important thing.	Show how different representations connect to each other.
Focus on getting the "one right" answer.	Recognize that there could be more than one right answer, as long as I can justify it.
Memorize the algorithm for every computation.	Use different strategies in different situations.
Show the steps of the algorithm I use.	Draw, build, model, or use gestures to show my thinking.

After students have examined their own thinking about their Points of Power, you can share how mathematicians developed their Points of Power. Students may want to revise their ideas about exploring these inspirational mathematicians. Note that we have included a diverse representation of mathematicians. Students feel empowered when they see themselves in their role models. The following Try It! uses literature to motivate and inspire your young mathematicians.

Try It! Windows and Mirrors on Mathematicians

Read *Hidden Figures: The True Story of Four Black Women and the Space Race* by Margot Lee Shetterly (2018) to the students. Other options are *The Girl With a Mind for Math: The Story of Raye Montague* (Mosca, 2018) or *Counting on Katherine: How Katherine Johnson Saved Apollo 13* (Becker, 2018) or *Ticktock Banneker's Clock* (Keller, 2016). Students could also read the brief biographies of Dorothy Vaughan, Katherine Johnson, Mary Jackson, and Christine Darden on the Berkley Library web page, *Women Who Figure: An Exhibit Inspired by the Mathematicians of Hidden Figures: Women of Hidden Figures* (https://guides .lib.berkeley.edu/c.php?g=642479&p=4592917). Arrange the students into pairs or small groups and assign each pair or group to one of the mathematicians. Ask the students to use the window to identify the mathematician's Points of Power and the evidence for those Points of Power (Figure 7.2). For example, students may note that each person persevered. Ask students to identify *how* they persevered. Finally, ask the students to identify another mathematics-related strength of one of the people from the stories and identify when they have demonstrated the same strength in learning mathematics. Recognizing how are they like these mathematicians is an important way for them to build a strong mathematical identity.

Describe the mathematician's Points of Power. Explain your thinking.

As we have discussed in prior chapters, our own experiences learning mathematics influence our own identity development as mathematics teachers. These experiences influence how we develop, support, build, and champion our students' Points of Power.

Turnaround Tip

Think about one mathematics teaching habit that you would like to change. Describe the habit. Where do you believe the habit originated? Identify a replacement behavior for the habit and let the students or a colleague know that you are working to change this habit. For example, perhaps you give directions and repeat yourself over and over as students begin asking questions. You decide to replace this habit by giving directions once, asking students to discuss the directions together, and soliciting student questions.

Our Teacher Mirror

How are your past memories, routines, and narratives possibly resulting in a rerun in your own classroom? When you go on "automatic pilot" in your teaching, are you falling into old habits or storylines from your own past experiences learning mathematics? What new habits should you develop? For example, how can you move from noticing what work students have not yet completed to the work they have finished? What shifts need to occur in the way you talk to the students or the directions you give? What clever strategies do you see students use that you can highlight?

Translation Task

**Translation Task:
A mathematics graphic organizer used to unpack student understanding.**

One way to develop new habits in your instructional approach rather than reruns is to explore the connections children have between multiple representations via the use of the Translation Task (Van de Walle, Karp, & Bay Williams, 2019). This simple structure unearths how flexibly students can think about the interplay between concepts and procedures and will help you notice and build your students' Points of Power.

 **Translation Task**

This task can be adapted for any grade level (see Figure 7.3). Students can decide on their own equation or you can give them an equation that matches the content you are teaching. Ask students to complete these sections on the sheet independently or in pairs. Then, have the students share their translation tasks with one another. Ask, "What do you notice about the word problems? Models? Explanations? What are the strengths that you see?"

FIGURE 7.3: Translation Task

Equation	Word Problem
Model/Illustration	Explain Your Thinking

Source: Adapted from Van de Walle, Karp, and Bay-Williams (2019).

 This feedback sort can be downloaded for use at resources.corwin.com/teachingturnarounds.

You can start by giving students an equation and asking them to solve it and then fill out the other boxes or give a word problem and have them generate the other representations. Another option is pulling together a pair or small group to work on the translation task as a team. This approach is particularly useful if you are able to group them by strengths, such as students who prefer making sketches. The Translation Task is also a perfect opportunity to share a "fictitious" student paper that they can review as they critique the reasoning of others looking for strengths and weaknesses. This paper can include mistakes such as the word problem is not a match or the explanation is weak. Then students can work to correct the word problem or enhance the details in the "Explain Your Thinking" section. Here is a sample of students' work that started with a word problem as a prompt (Figure 7.4).

FIGURE 7.4: Student Work Samples of the Translation Task

Equation	Word Problem
$6 \times 10 = 60$ $6 + 30 = 90$	Ari had 30 cents. Then he found 6 dimes on the ground. How much money does he have now?
Model/Illustration ⑩ ⑩ ⑩⑩⑩ ⑩ ⑩ ⑩ ⑩	Explain Your Thinking $30 + 60 = 90$ So he Started with thee Dimes and found Six more Dimes

Don't Miss an Opportunity to Recognize a Student's Points of Power

How can you be assured that you identify your students' Points of Power? What happens when you miss opportunities of finding those strengths in your students? Let's look at a situation from a classroom where that oversight occurred.

Jorge recently turned seven and is a first grader. He has spent the good portion of the year getting into "trouble" in class for talking and engaging in other activities, although his work is never incomplete. There has been no evidence of meanness or any negativity toward other students or the teacher. But on a scale posted on the wall that goes from a low of "Parental Contact" to a high of "On Fire," Jorge too often worries about falling into the "Parental Contact" zone as he knows that back at home, receiving that rating can result in lost privileges and parents who are sad. On one occasion, he was sent to the principal, who found out a few things by asking Jorge some questions. She identified that Jorge was finishing the tasks almost immediately and had time on his hands. She found he was curious and had an active imagination. When asked if he could identify good behavior in the class, Jorge suggested the teacher had two favorite children, "Tisa" and "Brandon." Then, the principal sent Jorge to the school psychologist as she suspected something more might be influencing the situation. After meeting and dialoging with Jorge, the school psychologist suggested to the parents that Jorge might be tested for "gifted." She felt from the evidence she gathered in their conversations that Jorge was not challenged and that he would start to talk to others when this boredom ensued. The timing of the school psychologist's meeting also aligned with the school talent show where she watched Jorge's comedy routine that he developed for his talent performance. In this presentation, he bantered and joked back and forth with a small robot via a coded program. He developed on his own the entire storyboard and program, including all the coding lines. Where others his age were doing cartwheels and magic tricks for their acts, the school psychologist realized that this act was the first time the school had a child who used "coding" as the talent. Jorge was observed engaging the entire audience, who heartily laughed at the jokes between the robot and the young boy, and few of the students or teachers knew exactly how he had coded his robotic friend.

Before formal aptitude testing was done, the school psychologist conducted some clinical interviews with Jorge to get a picture of his overall mathematical strengths and needs. First, she gave him sets of three rotating or changing patterns and asked him to draw the fourth figure. Repeatedly, he drew the correct response and immediately asked for another pattern. Next, she put several patterned figures in an array and asked him to select a set of three given several similarities or differences (like the card game SET). Within minutes, he went from basic matches of similar cards to sophisticated trios matched on multiple differences. Then she asked him to try some mathematics problems not in his grade level that he was never previously taught. She gave him some basic background about the meaning of the operations, and he was soon trying multiplication and division problems. In each case, he neither drew helping diagrams nor wrote down any numbers. When given the problem 12 × 12 orally, he was quiet for a few seconds and then wrote 124. The school psychologist asked, "How did you get that answer?" Jorge started to report that he was taking 12 groups of ten, and before he finished explaining, he grabbed the pen and rewrote the answer as 144. When she asked him, "Where did you get that changed answer?" he replied, "I have a little mathematician inside of me." This was something he had never said before.

After a few whole-number division problems, the interviewer gave him $2 \div \frac{1}{2} = ?$ and he immediately wrote down 4 and explained that his thinking related to how many one halves are in two whole circles. The next problem was $\frac{1}{2} \div \frac{1}{4} = ?$ and he stated 2 and dropped his pen to indicate he was sure that was correct. The interviewer asked Jorge to make up a division problem for her and write the answer in a secret place. He wrote $25 \div 10 =$ and in the top-secret location, he wrote the answer, $2\frac{1}{2}$. The problem Jorge generated and correctly answered would not be a common question to create, even by an adult, as it wouldn't have a whole number answer. Additionally, the answer format of $2\frac{1}{2}$ rather than 2 with 5 left over (or remaining) was unusual even for an upper elementary school child.

Given evidence from the school psychologist, the teacher gave Jorge several Ken Ken puzzles to try if he had free time. To her surprise, they were all finished that first day. The sad part of the story is that Jorge had been stressed all year, and the parents were worried he was not a "good boy" or a skillful listener. There were many tense conversations at home and many tears. But through conversations with the school psychologist, the teacher was saddened too, first that Jorge identified precisely the two students she truly did enjoy having in class and second that she probably missed one of the most uniquely gifted mathematics students she might ever have in her career.

So, what can we learn from this classroom vignette? We know we cannot wait for students to exhibit their mathematical strengths in very obvious ways, and instead, we must try to intentionally spot them. Strengths do not always mean that they can only be found in perfectly quiet students. Children who are not quiet may instead have a great deal to share. Results of examinations of teacher nominations of students for gifted programs have revealed that children with any behavioral issues are unlikely to be selected—when in reality those children may be the very students who need a challenge and have much to offer in class discussions (Plucker & Peters, 2016). Instead, every child should be screened for strengths every year. Find ways to have students complete diagnostic interviews to delve into the boundaries and possibilities of students' thinking. Plan ways to teach children how they can "grow their own" strengths and encourage them to actively develop perseverance and curiosity by presenting challenging tasks and inquiry-based instruction. Continually adjust your curriculum for students' strengths to consider the level, complexity, breadth, depth, and pace of the instruction (Assouline & Lupkowski-Shoplik, 2011; Johnsen & Sheffield, 2013; Renzulli, Gubbins, McMillen, Eckert, & Little, 2009; Renzulli & Reis, 2014).

SPOTLIGHT ON YOUR PRACTICE:
Looking for Opportunities

Select a student who currently may have you perplexed or could have diverted your attention from their strengths as Jorge did by talking in class. Perhaps your classroom observations indicate that this student does not seem to be engaged or interested in classroom activities in mathematics. Or perhaps the student is particularly inventive and curious, which may prevent the student from completing work. Here are three steps to consider:

1. **Describe the Student by Considering the Following Questions**

   - What does the student do when involved in mathematics learning?

   - What excites the student?

   - What frustrates the student?

   - When does the student shine?

   - Does the student exhibit learned helplessness, where they act as if they can't carry out the task?

2. **Find a Theme**

   Focusing on the moments when the student is excited, engaged, and shining in the mathematics classroom, which you identified in Step 1, is there a particular time (or times) during the lesson when the student seems to thrive? Why do you think the student is particularly engaged at this time?

3. **Look for Opportunities**

   Now that you have carefully observed the student and assessed the best timing during the lesson for building in a change, strategically construct an opportunity in your next mathematics lesson for the student to showcase a skill or share thoughts. Note how the student responds to this opportunity. Explore how you might repeat this reflection for another student.

Students' Productive Dispositions

Students' **productive dispositions** are one of the essential components of mathematical proficiency (National Research Council & Mathematics Learning Study Committee, 2001) as presented in Chapter 2. As students self-assess their strengths, there is an opportunity for them to share their dispositions as an avenue for you to determine their attitudinal Points of Power. The important part of identifying students' attitudes is that attitudes can be changed. Recognizing when students are anxious or nervous about mathematics can provide an impetus for you to provide an intervention. The following Try It! activity invites students to explore their attitudes about learning mathematics. Use any or all of the questions as you adapt for your grade level. Have students put a checkmark next to any of the following sentences that show how **they feel** about math (if you wish to use another recording sheet, you can also ask students to circle a smiley face, neutral face, or sad face for each as you read them aloud.

> **Productive Dispositions:** The inclination to see mathematics as important and useful, to engage meaningfully with mathematics, and to persevere while doing mathematics.

 **Try It!** Student Attitude Survey

☐ Math makes me curious.

☐ I enjoy doing math puzzles.

☐ I would rather avoid math classes.

☐ I never think about math unless I am in math class.

☐ Word problems are confusing.

☐ I am not very confident in math class.

☐ Working with numbers is fun.

☐ Using math materials helps me think about the problems.

☐ Math class makes me nervous.

☐ I have never liked math.

☐ I enjoy being challenged by math problems.

☐ Math tests are scary.

☐ When I get a hard math problem, I keep on working until I have a solution.

☐ My mind sometimes freezes up in math class.

Students Self-Analyze Their Strong Points

Students can begin to identify their strengths with a variety of nonmathematics activities as well, including those that involve reading nonfictional or fictional texts (or a mix of both). They can read a book such as *Stan and the Four Fantastic Powers* (Levy & Schiller, 2018) or *True You: Authentic Strengths for Kids* (Doman, 2018) as a launching point for a conversation about their strengths. Then segue to an emphasis on their mathematics strengths. You can also focus on the Mathematical Practices from the Common Core State Standards for Mathematics (National Governors Association Center for Best Practices & Council of Chief State School Officers, 2010) or your own state's version of these important characteristics as part of the conversation. Are students able to understand the problem? Do they persevere? Select an appropriate mathematical tool? Create a mathematical model? Find patterns? These are all considerations for their "super powers." By self-identifying their Points of Power, students can shed light on skills that may have gone unnoticed and now deserve attention. Then they try activities that formalize these findings such as the one described next.

Turnaround Tip

If you find that students are less confident about their mathematical skills, you can interview or conference with them individually and help them identify the moments when they are exhibiting the behaviors that are linked to success. For example, you might say, "I noticed that you were curious in math class when several classmates had different solutions."

You can also directly ask, "What could we do in mathematics class that would help you engage in or enjoy learning math more?" One of our colleagues asked this of a student and she replied, "I'd like to share my idea with you first before I share it with the whole class. Just to test it out." This small change in the routine transformed this student's experience in the classroom.

Using the book *My Head Is Full of Colors* (Friend, 1995), students communicate their mathematics strengths using fractional parts of a whole. The story is about a girl named Maria who awakes each morning to find her head is full of books, people, animals, and other things other than her hair. These visions become a precursor to her strengths for the day as she successfully reads stories, knows a great deal about animals, or can easily get to know and get along with many people. Using this opportunity to see themselves through children's literature, students were asked to write down several of their strengths in mathematics. The first day, they brainstormed as a group and many ideas were collected. Some students even suggested strengths for other students such as "Tisa is good at making models with place value materials." Once they decided how many strengths they were going to draw (either

4, 5 [made with three fourths and two eighths], 6, or 8), they then each picked the corresponding fractional parts of a whole (either fourths or eighths) to represent their strengths. Some said they would use the bigger portions to show their strongest assets. The next day, they translated these ideas into a circle using two pieces of multicultural construction paper to show their face on one circle and their mathematical strengths on the other. To show their strengths, they labeled the strength and drew in the section something to show that strength and colored the illustration. When finished with the coloring of these two circles, the circles were each cut on a straight line as a radius. They started at the top of the face, between the eyes, and continued cutting in a straight line to the center of the circle. They did the same to the other circle on a line that represented one of the sides of the fractional part. Finally, they slid the two circles together!

When the plates were slid together, they could be turned to expose the portions showing the mathematics strengths hidden beneath the child's face (see Figure 7.5). As they revealed an eighth or quarter by a turn, they talked with a partner about their strengths. Here are some options for questions:

- Share your plate with a partner. What do you notice about your partner's strengths? Do you share any strengths with your partner? If yes, what are they?

- Ask questions about your partner's strengths. What more information do you want to know?

FIGURE 7.5: Samples of Students' Head Full of Math Projects

Consider other pieces of children's literature as vehicles to help students develop strengths (see additional suggestions in Chapter 8). The children's book *How Full Is Your Bucket?* (Rath, 2009) focuses children's attention on thinking about others' strengths. As peers celebrate cool answers given by others, they begin to emphasize strengths rather than weaknesses as a way of looking at all classroom academic interactions. For example, when conducting a number talk, students are invited to share solutions as the teacher writes the strategy and solution on the board. Make sure that you record the student's name next to the strategy so that students can recognize one another's strengths. At the conclusion of the number talk, ask students to highlight one another's ideas and explanations. You might say, "Let's talk about the strengths we saw today in our number talk. Who can share a strength they saw?" Another example is during the lesson's closure. We routinely use gallery walks during the closure as a way to lift up students' strengths. For example, we ask students to take a blue sticky dot and place the dot on the student work that shows a strength and a green sticky dot on the student work that is most interesting to them. During the closure discussion, we ask students to explain why they placed their dots on the student work. Ensure that students are not privileging particular students over another by asking them to select a student they have not selected before. You will want to make sure that all students have an opportunity to be highlighted in these discussions. In the Spotlight on Your Practice, you can identify opportunities within a lesson you are planning to help students focus on one another's strengths. In the Try It!, you can design a Strengths Super Power Chart to highlight students' Points of Power.

Students' learning can be enhanced when they learn about and capitalize on the strengths of others. The following Try It! helps students identify the resources that reside right around them. Their PEERS!

SPOTLIGHT ON YOUR PRACTICE:
Planning to Support Students to Identify Strengths in Each Other

LESSON PLANNING COMPONENT (BRIEFLY DESCRIBE YOUR PLAN)	HOW WILL YOU PLAN FOR STUDENTS TO NOTICE PEERS' STRENGTHS?
Lesson Launch	
Facilitating the Lesson	
Closing the Lesson	

Reflect: How did it go? What will you try next time?

Try It!   Strengths Super Powers

Positioning the students as strengths leaders can help you keep the class running smoothly. Make a Strengths Super Power Chart for students to use as a resource to support one another while you are teaching. This resource will help you maximize your time during small-group instruction, position the students as strengths agents, and cultivate a positive learning environment. For example, you could make a *Strengths Super Power* list to post in the classroom. Develop this list with the students to ensure that each and every student is able to showcase a strength.

Strengths Super Power

PERSEVERANCE	CONSTRUCTING MODELS	COMMUNICATION
If I need someone to encourage me to keep working and not give up.	If I need someone to help me to show or explain my thinking using manipulatives or drawings.	If I need someone to help me understand the directions for the task. Or If I need someone to talk over an idea or possible strategy with me.
Then, I can go to . . . Mario Elena Max Tiffany Diamond	Then, I can go to . . . Jordyn Paris Jay	Then, I can go to . . . Bryce Hannah Sarita Jenna

Summary

Armed with the results of the activities you've tried from this chapter, we are hopeful that the children in your class can convey Points of Power when learning mathematics to others (and themselves). By turning what might be invisible to visible, we purposefully try to move the uncomfortable to the comfortable in the process. As their strengths are noticed and in some cases celebrated, they build resilience to the normal frustration we sometimes may experience when we are challenged. As you pursue students' strong points and talents, you may uncover a bunch of children like Jorge in your classroom. They are waiting for you!

Teaching Turnaround Five
Promote Strengths in the School Community

Teaching Turnaround Five: Promote Strengths in the School Community is the focus of Chapters 8 and 9. In this chapter, we explore how to promote strengths within the greater school community, including teachers, educational professionals within and across the broader school community, and school leaders. We believe that in promoting strengths-based work, all teachers are leaders as they emulate the strengths-based perspective.

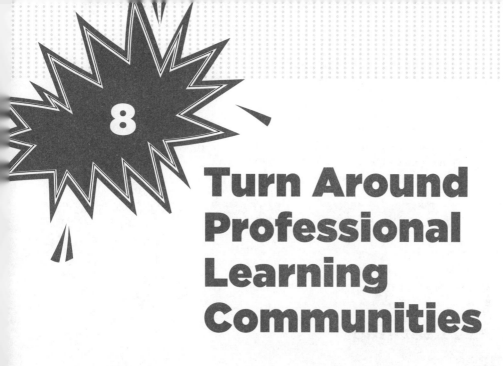

Turn Around Professional Learning Communities

Unity is strength . . . when there is teamwork and collaboration, wonderful things can be achieved.
—Mattie Stepanek

Sometimes we as teachers need supportive starting points to take on the leadership we know we want to express. We want

- a team approach to doing our work rather than coming to our workplace as individuals who "do their own thing,"
- a positive atmosphere where the forces outside our school or district are never as strong as our collective ability to make the best learning environments for children, and
- to harmonize in our approach to building consistency across the school and allowing students to see familiar learning tools and language rather than every year a new set of approaches or even new names or rules for what was learned previously.

Supporting Teachers' Strengths

A fresh approach to moving these desires to commonplace behaviors is possible and energizing. By creating a way to promote strengths in students and by acknowledging the strengths teachers have via their collective efficacy (Donohoo, 2017; Eells, 2011; Hattie et al., 2016), teachers can be more powerful levers in moving heavy loads. In the words of Alexander the Great, "Remember: upon the conduct of each depends the fate of all." Or those of Helen Keller, "Alone we can do so little: together we can do so much," or as basketball coach Phil Jackson said, "The strength of the team is each individual member. The strength of each member is the team."

The following Spotlight encourages you to examine and reflect upon which professional learning experiences best promote teaching practices that effectively support and build students' strengths.

SPOTLIGHT ON YOUR PRACTICE:
Professional Learning Experiences

1. What kinds of professional learning engages you the most productively? Describe.

2. What professional learning experiences have you participated in that have advanced your teaching expertise?

3. What professional learning experiences have positively impacted your understanding of mathematics content?

4. With whom do you most enjoy participating in professional learning? Why? How does this shared enjoyment connect to your learning? Your teaching?

5. If you could design your own professional learning, what would it look like? What would be the characteristics of the person delivering the professional development?

6. As you review your ideas, what themes do you notice?

 This Spotlight can be downloaded for use at resources.corwin.com/teachingturnarounds.

Consider your responses and the themes you identified in the Spotlight questions. As you explore professional learning opportunities that will support your students' mathematics growth, remember your vision of effective professional development. We suggest that you consider moving from thinking about teachers (and yourselves) as individual performers to working together as an ensemble through the use of either the Appreciative Inquiry (AI) framework or the Whole-School Agreement (or both). Combining teachers' capacity for making lasting change more than doubles the potential for satisfying outcomes for children (Hattie et al., 2016). Bandura (1997) calls this comprehensive effort **collective efficacy**, which increases student achievement and teachers' confidence to teach effectively (Goddard, Hoy, & Woolfolk Hoy, 2004).

> **Collective Efficacy:**
> A group's shared belief in its conjoint capability to organize and execute the courses of action required to produce given levels of students' attainment (Bandura, 1997, p. 477).

The Appreciative Inquiry (AI) Framework

In Chapter 2, we explored the **Appreciative Inquiry** process to uncover teachers' strengths. In this chapter, we turn again to Appreciative Inquiry to discover students' strengths through a collaborative effort. Furthermore, we encourage you to use Appreciative Inquiry as a regular format for engaging in professional learning.

> **Appreciative Inquiry:**
> A change process to find the best of what works in people and organizations.

Let's imagine for a moment two different **professional learning communities**. In the first community, a leader has collected a group of teachers to discuss students who are having difficulties learning mathematics. Designed to support students, teachers bring forward their concerns about the students, show evidence of the problems, and make recommendations about how to help the students. In this professional community, the focus is on each student's deficits, evidence for the deficit, and planning for ways to fix the deficit.

> **Professional Learning Communities:** A group of educators who regularly work together to improve learning for students.

In the second community, teachers have been gathered together because a leader has noted that there is limited evidence of student discourse in the mathematic instruction. The professional learning focus is on the lack of student discourse, which results in conversations about the dearth of discourse opportunities provided by the teacher and progresses to how students do not know how to productively talk with one another.

We share these scenarios to illustrate how draining these conversations can be on our outlook and our abilities to imagine and design thoughtful teaching moments. Notice how you feel after you have participated in one of these conversations about students or attended professional learning that was targeted at "fixing" deficits in your own teaching. Most of us feel defensive and depleted by negative conversations, even when we are engaged in attempting to identify positive solutions.

> **"** ·
>
> Combining teachers'
> capacity for making lasting
> change more than doubles
> the potential for satisfying
> outcomes for children.

Moreover, these kinds of negative conversations—particularly when they focus on the deficits of students—often lead to stereotyping (Bernard, 1997). Labels such as "at risk" focus attention on all that is wrong with the student, further separates the student from other students who do not share the label, creates a particular identity (Southeast Educational Development Laboratory, 2005), and distracts educators from seeing the students' assets (Schonert-Reichl, 2000).

By contrast, Appreciative Inquiry (AI) is the collective and cooperative uncovering, through inquiry, of the very best in people and their organizations (Cooperrider & Whitney, 2005). While the traditional approach to making change is to search for a problem, analyze it, and select a solution pathway, AI focuses on what is going well so that the successes can be repeated, cultivated, and grown (Hammond, 1998). More recently, research demonstrates that using the AI approach through a professional learning community can help teachers, administrators, and students build positive relationships, find creative ways to support students who struggle, and positively influence academic outcomes (Calabrese, Hummel, & San Martin, 2007; Kobett, 2016).

Let's take a look at the AI process, including specific questions that a professional learning community can use to frame their conversations and action planning for supporting students who struggle. The progression includes five steps (Cooperrider & Whitney, 2005; Figure 8.1), with each step focusing on a particular aspect of the AI cycle.

FIGURE 8.1: Five Steps of the AI Cycle

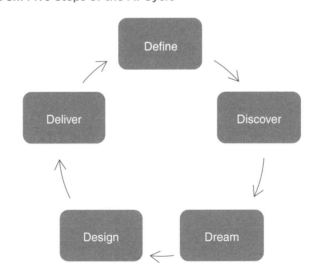

Source: Cooperrider and Whitney (2005).

1. **Define:** In the first step of the process, participants ask and answer provocative questions such as the following:

    - What does a successful mathematics learner look like in your classroom, grade, and school?

    - How do you know when students are successful mathematics learners in your classroom, grade, and school? Or beyond?

2. **Discover:**

    - Describe a time when (insert student name) was at his most successful in learning mathematics.

    - What was he learning?

    - What was he doing?

    - How do you know that he was successful?

    - Was he energized by the success? What did you notice?

    - How did you respond to his learning?

    - How did he respond after his success on the next tasks?

    - Are there any themes that you notice?

3. **Dream:**

    - If you could imagine that (insert student name) experiences the same success every day that he experienced during the successful learning example you provided, what would he be doing? What would you be doing? What would your team or school be doing to support the continuation of this level of performance?

    - Discuss with your professional learning community your thoughts and ideas from this imagining.

    - What do you notice?

    - Is this dream within your grasp? Is part of this dream within your grasp? How do you know?

4. **Design:**

    - Using your ideas and the ideas from the group conversation and the discussion of the themes that you noticed, design a teaching experiment to capitalize on (insert student name)'s success. The idea should focus on his strengths, connect to your dream, and be something you can try the very next day. If you had to give a rating from 0 to 10 representing your confidence for implementing the design, your score must be 8, 9, or 10. Otherwise, you need to go back and design something more attainable.

5. **Deliver:**

    - How will you deliver your teaching experiment?

    - How will you determine the success of your experiment?

    - When and how will you share the results of your experiment?

While a focus on student success is important, the approach does not diminish the very real mathematics learning difficulties of individual students. In this process, AI challenges the professional learning community to rethink our ideas about how growth can be fostered and implemented.

We recently facilitated a session just like this one, and the process and results were empowering. Teachers used words like *wonderful, persistent,* and *curious* to describe the students who were having difficulties learning mathematics. A student called Mario was brought up for group discussion because of his lack of engagement in the classroom. He rarely completed assignments and had to be consistently prodded to get any work done. After participating in the AI process, the teachers identified that Mario loved to work with a particular student partner, although the students rarely got the opportunity to work together because they received instruction in different small groups. After some discussion, the teachers designed an experiment for all of the students to work on a problem-based task in pairs. They would assign Mario to his preferred partner and see if that increased his productivity, engagement, and mathematical understanding. They also decided that they would have the pair share their work with the whole class to give Mario an opportunity to showcase his understanding. This grade-level professional learning community buzzed with excitement about this new experimental plan and the potential results. Just as we were leaving, his teacher exclaimed, "I can't wait to see Mario tomorrow!" The group responded, "We can't wait to find out what happens."

The Appreciative Inquiry process changes the ways we

- think and talk *about* our students,
- think and talk *with* our students,
- interact *with* our students, and
- interact *with* one another.

Whole-School Agreement

> There is often more group unity agreed upon in the area of student discipline than in content area instruction. That doesn't make sense.

Many schools have engaged in rallying around a single system of classroom management for the school to implement. For example, using these approaches, teachers employ a common way for students to ask for help, provide similar rules for movement around the classroom, and develop shared expectations for student behavior. But what about academic endeavors? Why don't we strive for the same level of organized unity? When teaching mathematics, are teachers using the same models each year with increasing sophistication, the identical problem-solving mnemonic across the entire school, and the same terminology? Probably not! Often such clarity and cohesiveness have not even been raised as issues of concern. There is often more group unity agreed upon in the area of student discipline than in content area instruction. That doesn't make sense.

The Whole-School Agreement (WSA) is developed around the idea that students learn mathematics more effectively when all people who engage with students in the school who are learning mathematics come to an understanding about precisely what rules, language, notation, models, and problem-solving approaches will be used (Karp, Bush, & Dougherty, 2016). The WSA process includes everyone on the "team," including family members or caregivers, staff, substitute teachers, volunteers, student teachers, principals, and of course all teachers. Yes, all. This WSA process links to a strengths-based approach as it provides the consistent message of unified faculty and family voices about the mathematics being learned. When all groups are working in concert with vocabulary, rules, notation, and generalizations over multiple grades, the instruction is reinforced rather than scattered and fragmented. This approach builds strengths and fortifies the most critical aspects of the discipline of mathematics.

> "
> When all groups are working in concert with vocabulary, rules, notation, and generalizations over multiple grades, the instruction is reinforced rather than scattered and fragmented.

Let's start with mathematics vocabulary. In an effort to find instructional ideas and activities to help their students, individual teachers often head to Pinterest or Teachers Pay Teachers. Unfortunately, these sites carry a very mixed bag of resources in terms of quality, with often weird and incorrect instructional resources. Here is what we found there. Suggested for teachers to use when students look at a way to describe the relationship demonstrated by 4 + 6 = 6 + 4 are the "Ring around the Rosie" property, the "Flip-Flop" property, the "Peanut Butter and Jelly" property, or the "Commuter (travel back and forth)" property. Do these resonate with the desire to have students develop a meaningful collection of mathematical ideas? Not at all! Although perhaps developed with the good intentions of engaging students or making mathematics learning "fun" or "memorable," these approaches quickly lead to students' failure to align with more sophisticated but connected ideas in subsequent years. This situation occurs when their third-grade teacher has no idea what the "Flip-Flop" property is and the sixth-grade teacher cannot see the connection between the distributive property and the BABY property (you get it; B(A + Y) = BABY!). So, what's a better step toward student success? Yes, the WSA. Figure 8.2 offers a beginning collection of terms that need to be jettisoned for more meaningful and interconnected words that will play an important role in students' learning of mathematics. Add more of your own suggestions. What mathematical words did you learn as a child that need an update to emphasize meaning and students' ability to have a solid grounding? What terms should you use instead?

FIGURE 8.2: Mathematics Vocabulary

TERMS FROM THE PAST	AGREED-UPON TERMS
Borrowing or Carrying	Trading or Regrouping
Plug a number in the equation	Substitute a number in the equation
Reducing fractions	Putting fractions in lowest terms or simplifying fractions
Times it	Multiplying
Plussing	Adding
2 + 2 makes 4	2 + 2 equals 4

online resources ⬆ This figure can be downloaded for use at resources.corwin.com/teachingturnarounds.

When we say agreed-upon terms here, we mean the whole school agrees. That is all parents and all those who enter the building who may interact with children. What handout should you make for substitute teachers and volunteers? Family members? What do they need to know so they don't unintentionally reinforce some terms or phrases that are different from precise mathematical language? Set those boundaries as a cohesive whole. The students who struggle with mathematics need a consistent message. How can the table (Figure 8.2) shown above be used as a basis for the handout? This example of a component of a WSA builds students' strengths by reinforcing the same words, notation, and ideas over and over in a unified and unwavering approach.

Let's look at another example. In a study by Andrews and Kobett reported in 2017, they found when visiting a single school, confusion reigned in the use of problem-solving posters. Here is what they saw (see Figure 8.3).

Notice that we cross out the Key Words poster as it should be thrown away, as a key words strategy is not an appropriate or useful approach (see Karp, Bush, & Dougherty, 2019).

FIGURE 8.3: Various Problem-Solving Posters Found in One School

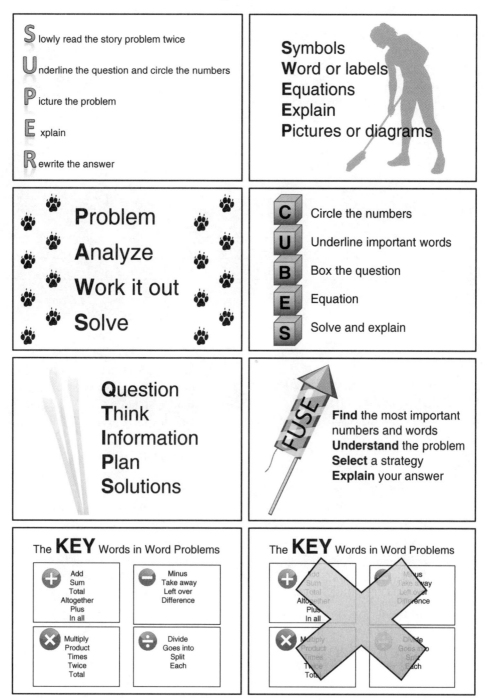

Image sources: Sweeping: A-Digit/iStock.com; Cotton swab: eldadcarin/iStock.com; Rocket: Olga Andreevna Shevchenko/iStock.com.

If you look at these posters, which may be colorful and attractive (or even free), what is the overall instructional effect? Let's look at Andrews and Kobett's careful analysis in the following table that was documented by traveling grade by grade throughout an elementary school (Figure 8.4).

FIGURE 8.4: An Analysis of Problem-Solving (PS) Process Posters

GRADE	PS PROCESS	E MEANS	P MEANS	S MEANS	U MEANS
1	CUBES	Equation		Solve	Underline important words
2	SUPER	Explain with a number sentence	Picture	Slowly read the problem	Underline the question
3	FUSE	Explain thinking		Select a strategy	Understand
4	QTIPS		Plan	Solution	
5	SWEEP	Equation	Pictures	Symbols	

Source: Created by Beth Kobett and Delise Andrews.

Turnaround Tip

Help families think about ways to become involved in the mathematics their children are learning during homework experiences.

- Share the problem-solving poster for them to use at home.

- Encourage a home word wall for math on the back of a door for students to add new words.

- Give them the new vocabulary to expect their child to know.

- For homework, ask the child to create a word problem with the family's names or about a family event to share with a partner.

As you might notice, the S on a poster in one year means solve, means slowly read the problem the next year, and later can mean strategy, solution, or symbols. How does learning a new mnemonic every year help children who need support in solving problems? A better way to engage students' strengths would be the use of a single problem-solving poster agreed upon by the whole school. Then students are reinforcing what they know, finding familiar patterns year after year, and no longer needing to remember what "S" means this year. What started as an attempt to help students with a visual guide for problem solving, coupled with a mnemonic, ended up being a confusing and ever-changing set of words that became arbitrary rather than infused with meaning and supportive of sense making.

Another great topic for the WSA is to consider how to develop a vetting process for outside resources. Unintentionally, teachers select print, web, or application resources from educational websites that may not be pedagogically sound and, in fact may promote the exact opposite mathematics message that the school wants to encourage. In a recent WSA school meeting discussing fluency, teachers from every grade level discovered that they were all using different web applications, websites, and programs. They developed a list of criteria for their WSA (Figure 8.5) and then put their resources to the test. They were surprised to discover that only one of the applications they reviewed aligned with their philosophy for developing mathematically fluent students.

FIGURE 8.5: Fluency Web Resources Criteria

FLUENCY WEB RESOURCES			
Criteria	Yes	No	Notes
Untimed			
Gives targeted feedback			
Promotes flexible strategy use			

In the Spotlight on the next page, consider topics for your school to explore as you consider developing your own WSA.

Summary

In the words of Margaret Mead, the noted anthropologist, "never doubt that a small group of thoughtful, committed people can change the world. Indeed, it is the only thing that ever has." This chapter led you to two specific steps that can engage your school in vital changes. First, through the use of an Appreciative Inquiry model, you can organize a shift toward what is successful and how it can be replicated rather than a focus on what weaknesses you see in students. Second, the Whole-School Agreement focuses on how you can strengthen all students' Points of Power by moving as a unified force. By trialing these approaches, you can summon the collective efficacy of the teaching faculty, administration, families, and students. This combined and concentrated effort builds a shared passion for seeking the best approaches for teaching mathematics to each and every child in your school community.

SPOTLIGHT ON YOUR PRACTICE:
Whole-School Agreement

What topics keep coming up in your school that could support your students' mathematical success? Here are some ideas for a full faculty discussion.

1. What words do teachers and students use to describe the mathematics they are learning?

2. What rules are being introduced to students?

3. What are the beliefs about basic fact practice? What should be the agreed-upon use of timed tests?

4. How are students' strengths being supported?

5. What kinds of mathematics homework do students complete? What is the homework policy? How could homework be more engaging, motivating, and relevant?

6. What kinds of representations are students expected to use and know at each grade level?

For more information to support the development of a Whole-School Agreement, check out these references:

Karp, K. S., Bush, S. B., & Dougherty, B. J. (2014). 13 Rules that expire. *Teaching Children Mathematics, 21*(1), 18–25.

Karp, K. S., Bush, S. B., & Dougherty, B. J. (2015). 12 Math rules that expire in middle grades. *Teaching Children Mathematics, 21*(4), 208–215.

Karp, K. S., Bush, S. B., & Dougherty, B. J. (2019). Avoiding the ineffective key-word strategy. *Teaching Children Mathematics, 25*(7), 428–435.

Yagi, S., & Venenciano, L. (2017). Math "rules" prompt reflection on teachers' identity. *Mathematics Teaching in the Middle School, 22*(9), 555–557.

 This Spotlight can be downloaded for use at resources.corwin.com/teachingturnarounds.

Notes

_____

_____

_____

_____

_____

_____

_____

_____

_____

_____

_____

_____

_____

_____

_____

_____

_____

_____

_____

_____

_____

_____

Teaching Turnaround Five

Promote Strengths in the School Community

In this second chapter for Teaching Turnaround Five: Promote Strengths in the School Community, we continue to explore how to promote strengths within the greater school community by turning to our treasured and important educational partners— our families.

Turn Around Family Communication

The key ingredient in family communication is listening, really listening.

—Zig Ziglar

In this chapter, we turn to the families as a critical and essential component for supporting strengths finding within the school community. When schools foster positive and open communication with families, all relationships are strengthened. Making the mathematics curriculum visible and accessible from a strengths-based perspective promotes positive connections and access to the mathematics classroom.

Here's a recollection from a colleague about her emotional reaction to a note from her son Owen's teacher. The teacher's communication stated,

> Hi, Owen did not complete his in-class math assignment today. He continues to struggle with division. We are learning that division is multiplication backwards, but he is still having difficulties making that connection. Please have him complete all the odd problems on pages 198 and 199. Thank you for your support.

Our colleague shared this message with a group of close friends, bringing up how all the deficit language used in the note made both her as a parent and Owen as student feel. She described how the short message completely shaped how she and Owen worked together on homework that night "with Owen in tears and feeling like a failure because it's the same messaging he got routinely at school . . . even asking if I thought he was still a good person because he was struggling with math." This mother felt just as defeated and crushed as her son, evoking the sensation that matches the late comedian Joan Rivers' well-known saying, "You can only be as happy as your least happy child."

Several other colleagues jumped in with their own stories. One had similar experiences with notes from both her boys' teachers. Another in the group described a time where her generally high-achieving daughter failed a math test and nearly gave up on herself, but her positive, strengths-based teacher helped her through it and now she's going on to advanced math classes. One friend remembered his own report card with a written comment that read "algebra just isn't your cup of tea." That was enough to lead him to become an English major, thereby avoiding mathematics and totally shaping his long-term career choices. The memory still sticks with him 45 years later.

We think that there are likely more stories like these—and hopefully as teachers we can see that even if a message went home to families in the past that we'd like to retract, there are numerous ones in the future that can change families' lives for the better. Our interactions can lead families to be more interested and excited about mathematics—as a team. Try sharing a strength or positive approach in each note or communication you have with families (Figure 9.1). The strengths-based perspective is the foundation of a powerful action plan to build family connections. Let's think differently.

FIGURE 9.1: Notes to Families From Past to Present

NOTES THAT WENT HOME IN THE PAST	NOTES GOING HOME FROM NOW ON
Crystal is having trouble with her multiplication facts. Can you help her at home?	Here's a game we think your family will enjoy playing. The best part about this game is that it helps with multiplication facts. Notice how Crystal uses her skip counting to figure out the problems with a 5 as a factor.
Rory has expressed to me that he doesn't like mathematics. This tends to play out in his low energy and interest during math instruction. Can you talk to him?	There are many ways that math can be used in the real world! Can you help Rory make a list of "math around the house" this week? How many ways can he notice math being used?
Rena isn't measuring accurately with a ruler. Can you practice this skill with her?	Here is a scavenger hunt sheet to try with Rena. Find some objects in the house that appear to be the same size as these objects: cotton swab (provide one), fork, chair height. Then measure each with this paper ruler.

These notes are strengths-based because they promote activities that provide opportunities for students and families to engage with mathematics in specific, friendly, and accessible ways.

SPOTLIGHT ON YOUR PRACTICE:
Notes to Families

Looking forward, consider a short note that you want to send home to a family about a student who is currently struggling in your classroom. Write your first draft in the first section of the table. Then, using the samples provided, rewrite the note using strengths-based language.

What do you want to communicate to the family?
Strengths-Based Note

Reflect: What did you notice about this process? What do you anticipate the families' response will be?

 This template can be downloaded for use at resources.corwin.com/teachingturnarounds.

We need to change the content of these stories noted earlier in this chapter from descriptions of turning a family evening into a conflict zone to easing the entry of families seeing mathematics as a necessity for everyone's future. By making this shift, we can open up the path for students to thinking differently—maybe actually loving mathematics. For what we do know is that there is a deep connection between emotions and reasoning (Brooks, 2019). Brooks (2019) suggests that it is the work of schools to provide children with new "things to love" (p. 8). Good relationships all around among teachers, students, and families reduce the fear that can have a negative effect on learning and demonstrate the caring that generates the climate for powerful learning (Aspen Institute, 2019).

Engaging Families in Strengths-Based Talk

Margaret Drabble (*The Guardian,* August 5, 1975), a famous British author, once wrote,

> *I dropped maths with a sigh of relief, for I had always loathed it, always felt uncomprehending even while getting tolerable marks, didn't like subjects I wasn't good at, and had no notion of this subject's appeal or significance . . . I am not really as innumerate as I pretend, and suspect there is little wrong with the basic equipment, but I shall never know. . . .*
>
> *And that effectively, though I did not appreciate it at the time, closed most careers and half of culture to me forever. (p. 16)*

> **Maths: The international term for math.**

Many people are not afraid to publicly share their dislike of mathematics. Even for those family members who may have liked the subject of mathematics as students, they may be uncomfortable when faced with new ways of teaching mathematics. Many family members believe their strengths in mathematics are grounded in the methods they use, and when we take those comfortable approaches away from them, they feel untethered and "disempowered" (Remillard & Jackson, 2006, p. 254). Algorithms are their superpowers. These uneasy feelings often emerge during homework interactions with their children. Not only are these times when emotions can run high, but research also suggests that it is the homework experience that often facilitates the transfer of mathematics anxiety from family member to child (Maloney, Ramirez, Gunderson, Levine, & Beilock, 2015; Soni & Kumari, 2015). These researchers found that if family members are anxious when helping their child with the evening's homework, this reaction feeds into not only their children's feelings toward the subject of mathematics but also their children's performance in math. The findings revealed that the students with mathematics-anxious family members who frequently helped them do homework were falling, on average, a third of a year behind others; we

> " . . . .
>
> The findings revealed that the students with mathematics-anxious family members who frequently helped them do homework were falling, on average, a third of a year behind others.

just can't afford that. Unfortunately, family members' challenges with trying to independently understand mathematics instructional approaches they are not familiar with have been linked to math anxiety (Antolin, Lipovec, & Lipovec, 2017; Jay, Rose, & Simmons, 2017). In Elizabeth Green's (2014) article for the *New York Times Magazine* called "Why Do Americans Stink at Math," she discusses family members' perceptions that they sense many barriers in helping their child do well in mathematics.

Teachers are the best people to support families in learning about the newer strategies for teaching mathematics. We need to remember that what was prized in mathematical performance and what was perceived as a "brainy" child in mathematics may have changed over the years. Although we don't always talk about this, other countries faced similar initial reactions to their changes in mathematics and instructional focus, but over a long time and with teacher support, the family members shifted their thinking from "Why are you doing this?" to "Let's do this!" The Turnaround Tips help you think about

Turnaround Tip

Help families think about ways to change the language they use when engaging in the homework experience.

PLEASE DON'T SAY . . .	PLEASE DO SAY . . .
I could never do math.	I love how hard you are working to learn math.
I never did math this way.	It is exciting that you are learning new ways to understand math.
This new way doesn't make any sense.	Explain to me how you are learning . . .
What family message might you add?	

Turnaround Tip

Check in with family members about how the homework experience is going. Consider sending home a Homework Encouragement Checklist with students' homework to encourage family members to engage positively with their children. For example,

- I encouraged my child's effort.

- I expressed positive messages about learning mathematics.

- I asked my child to teach me a new mathematics strategy.

One way to get families on board is to communicate early in the school year about your approach to mathematics teaching. This will ideally help them want to be your ally in your quest to focus on strengths and avoid negative stereotypes (about themselves and others!) when it comes to mathematics.

engaging with families from a strengths-based perspective, particularly as we focus on the ways that we communicate with these home-based learning coaches and the way they are invited to communicate with us.

On the next page, you'll find sample letter to send home to families before your Family Math Night, Back-to-School Night, or How-We-Are-Teaching-Your-Child-Math Night. Please make sure you translate this letter for families whose home language is not English. For this and many of the resources in this chapter, we have provided copies in English and Spanish on the companion website, resources.corwin.com/teachingturnarounds.

Incorporating Family and Community Strengths

When communication between the families and schools is reciprocal, students, teachers, families, and communities benefit (Teaching Tolerance, 2019). Facilitating positive mathematics conversations and providing space for each member of the community to participate and share experiential knowledge supports students to develop positive mathematical identities. You can do this by asking students to conduct family interviews to share mathematics strengths and inviting diverse guest speakers from the community to the classroom to share their mathematics strengths. For example, Tiffany brought her class together to conduct oral interviews with family and community members. The class posed an overarching inquiry question, "How do our families use mathematics?" The students brainstormed more questions to ask their families, designed a recording sheet, and set a deadline for all of the interviews to be conducted. The students also asked, "Why is math important in your life?" and "How does math help the world?" Next, they shared what they learned from their families and community partners.

> " Facilitating positive mathematics conversations and providing space for each member of the community to participate and share experiential knowledge supports students to develop positive mathematical identities.

SPOTLIGHT ON YOUR PRACTICE:
Sample Family Letter

Hello Families,

I want to let you know more about an approach we are using in class to talk about your child's mathematics learning. I am focusing on an approach that is called a Strengths-Based Perspective. Rather than just talking about what is lacking in your child's understanding of mathematical ideas, I will try to focus on the strengths I see such as what they do well and how they have used ideas they already know to build new ideas. Expect that I may share homework that is a game to play or a puzzle to solve. I may ask your child to teach you something we are learning during mathematics instruction—please be well behaved!

I want you to know that we are partners in helping your child become a mathematically literate member of a democratic society, who won't be scammed by people trying to trick them out of their money or confused by numbers. Instead, your child will be able to know the mathematics that will get jobs and help them be successful with their finances.

One thing we do request in this process is that you do not say to your child any of the following (even if you may have felt this way at some point in your life): *I never understood math, math was always my worst subject, I don't use math at my workplace,* and *you may have gotten your dislike of math from my side of the family*! Research shows your words have the greatest power with your child. Instead, tell them how mathematics will help them now and in the future. Maybe you too will share your math strengths with your child. I appreciate your help and your positive energy. Together, let's make your child ready for any future they can imagine.

Your child's teacher,

 You can find English and Spanish versions of this letter at resources.corwin.com/teachingturnarounds.

Tiffany asked each student to select a quotation from their interview to post.

"Math helps the world because people use math to find cures for sickness."

"I use math in my job as a cashier. I make sure the prices add up!"

"I use math to design and plant landscapes."

Students then reflected on the comments that their families contributed. Tiffany asked, "What do you notice about the comments?" Students noticed that all their families used mathematics in their homes, on the job, and in the community. Throughout the year, Tiffany invited families to contribute more items for students to reflect upon.

Working Together to Share Mathematical Ideas

Sharing the responsibility of teaching mathematical ideas to children with their families involves sharing the changes in the mathematics curriculum, new approaches to teaching, and new connections to other subjects and the real world. This level of partnership with family members is particularly important as young children have suggested that when their families help them with strategies that differ from what is being learned in school, they are distressed (Lange & Meaney, 2011). Families *always* want their child to be successful, and helping them connect new approaches and habits of mind with the mathematical learning and knowledge they already have benefits (Knapp, Landers, Liang, & Jefferson, 2017). Knapp et al. (2017) call this emphasis "mathematical knowledge for parental involvement" (p. 70).

You can also start building family members' strengths and confidence in mathematics with easy-to-access activities they can try together with their children. Wherever possible, translate the activities for families that speak languages besides English. The following lively activities will engage families in mathematical thinking. Exploring the Problem of Nines (Dougherty, 2018) is a great way to begin.

 **Try It!**   Exploring the Problem of Nines

- Take out nine sticky notes for you and your partner (or group of three).
- Number them boldly with the digits 1 to 9.
- Place the sticky notes into the form of an addition problem with two three-digit addends (Figure 9.2), so that the answer uses the remaining sticky notes (all nine sticky notes are used).

FIGURE 9.2: Sticky Note Template for the Problem of Nines

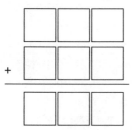

- Make as many different successful problems as you can.
- Record your findings on paper.

Look at the problems you found that work. Can you identify any patterns?

- What's the smallest possible digit in the hundreds place of the sum?
- What's the smallest possible digit in the hundreds place of the addends?
- Are there solutions you can find that don't require regrouping?

Source: Adapted from Dougherty (2018).

 This Exploring the Problems of Nines page can be downloaded for use in Spanish and English at resources.corwin.com/teachingturnarounds.

Why is the problem of nines a good problem to use? How is it different from the way family members learned when they were in school but not as stressful as facing new approaches to learning mathematics?

 **Try It!** Play SALUTE!

Remove all picture cards from a regular deck of playing cards and shuffle. Then, using a group of three people, have two players draw the top card from the deck and place the card on their foreheads without looking at the card on their own head. Instead, they must look at the cards on the other player's forehead. Then, the third person calls out either the sum or the product of the two numbers, whatever the group decides in advance. Each player then calls out the number that is on their head. For example, if the group decided they were adding and one person had a 5 and the other a 3 on their foreheads, the third person would call out 8, and each player would look at the other person's card to figure out what they had on their head. This game can be played competitively (who states their number first) or collaboratively (where both just state what they have without a time element). Be prepared! When family members have the cards on their foreheads and the child is calling out the answers, there are usually a lot of laughs.

Source: Adapted from Van de Walle, Karp, and Bay-Williams (2019).

 Instructions to play SALUTE! can be downloaded in English and Spanish at resources.corwin.com/teachingturnarounds.

Build a culture of family mathematics by sending home baggies with a game inside for families to play and, when done, they return it to trade for another choice or it can be homework if you have enough for the entire class. Students often enjoy including a favorite classroom game in the rotation. Here are a couple to try.

 **Try It!** Area Game

The Area Game is a perfect choice for children in Grades 3 and beyond who need practice with multiplication basic facts and who are also learning about the concept of area as covering space. The baggie should include at least one piece of 1-cm grid paper folded in half (hamburger fold) and two dice. Have two players position themselves on either side of the grid paper. Then, the first player rolls the dice. If the child gets a 2 and 3, they start from the bottom-right corner of the paper on their side and create a 2 × 3 array (two rows of 3). Inside the array, they write the equation (2 × 3 = 6). Then it is the family member's turn. They roll the dice and put their array on the bottom-right corner of their space closest to them. Arrays must touch a side of another array. As players continue to roll and cover spaces, they will want to fill in the grid paper by attaching the arrays as closely as possible— as the first player who is forced to cross into the other player's territory (that is, they don't have a place for their array on their half of the gameboard) loses (Figure 9.3). A lot of multiplication will occur! If you want to change the game, use dice that go from 4 to 9 or use only one die that goes to higher numbers with a regular die. Have students bring the completed gameboard(s) back to class.

FIGURE 9.3: Partially Completed Area Game

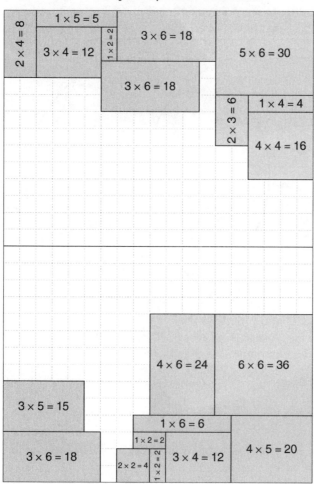

Source: Created by Bob Ronau.

 Family Venn Diagram

Here, provide a handout with a two-circle Venn diagram. The child and a family member put their names above one of the circles. The idea is to find either math interests or strengths and write them inside the circle such as "I love math" or "I know all the multiplication facts for 10." Of course, there are things each person does well, but also what do they have in common? Put those in the overlap (Figure 9.4). If you collect these, the data can inform the creation of engaging word problems that includes information about families and even strengths that classmates share.

FIGURE 9.4: Students' Venn Diagrams With Family Members

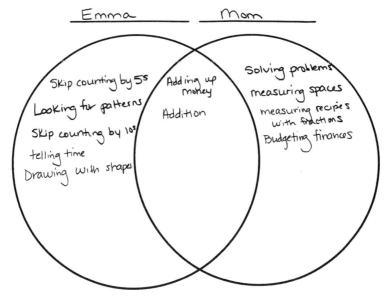

online resources 🔖 This Venn Diagram page can be downloaded for use at resources.corwin.com/teachingturnarounds.

Family Math Resources

Families often ask for resources to use with their children. In addition to the letter or checklists mentioned earlier, you can send home this handout of other resources or distribute it at Family Math Night, Back-to-School Night, or How-We-Are-Teaching-Your-Child-Math Night.

Try It!   Family Math Letter

Hello Families,

One of the important goals of this year is to have families get involved in the math your child is learning in school. I will be sending home great activities to try and fun homework, but I know some of you may want to think about books for your own reading, books that will engage your children, and websites with ideas for things to try. There are also math games to play that might make a good gift. Try out some of these resources for ideas about how to support your child to learn mathematics with a positive attitude.

Books for Adults

AUTHOR	TITLE	TOPIC
Boaler	*What's Math Got to Do With It?*	Ideas for teachers and families to improve children's learning of mathematics
Kellison & Fosnot	*Parent's Guide to Understanding Math Education in Today's Schools*	What families can do at home to help students in mathematics
Kenshaft	*Math Power: How to Help Your Child Love Math, Even If You Don't*	Strategies for teaching math concepts that families can try
Kreisberg & Beyranevand	*Adding Parents Into the Equation: Understanding Your Child's Elementary School Math*	Support for families who want to understand the approaches children are using in math class
Overdeck	*Bedtime Math* (there is also a matching app)	Stories and problems to share with children at bedtime
Zahler	*50 Simple Things You Can Do to Raise a Child Who Loves Math*	Activities for families to do with children to develop an interest in math

Children's Literature

AUTHOR	TITLE	STRENGTH/MATH CONCEPT
Alber	*Snippets: A Story About Paper Shapes*	Geometry/uniqueness
Beaty	*Ada Twist, Scientist*	Perseverance/creativity
Beaty	*Iggy Peck, Architect*	Perseverance/creativity
Beaty	*Rosie Revere, Engineer*	Perseverance/creativity
Becker	*Counting on Katherine: How Katherine Johnson Saved Apollo 13*	Computation/ perseverance
Bunting	*Yard Sale*	Money/computation
Burr	*1% Clean*	Fractions/percents
Clement	*Counting on Frank*	Estimation/volume
Coates	*Nigel's Numberless World*	Importance of numbers
Cuyler	*Guinea Pigs Add Up*	Addition/subtraction
Danielson	*How Many?*	Counting
Danielson	*Which One Doesn't Belong? A Shapes Book*	Classifying/2D shapes
Dean	*Pete the Cat and His Four Groovy Buttons*	Counting/subtraction
DiSalvo-Ryan	*City Green*	Area/Collaboration
Esham	*Last to Finish: A Story About the Smartest Boy in Math Class*	Perseverance/learning using different strategies
Finley Mosca	*The Girl With a Mind for Math: The Story of Ray Montague*	Perseverance
Finley Mosca	*The Girl Who Thought in Pictures: The Story of Dr. Temple Grandin*	Perseverance/creativity
Fisher	*How High Can a Dinosaur Count and Other Math Mysteries*	Problem solving/ subtraction
Gehl	*One Big Pair of Underwear*	Counting/subtraction
Hong	*Two of Everything*	Doubles/multiplication
Isaacs	*Swamp Angel*	Averages/measurement
Jacobsen	*Mighty Mommies and Their Amazing Jobs*	STEM careers/role models

Jenkins	*Lemonade in Winter: A Book About Two Kids Counting Money*	Computation/money/ perseverance
Khan	*Crescent Moons and Pointed Minarets: A Muslim Book of Shapes*	Geometry
Lamer	*Kid Chef Junior Cookbook: Children Enjoy Cooking With Their Parents*	Measurement
Lasky	*Librarian Who Measured the Earth*	Geometry/measurement
Leedy	*Measuring Penny*	Measurement
McKellar	*Ten Magic Butterflies*	Counting/place value
Nagara	*Counting on Community*	Counting/value of community
Otoshi	*Zero*	Numbers/self-esteem
Oxley	*Peg + Cat: The Racecar Problem*	Geometry/measurement
Pinces	*Remainder of One*	Division
Rosen Schwartz	*Twinderella: A Fractioned Fairy-Tale*	Fractions/division
Scieszka	*Math Curse*	Problem solving/ importance of mathematics
Shannon	*One Family*	Counting/units
Swiatkowska	*Infinity and Me*	Large numbers
Winter	*The World Is Not a Rectangle: A Portrait of Architect Zaha Hadid*	Shapes/patterns

Websites

WEBSITE	URL	TOPIC
A Maths Dictionary for Kids	http:// mathsdictionaryforkids .com	Definitions and mathematics support
A Mighty Girl	https://www.amightygirl .com/	Women mathematicians, STEM books, blog
Calculation Nation	https://calculationnation .nctm.org/	Mathematics games to be played alone or with other kids across the country

WEBSITE	URL	TOPIC
Cyberchase	https://pbskids.org/cyberchase/	Games and activities on math topics, info for families
Education.com	www.education.com/games/math	Choices of online games by grade level and mathematics topic
Family Math Night	http://familymathnight.com/resources/	Ideas for family–school engagement
Figure This!	www.figurethis.org	Math challenges for families
Guided Dynamic Knowledge	https://gdkmath.com/	Videos to support sense making in mathematics
HCPSS Family Mathematics Support Center	http://hcpssfamilymath.weebly.com/	Howard County MD school's support for different grade levels
Math and Mind	https://mathandmind.com/	Recreational math activities
Math and Parent Partners Program (MAPPS)	http://mapps.math.arizona.edu/	Helps family members learn the new mathematics strategies used in schools
Math Before Bed	https://mathbeforebed.com/	Prompts that lead to discussions about mathematics topics
NCTM Illuminations	https://illuminations.nctm.org/	Games and brain teasers
PBS Parents—Early Math	www.pbs.org/parents/earlymath/about.html	How to explore mathematics with young children

Games

GAME	DESCRIPTION
Blokus	A strategy game for players who have good spatial sense or want to develop it. Pieces made from connected squares are fit tightly onto the board by players in turn. The game ends when no more pieces fit. The player with the fewest pieces left wins.
Mancala	This game originated in Africa and involves strategy and counting. Players take turns dropping pieces in the cup like spaces. By thinking ahead, you can take the pieces of your partner. Player who has the most pieces at the end wins.
Prime Climb	Focusing on the four whole-number operations, students work to the center of the board and sometimes they send other players back to start.

Qwirkle	This is a great game for young players to adults where you try to strategically place tiles down by grouping colors or shapes. Scores are tallied by the number of tiles involved with each play. Logic and decision making are critical skills.
Set	An award-winning card game that involves the whole family in using their visual perception to find a "set" of three cards. It involves matching, classifying, logical thinking, and reasoning.
Shut the Box	There are several versions of this classic game for one two or four players. A player rolls a pair of dice and then must knock down wooden pieces that add up to (or are) the sum. It involves counting, number recognition, and strategy use.
Zoo Logic	At first there seem like a lot of rules, but they are slowly shown in a set of 60 increasingly difficult puzzles. For example, a dog can't be next to a cat and a cat can't be next to a mouse and so on. Placing the tiles involves strategic thinking and of course logical deduction. Children as young as five can enjoy these brain busters!

 This Family Math Resource list can be downloaded for use in Spanish and English at resources.corwin.com/teachingturnarounds.

Conferences With Family Members From a Strengths-Based Perspective

Conferences are key times to build positive relationships with families. As children are ready and as schools allow, include them in on the conference (as in the following suggestion). The child can take part in sharing their work samples and providing evidence of their strengths. Keep in mind that in the same way some people are tense entering a hospital due to memories of past experiences that may not be positive, family members may similarly feel that tension and anxiety about schools. Changing those recollections to a welcoming and safe environment where their child can be celebrated and where plans for growth can be made is a critical and necessary shift.

1. Arrange in advance for an interpreter if there is a language difference. Send any materials in advance to look over before the conference.

2. Start the conference with a look at the child's strengths in mathematics, both in cognitive and noncognitive aspects.

3. Talk about how their child's strengths are important for improving performance in specific areas with next instructional steps.

4. Explain how the focus in mathematics instruction is on the child "doing" mathematics and sometimes their student will be bringing that work home to engage the family.

5. Enlist families' support by sharing something you'd like them to try at home and show them specifically what you want them to do (like a Number Talk). Tell them you will sharing a Number Talk or other activity for them to try each week on the class website.

6. Offer a Monday Morning Math session where family members/guardians and children can come in and either move through stations or you can answer questions on work from the week.

7. Hold a student-led conference.

Summary

Imagine sitting on a three-legged stool. Now, imagine that one of the legs is shorter or broken in some way. Each leg needs to be equal in strength. The three-legged stool is a perfect metaphor for what you are aiming to have happen in conferences and through letters and communications home. There is no real support without the teacher, child, and family working together on learning mathematics.

Epilogue

Turn Around Reflection

In these pages, we hoped to convince you to boldly test the strengths-based model to see and feel the marvelous impact of this effort on your students, their families, your colleagues, and yourself. We aren't going to soft-sell this approach, as changing the way we teach mathematics from what might be a deficit approach to an asset approach takes dedication and daily diligence. In this way, we recognize and value the gifts and talents that our students, families, and colleagues carry with them every day into our learning community. Your effort will support your students and those around you, creating an energetic strengths-based force field. As we close this book, we again return to the message by Sufi poet Shams-ud-din Muhammad Hafiz:

The words you speak become the house you live in.

We humbly offer,

The words you speak become the classroom your students learn in.

And ask,

What kind of classroom do you want to teach in?

References

Aguirre, J., Mayfield-Ingram, K., & Martin, D. (2013). *The impact of identity in K–8 mathematics: Rethinking equity-based practices*. Reston, VA: The National Council of Teachers of Mathematics.

Alvidrez, J., & Weinstein, R. S. (1999). Early teacher perceptions and later student academic achievement. *Journal of Educational Psychology, 91*(4), 731–746.

Anderson, E. C. (2000, February). *Affirming students' strengths in the critical years*. Paper presented at the National Conference on the First Year Experience, Columbia, SC.

Andrews, D., & Kobett, B. M. (2017, July). *Connection to discourse: Word problems*. Presentation at the NCTM Discourse Institute, Baltimore, MD.

Annenberg Learner. (2018). Teaching math: Session 5, representation. Retrieved from https://www.learner.org/courses/teachingmath/grades3_5/session_05/index.html

Antolin, D., Lipovec, D., & Lipovec, A. (2017). Mathematical experiences and parental involvement of parents who are and who are not mathematicians. *Irish Educational Studies, 36*(3), 357–374.

Arcavi, A. (2003). The role of visual representations in the learning of mathematics. *Educational Studies in Mathematics, 52*(3), 215–241.

Arcavi, A., & Isoda, M. (2007). Learning to listen: From historical sources to classroom practice. *Educational Studies in Mathematics, 66*(2), 111–129.

Ascher, C. (1992). *Successful detracking in middle and senior high schools* (ERIC/CUE Digest No. 82). New York, NY: ERIC Clearinghouse on Urban Education.

Aspen Institute. (2019). *From a nation at risk to a nation at hope*. Washington, DC: National Commission on Social, Emotional & Academic Development.

Assouline, S. G., & Lupkowski-Shoplik, A. (2011). *Developing math talent: A comprehensive guide to math education for gifted students in elementary and middle school* (2nd ed.). Waco, TX: Prufrock Press.

Bandura, A. (1977). Self-efficacy: Toward a unifying theory of behavioral change. *Psychological Review, 84*(2), 191–215.

Bargh, J. A., Gollwitzer, P. M., Lee-Chai, A., Barndollar, K., & Trötschel, R. (2001). The automated will: nonconscious activation and pursuit of behavioral goals. *Journal of Personality and Social Psychology, 81*(6), 1014–1027.

Barnes, D. (2008). Exploratory talk for learning. In N. Mercer & S. Hodgkinson (Eds.), *Exploring talk in school* (pp. 1–15). London, UK: Sage.

Becker, H. (2018). *Counting on Katherine: How Katherine Johnson saved Apollo 13.* New York, NY: Holt.

Bernacki, M., & Walkington, C. (2014, July). *The impact of a personalization intervention for mathematics on learning and non-cognitive factors.* Paper presented at the 7th International Conference on Educational Data Mining, London, UK.

Bernacki, M. L., & Walkington, C. (2018). The role of situational interest in personalized learning. *Journal of Educational Psychology, 110*(6), 864–881.

Bernard, B. (1997). *Turning it around for all youth: From risk to resilience* (ERIC/CUE Digest No. 16). New York, NY: ERIC Clearinghouse on Urban Education. ERIC Document Reproduction Service No. ED4123091.

Berry, R. Q., III. (2008). Access to upper-level mathematics: The stories of successful African American middle school boys. *Journal for Research in Mathematics Education, 39*(5), 464–488.

Birch, S. H., & Ladd, G. W. (1997). The teacher-child relationship and children's early school adjustment. *Journal of School Psychology, 35*(1), 61–79.

Black, P., & Wiliam, D. (1998). Assessment and classroom learning. *Assessment in Education: Principles, Policy & Practice, 5*(1), 7–74.

Boaler, J. (1997). Setting, social class and survival of the quickest. *British Educational Research Journal, 23*(5), 575–595.

Boaler, J. (2007, July). *Promoting relational equity in mathematics classrooms—Important teaching practices and their impact on student learning.* Text of a "regular lecture" given at the 10th International Congress of Mathematics Education (ICME X), Copenhagen, Denmark.

Boaler, J. (2013). Ability and mathematics: The mindset revolution that is reshaping education. *Forum, 55,* 143–152.

Boaler, J. (2015). *What's math got to do with it? How teachers and parents can transform mathematics learning and inspire success.* New York, NY: Penguin.

Boaler, J., & Staples, M. (2008). Creating mathematical futures through an equitable teaching approach: The case of Railside school. *Teacher College Record, 110*(3), 608–645.

Brooks, C. F., & Young, S. L. (2011). Are choice-making opportunities needed in the classroom? Using self-determination theory to consider student motivation and learner empowerment. *International Journal of Teaching and Learning in Higher Education, 23*(1), 48–59.

Brooks, D. (January 18, 2019). Learning and love. *New York Times,* p. 8.

Bull, R., & Lee, K. (2014). Executive functioning and mathematics achievement. *Child Development Perspectives, 8*(1), 36–41.

Burris, C., & Welner, K. (2005). Closing the achievement gap by detracking. *Phi Delta Kappan, 86*(8), 594–598.

Burris, C. C., Heubert, J. P., & Levin, H. M. (2006). Accelerating mathematics achievement using heterogeneous grouping. *American Educational Research Journal, 43*(1), 137–154.

Calabrese, R., Hummel, C., & San Martin, T. (2007). Learning to appreciate at-risk students: Challenging the beliefs and attitudes of teachers and administrators. *International Journal of Educational Management, 21*(4), 275–291.

Caldwell, J. H., Kobett, B., & Karp, K. (2014). *Putting essential understanding of addition and subtraction into practice: Pre-K–2.* Reston, VA: National Council of Teachers of Mathematics.

Caviola, S., Carey, E., Mammarella, I. C., & Szucs, D. (2017). Stress, time pressure, strategy selection and math anxiety in mathematics: A review of the literature. *Frontiers in Psychology, 8,* 1488. doi:10.3389/fpsyg.2017.01488

Clements, D. H., & Sarama, J. (2004). Learning trajectories in mathematics education. *Mathematical Thinking and Learning, 6*(2), 81–89.

Clifton, D. O., & Harter, J. K. (2003). Investing in strengths. In K. S. Cameron, J. E. Dutton, & R. E. Quinn (Eds.), *Positive organizational scholarship: Foundations of a new discipline* (pp. 111–121). San Francisco, CA: Berrett-Koehler.

Cooperrider, D. L., & Whitney, D. (2005). Appreciative inquiry: A positive revolution in change. In P. Holman & T. Devane (Eds.), *The change handbook* (pp. 245–263). Oakland, CA: Berrett-Koehler.

Cuyler, M. (2010). *Guinea pigs add up.* New York, NY: Walker and Company.

Daniels, D. H., Kalkman, D. L., & McCombs, B. L. (2001). Young children's perspectives on learning and teacher practices in different classroom contexts: Implications for motivation. *Early Education and Development, 12*(2), 253–273.

Daniels, D. H., & Perry, K. E. (2003). "Learner-centered" according to children. *Theory Into Practice, 42*(2), 102–108.

Daniels, H. (2016). *Vygotsky and pedagogy.* London, UK: Routledge.

Danielson, C. (2016). *Which one doesn't belong?* Portsmouth, NH: Stenhouse.

Dean, J. (2012). *Pete the cat and his four groovy buttons.* New York, NY: HarperCollins.

Dean, J. (2016). *Pete the cat and the missing cupcakes.* New York, NY: HarperCollins.

Decker, D. M., Dona, D. P., & Christenson, S. L. (2007). Behaviorally at-risk African American students: The importance of student–teacher relationships for student outcomes. *Journal of School Psychology, 45*(1), 83–109.

Doman, F. (2018). *True you: Authentic strengths for kids*. Austin, TX: Next Century Publishing.

Donohoo, J. (2017). *Collective efficacy: How educators' beliefs impact student learning*. Thousand Oaks, CA: Corwin.

Dougherty, B. (2018, April). *MTSS: Effective interventions and assessments*. Institute given at the NCTM Annual Conference, Washington, DC.

Doyle, W. (1988). Work in mathematics classes: The context of students' thinking during instruction. *Educational Psychologist, 23*(2), 167–180.

Drucker, P. F. (2005). Managing oneself. *Harvard Business Review, 83*(1), 100–109.

Eells, R. (2011). *Meta-analysis of the relationship between collective teacher efficacy and student achievement*. Dissertations, 133. Retrieved from https://ecommons.luc.edu/luc_diss/133

Entwisle, D. R., Karl, L. A., & Olson, L. S. (1997). *Children, schools and inequality*. Boulder, CO: Westview.

Falwell, C. (2003). *Feast for 10*. New York, NY: Houghton Mifflin Harcourt.

Fennell, F. (2006). *President's message: Representation—Show me the math* (NCTM News Bulletin). Reston, VA: National Council of Teachers of Mathematics.

Fennell, F., Kobett, B. M., & Wray, J. A. (2017). *The formative 5: Everyday assessment techniques for every math classroom*. Thousand Oaks, CA: Corwin.

Fennell, F., Kobett, B. M., & Wray, J. A. (2018, November). *Formative assessment: Using hinge questions, providing feedback, and informing instruction*. Presentation for the National Council of Teachers of Mathematics Regional Conference, Kansas City, MO.

Finley-Mosca, J. (2018) *The girl with a mind for math: The story of Raye Montague*. Seattle, WA: The Innovation Press.

Flores, A. (2007). Examining disparities in mathematics education: Achievement gap or opportunity gap? *The High School Journal, 91*(1),29–42.

Flowerday, T., & Schraw, G. (2000). Teacher beliefs about instructional choice: A phenomenological study. *Journal of Educational Psychology, 92*(4), 634–645.

Freire, P. (1972). *Pedagogy of the oppressed*. Harmondsworth, UK: Penguin.

Friend, C. (1995). *My head is full of colors*. New York, NY: Hyperion Books for Children.

Goddard, R. D., Hoy, W. K., & Woolfolk Hoy, A. (2004). Collective efficacy beliefs: Theoretical developments, empirical evidence, and future directions. *Educational Researcher, 33*(3), 3–13.

González, N., Moll, L., & Amanti, C. (Eds.). (2005). *Funds of knowledge: Theorizing practices in households, communities and classrooms*. Mahwah, NJ: Erlbaum.

Green, E. (2014, July 23). Why do Americans stink at math? *New York Times*, p. 23.

Gutiérrez, R. (2017). Living mathematx: Towards a vision for the future. *Philosophy of Mathematics Education Journal, 32.*

Hammond, S. (1998). *The thin book of appreciative inquiry.* Plano, TX: Thin Book Publishing.

Hattie, J. (2009). The black box of tertiary assessment: An impending revolution. In L. H. Meyer, S. Davidson, H. Anderson, R. Fletcher, P. M. Johnston, & M. Rees (Eds.), *Tertiary assessment and higher education student outcomes: Policy, practice and research* (pp. 259–275). Wellington, New Zealand: Ako Aotearoa.

Hattie, J. (2012). *Visible learning for teachers: Maximizing impact on learning.* New York, NY: Routledge.

Hattie, J., Fisher, D., Frey, N., Gojak, L. M., Moore, S. D., & Mellman, W. (2016). *Visible learning for mathematics, grades K–12: What works best to optimize student learning.* Thousand Oaks, CA: Corwin.

Hattie, J., & Timperley, H. (2007). The power of feedback. *Review of Educational Research, 77*(1), 81–112.

Heinze, A., Star, J. R., & Verschaffel, L. (2009). Flexible and adaptive use of strategies and representations in mathematics education. *ZDM The International Journal of Mathematics Education, 41*, 535–540.

Herbel-Eisenmann, B. A., & Breyfogle, M. L. (2005). Questioning our patterns of questioning. *Teaching Mathematics in the Middle School, 10*(9), 484–489.

Heubert, J. P., & Hauser, R. M. (Eds.). (1999). *High stakes: Testing for tracking, promotion and graduation.* Washington, DC: National Academies Press.

Hiebert, J. (1997). *Making sense: Teaching and learning mathematics with understanding.* Portsmouth, NH: Heinemann.

Jansen, A. (2020). *Rough draft talk.* Portland, ME: Stenhouse.

Jansen, A., Cooper, B., Vascellaro, S., & Wandless, P. (2016). Rough-draft talk in mathematics classrooms. *Mathematics Teaching in the Middle School, 22*(5), 304–307.

Jay, T., Rose, J., & Simmons., B. (2017). Finding "mathematics": Parents questioning school-centered approaches to involvement in children's mathematics learning. *School Community Journal, 27*(1), 201–230.

Jensen, E. (2005). *Teaching with the brain in mind.* Alexandria, VA: ASCD.

Jilk, L. (2016). Supporting teacher noticing of students. *Mathematics Teacher Educator, 4*(2), 188–199.

Johnsen, S. K., & Sheffield, L. J. (Eds.). (2013). *Using the common core state standards for mathematics with gifted and advanced learners.* Reston, VA: NCTM.

Karp, K., Bush, S., & Dougherty, B. (2016). Establishing a mathematics whole school agreement. *Teaching Children Mathematics, 23*, 69–71.

Karp, K. S., Bush, S. B., & Dougherty, B. (2014). 13 Rules that expire. *Teaching Children Mathematics, 21*(1), 18–25.

Karp, K. S., Bush, S. B., & Dougherty, B. J. (2015). 12 Math rules that expire in middle grades. *Teaching Children Mathematics, 21*(4), 208–215.

Karp, K. S., Bush, S. B., & Dougherty, B. J. (2019). Avoiding the ineffective key-word strategy. *Teaching Children Mathematics, 25*(7), 428–435.

Keller, S. (2016). *Ticktock Banneker's clock.* Chelsea, MI: Sleeping Pear Press.

Kellison, C., & Fosnot, C. T. (2012). *A parent's guide to understanding math education in today's schools.* Scotts Valley, CA: CreateSpace Independent Publishing Platform.

Kelly, S. (2009). The Black-White gap in mathematics course taking. *Sociology of Education, 82,* 47–69.

Klehm, M. (2014). The effects of teacher beliefs on teaching practices and achievement of students with disabilities. *Teacher Education and Special Education, 37*(3), 216–240.

Klem, A. M., & Connell, J. P. (2004). Relationships matter: Linking teacher support to student engagement and achievement. *Journal of School Health, 74*(7), 262–273.

Knapp, A., Landers, R., Liang, S., & Jefferson, V. (2017). We all as a family are graduating tonight: A case for mathematical knowledge for parental involvement. *Educational Studies in Mathematics, 95*(1), 79–95.

Kobett, B. (2016, July). *Strengths-based instructional design for students who struggle.* Presentation for the Maryland Council of Teachers of Mathematics, Baltimore, MD.

Kobett, B., & Karp, K. (2018). Using formative assessment to guide the effective implementation of response to intervention (RtI). In E. Silver & V. Mills (Eds.), *A fresh look at formative assessment in mathematics teaching* (pp. 127–144). Reston, VA: NCTM.

Kral, R. (1995). *Strategies that work: Techniques for solution in the schools.* Milwaukee: Brief Family Therapy Center, Wisconsin Institute on Family Studies.

Kramer, K. (1966). *The teaching of elementary school mathematics.* Boston, MA: Allyn & Bacon.

Kreisberg, H., & Beyranevand, M. (2019). *Adding parents into the equation: Understanding your child's elementary school math.* Lanham, MD: Rowman & Littlefield.

Ladinsky, D. (Trans.). (1999). *The gift: Poems by Hafiz, the great Sufi master.* New York, NY: Penguin.

Lange, T., & Meaney, T. (2011). I actually started to scream: Emotional and mathematical trauma from doing school mathematics homework. *Educational Studies in Mathematics, 77*(1), 35–51.

Levy, S., & Schiller, M. (2018). *Stan and the four fantastic powers.* Chagrin Falls, OH: Taos Institute.

Maloney, E. A., Ramirez, G., Gunderson, E. A., Levine, S. C., & Beilock, S. L. (2015). Intergenerational effects of parents' math anxiety on children's math achievement and anxiety. *Psychological Science, 26*(9), 1480–1488.

McKenzie, K. B., & Scheurich, J. J. (2004). Equity traps: A useful construct for preparing principals to lead schools that are successful with racially diverse students. *Educational Administration Quarterly, 40*(5), 601–632.

McLeod, S. (1995). Pygmalion or Golem? Teacher affect and efficacy. *College Composition and Communication, 46*(3), 369–386.

Measures of Effective Teaching Project. (2010). *Learning about teaching: Initial findings from the Measures of Effective Teaching project.* Seattle, WA: Bill and Melinda Gates Foundation.

Moll, L. C., Amanti, C., Neff, D., & Gonzalez, N. (1992). Funds of knowledge for teaching: Using a qualitative approach to connect homes and classrooms. *Theory Into Practice, 31*(2), 132–141.

Moll, L. C., Vélez-Ibañez, C. G., & Greenberg, J. (1990). *Community knowledge and classroom practice combining resources for literacy instruction: A technical report from the Innovative Approaches Research Project.* Washington, DC: US Department of Education, Office of Educational Research and Improvement, Educational Resources Information Center.

Mosca, J. F. (2018). *The girl with a mind for math: The story of Raye Montague.* Seattle, WA: Innovation Press.

National Council of Teachers of Mathematics. (1991). *Professional standards for teaching mathematics.* Reston, VA: Author.

National Council of Teachers of Mathematics. (2000). *Principles and standards for school mathematics.* Reston, VA: Author.

National Council of Teachers of Mathematics. (2014). *Principles to actions: Ensuring mathematical success for all.* Reston, VA: Author.

National Council of Teachers of Mathematics. (2018). *Catalyzing change in high school mathematics: Initiating critical conversations.* Reston, VA: Author.

National Governors Association Center for Best Practices & Council of Chief State School Officers. (2010). *Common core state standards for mathematics.* Retrieved from http://www.corestandards.org/Math

National Research Council & Mathematics Learning Study Committee. (2001). *Adding it up: Helping children learn mathematics.* Washington, DC: National Academies Press.

Oakes, J., & Lipton, M. (1999). *Teaching to change the world.* Boston, MA: McGraw-Hill.

Overdeck, L. (2013). *BEDTIME MATH, a fun excuse to stay up late.* New York, NY: Feiwel & Friends.

Owens, M. T., & Tanner, K. D. (2017). Teaching as brain changing: Exploring connections between neuroscience and innovative teaching. *CBE Life Sciences Education, 16*(2), fe2. doi:10.1187/cbe.17–01–0005

Parrish, S. (2014). *Number talks: Helping children build mental math and computation strategies, grades K–5.* Sausalito, CA: Math Solutions.

Plucker, J. A., & Peters, S. J. (2016). *Excellence gaps in education: Expanding opportunities for talented students.* Cambridge, MA: Harvard Education Press.

Rath, T. (2009). *How full is your bucket?* Washington, DC: Gallup Press.

Remillard, J. T., & Jackson, K. (2006). Old math, new math: Parents' experiences with Standards-based reform. *Mathematical Thinking and Learning, 8*(3), 231–259.

Renzulli, J. S., Gubbins, E. J., McMillen, K. S., Eckert, R. D., & Little, C. A. (Eds.). (2009). *Systems & models for developing programs for the gifted & talented* (2nd ed.). Mansfield Center, CT: Creative Learning Press.

Renzulli, J. S., & Reis, A. (2014). *The schoolwide enrichment model: A how to guide for talent development* (3rd ed.). Mansfield Center, CT: Creative Learning Press.

Resnick, L. B. (1987). *Education and learning to think.* Washington DC: National Academies Press.

Reys, B. J. (1991). *Developing number sense: Curriculum and evaluation standards for school mathematics Addenda series, grades 5–8.* Reston, VA: National Council of Teachers of Mathematics.

Riener, C., & Willingham, D. (2010). The myth of learning styles. *Change: The Magazine of Higher Learning, 42*(5), 32–35.

Ritchhart, R., Church, M., & Morrison, K. (2011). *Making thinking visible: How to promote engagement, understanding, and independence for all learners.* San Francisco, CA: Jossey-Bass.

Ritchhart, R., Turner, T., & Hadar, L. (2009). Uncovering students' thinking about thinking using concept maps. *Metacognition and Learning, 4*(2), 145–159.

Rodriguez, G. (2013). Power and agency in education: Exploring the pedagogical dimensions of funds of knowledge. *Review of Research in Education, 37*(1), 87–120.

Rosenthal, R., & Jacobsen, L. (1968). *Pygmalion in the classroom: Teacher expectation and pupils' intellectual development.* New York, NY: Holt, Rinehart and Winston.

Rösken, B., & Rolka, K. (2006). A picture is worth a 1000 words: The role of visualization in mathematics learning. In J. Novotná, H. Moraová, M. Krátká, & N. Stehlíková (Eds.), *Proceedings of the 30th Conference of the International Group for the Psychology of Mathematics Education* (Vol. 3, pp. 233–240). Prague, Czech Republic: PME.

Rowe, M. B. (1974). Wait time and rewards as instructional variables, their influence on language, logic, and fate control—Part One: Wait time. *Journal of Research on Science Teaching, 11,* 81–94.

Rowe, M. B. (1986). Wait time: Slowing down may be a way of speeding up. *Journal of Teacher Education, 37*(1). https://journals.sagepub.com/doi/pdf/10.1177/002248718603700110

Schoenfeld, A. (1995). Is thinking about algebra a misdirection? In C. Lacampagne, W. Blair, & J. Kaput (Eds.), *The Algebra Colloquium: Vol. 2. Working group papers* (pp. 83–86). Washington, DC: U.S. Department of Education.

Schonert-Reichl, K. A. (2000). *Children and youth at risk: Some conceptual considerations.* Refereed paper prepared for the Pan-Canadian Education Research Agenda Symposium, Ottawa, Ontario. Sponsored by the Canadian Education Statistics Council with the assistance of Human Resources Development Canada.

Schulz, C. (1963). Sally's problem. *Peanuts* [Cartoon].

Seeley, C. L. (2009). *Faster isn't smarter: Messages about math, teaching, and learning in the 21st century: A resource for teachers, leaders, policy makers, and families.* Sausalito, CA: Math Solutions.

Shetterly, M. L. (2018). *Hidden figures: The true story of four Black women and the space race.* New York, NY: HarperCollins.

Siegler, R. S., & Lemaire, P. (1997). Older and younger adults' strategy choices in multiplication: Testing predictions of ASCM using the choice/no-choice method. *Journal of Experimental Psychology: General, 126,* 71–92.

Simmons, A. M., & Page, M. (2010). Motivating students through power and choice. *English Journal, 100*(1), 65–69.

Small, M. (2009). *Good questions: Great ways to differentiate mathematics instruction.* New York, NY: Teachers College Press.

Smith, M. S., & Stein, M. K. (1998). Selecting and creating mathematical tasks: From research to practice. *Mathematics Teaching in the Middle School, 3*(5), 344–350.

Smith, N. (2017). *Every math learner, grades 6–12: A doable approach to teaching with learning differences in mind.* Thousand Oaks, CA: Corwin.

Soni, A., & Kumari, S. (2015). The role of parental math attitude in their children math achievement. *International Journal of Applied Sociology, 5*(4), 159–163.

Southwest Educational Development Laboratory. (2005). *Evolution of the concept "at-risk"* [PDF]. Washington, DC: Author.

Sparks, S. (2018, June). Getting feedback right: A Q & A with John Hattie. *Education Week.*

Stahl, R. J. (1994). *Using "Think-Time" and "Wait-Time" skillfully in the classroom.* Bloomington, IN: ERIC Clearinghouse for Social Studies and Social Science Education.

Stamper, J., Pardos, Z., Mavrikis, M., & McLaren, B. M. (2014). *Proceedings of the Seventh International Conference on Educational Data Mining (EDM).* London, UK: International Educational Data Mining Society.

Stein, M. K., Grover, B. W., & Henningsen, M. (1996). Building student capacity for mathematical thinking and reasoning: An analysis of mathematical tasks used in reform classrooms. *American Educational Research Journal, 33*(2), 455–488.

Stein, M. K., & Lane, S. (1996). Instructional tasks and the development of student capacity to think and reason: An analysis of the relationship between teaching and learning in a reform mathematics project. *Educational Research and Evaluation, 2*(1), 50–80.

Stein, M. K., Lane, S., & Silver, E. A. (1996, April). *Classrooms in which students successfully acquire mathematical proficiency: What are the critical features of teachers' instructional practice.* Paper presented at the annual meeting of the American Educational Research Association, New York, NY.

Stein, M. K., & Smith, M. S. (1998). Mathematical tasks as a framework for reflection: From research to practice. *Mathematics Teaching in the Middle School, 3*(4), 268–275.

Stein, M. K., Smith, M. S., Henningsen, M. A., & Silver, E. A. (2009). *Implementing standards-based mathematics instruction: A casebook for professional development* (2nd ed.). New York, NY: Teachers College Press.

Stratton-Berkessel, R. (2010). *Appreciative inquiry for collaborative solutions: 21 strength-based workshops.* New York, NY: John Wiley & Sons.

Strayton, M. V., & Lawton, L. W. (2019). Acorns to oaks: Nurturing growth through strengths-based practices. *Teaching Children Mathematics, 25*(6), 355–360.

Style, E. (1988). Curriculum as window and mirror. In M. S. Crocco (Ed.), *Listening for all voices: Gender balancing the school curriculum* (pp. 6–12). Summit, NJ: Oak Knoll School.

Teaching Tolerance. (2019). Family engagement. Retrieved from https://www.tolerance.org/professional-development/family-engagement

Van de Walle, J., Karp, K., & Bay-Williams, J. (2019). *Elementary and middle school mathematics: Teaching developmentally.* New York, NY: Pearson.

van Hiele, P. M. (1984). The child's thought and geometry. In D. Fuys, D. Geddes, & R. Welchman Tischler (Eds.), *English translation of selected writings of Dina van Hiele-Geldof and Pierre M. van Hiele* (pp. 243–252). Brooklyn, NY: City University of New York.

Walkington, C. (2013). Using learning technologies to personalize instruction to student interests: The impact of relevant contexts on performance and learning outcomes. *Journal of Educational Psychology, 105*(4), 932–945.

Walkington, C., Clinton, V., & Shivraj, P. (2018). How readability factors are differentially associated with performance for students of different backgrounds when solving mathematics word problems. *American Educational Research Journal, 55*(2), 362–414.

Weaver, J. F. (1970). Differentiated instruction in arithmetic: An overview and a promising trend. In K. Kramer (Ed.), *Problems in the teaching of elementary school mathematics* (pp. 334–335). Boston, MA: Allyn & Bacon. (Original work published 1954)

Welner, K. G. (2001). *When community control collides with educational equity*. Albany, NY: SUNY Press.

White, T. W. (1996). Working in interesting times. *Vital Speeches of the Day, 62*(15), 472–474.

Wiliam, D. (2011). *Embedded formative assessment*. Bloomington, IN: Solution Tree Press.

Wiliam, D., Lee, C., Harrison, C., & Black, P. (2004). Teachers developing assessment for learning: Impact on student achievement. *Assessment in Education: Principles, Policy & Practice, 11*(1), 49–65.

Williams, L., Kobett, B., & Harbin Miles, R. (2018). *The lesson planning handbook, grades 6–8: Your blueprint for building cohesive lessons*. Thousand Oaks, CA: Corwin.

Wood, T. (1998). Alternative patterns of communication in mathematics classes: Funneling or Focusing? In H. Steinbring, M. G. Bartolini Bussi, & A. Sierpinska (Eds.), *Language and communication in the mathematics classroom* (pp. 167–178). Reston, VA: National Council of Teachers of Mathematics.

Wyner, J. S., Bridgeland, J. M., & DiIulio, J. J., Jr. (2007). *Achievement trap: How America is failing millions of high-achieving students from lower-income families*. Lansdowne, VA: Jack Kent Cooke Foundation.

Yagi, S., & Venenciano, L. (2017). Math "Rules" prompt reflection on teachers' identity. *Mathematics Teaching in the Middle School, 22*(9), 555–557.

Index

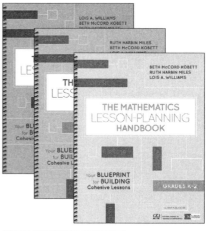

ALL students should have the opportunity to be successful in mathematics!

Trusted experts in mathematics education offer clear and practical guidance to help students move from surface to deep mathematical understanding, from procedural to conceptual learning, and from rote memorization to true comprehension. Through books, videos, consulting, and online tools, we offer a truly blended learning experience that helps you demystify mathematics for students.

JOHN HATTIE, DOUGLAS FISHER, NANCY FREY, LINDA M. GOJAK, SARA DELANO MOORE, WILLIAM MELLMAN

The what, when, and how of teaching practices that evidence shows work best for student learning in mathematics.

Grades K–12

JOHN ALMARODE, DOUGLAS FISHER, JOSEPH ASSOF, SARA DELANO MOORE, KATERI THUNDER, JOHN HATTIE, NANCY FREY

In this sequel to the best-selling *Visible Learning for Mathematics*, these grade-banded companions show Visible Learning strategies in action in Grades K–2, 3–5, 6–8, and high school mathematics classrooms.

Grades K–2, 3–5, 6–8, and High School

JOHN J. SANGIOVANNI, SUSIE KATT, KEVIN J. DYKEMA

Guiding teachers through six specific actions—valuing, fostering, building, planning, supporting, and reflecting on struggle—this book provides an essential plan for embracing productive perseverance in mathematics.

Grades K–12

SARAH BUSH, KRISTIN COOK

Build cohesive and sustainable STEAM infrastructures—grounded in grade-level standards and purposeful assessment—to deepen the mathematics and science learning of each and every student.

Grades K–5

A SAGE Publishing Company

Helping educators make the greatest impact

CORWIN HAS ONE MISSION: to enhance education through intentional professional learning.

We build long-term relationships with our authors, educators, clients, and associations who partner with us to develop and continuously improve the best evidence-based practices that establish and support lifelong learning.

NATIONAL COUNCIL OF
TEACHERS OF MATHEMATICS

The National Council of Teachers of Mathematics supports and advocates for the highest-quality mathematics teaching and learning for each and every student.